Human Dignity
and the
Great Victorians

Human Dignity and the Great Victorians

By BERNARD N. SCHILLING

ARCHON BOOKS

1972

TO MY MOTHER

Acknowledgments

THE OPPORTUNITY TO THANK my teachers and colleagues for their assistance is most welcome. My first thanks are due to Professor Lewis P. Curtis, of the Department of History at Yale, who has generously allowed me to draw upon his learning and critical judgment and has protected me from many of the dangers of historical generalization. I am much in debt to Professor David E. Owen, now of the Department of History at Harvard, who collaborated with Professor Curtis in directing my work as a graduate student at Yale and has subsequently given expert advice. These men placed at my disposal their prodigious grasp of nineteenth-century England, permitting me to lay the foundation for whatever is valuable in the present study. For the exceptional freedom, and breadth of opportunity which I enjoyed as a graduate student I am much indebted to Professor Stanley T. Williams and Professor Robert D. French, of the Department of English at Yale. Their encouragement and help opened to me more possibilities than I shall ever be able to exhaust.

To my associates at Northwestern University I am much indebted for generous help. Professor Bergen Evans read the entire first draft of the manuscript; his sharp and uncompromisingly honest criticism enabled me to improve my work both in style and in content. Professor Frederick Faverty read the manuscript in an early form and gave much useful criticism. Dr. Frederick Mulhauser, now of Pomona College, provided much bibliographical material and gave valuable help in the manuscript's early stages. I am obliged also to Professor E. B. Hungerford, who suggested that my work should take something like its present form, and to Professor M. E. Prior for advice and encouragement. Professor Daniel Boughner was helpful through reading the manuscript with his characteristic thoroughness.

President Samuel N. Stevens of Grinnell College has offered such varied help—personal, financial, and critical—that the project could not have been completed without his coöperation. Professor Stuart Gerry Brown, of the Department of English at Grinnell, was good enough to read the whole manuscript and to offer a number of invaluable suggestions for its improvement. Professor Charles E. Payne, of the Department of History, and Professor Paul S. Wood, of the Department of English, read various chapters and made useful criticisms.

Professor W. S. Knickerbocker and Mr. Joseph Shipley, editors of *The American Bookman*, read the chapter on Matthew Arnold. I am much indebted to them not only for helping with the analysis of Arnold but also for providing me with a principle which, when applied to the manuscript as a whole, enabled me to shorten it, and therefore to improve it, considerably. My thanks are due finally to the editorial assistance of Miss Ida M. Lynn, of the Columbia University Press.

BERNARD N. SCHILLING

Grinnell, Iowa
January, 1946

Contents

Introduction

Thomas Mann has recorded for us his early belief that "life and intellect, art and politics" are "totally separate worlds," that it is possible and even appropriate for the man of letters "to isolate himself within the ivory tower" of his own special concerns. But the world and the life of man within it were shortly visited by so terrible a disaster that Thomas Mann was forced, like Carlyle, to accept the travail of his embassy. He declared the general ethical significance of the Word, its immense human responsibility. "In the Word is involved the unity of humanity, the wholeness of the human problem, which permits nobody, today less than ever, to separate the intellectual and artistic from the political and social." The artist could not be silent when evil was being done "to bodies, souls and minds, to right and truth, to men and mankind." So once again the man of letters was aroused by the spectacle of human suffering. For generations he had been forced to speak in defense of man and the preciousness of human life. He had left his isolation whenever there seemed to be a widespread danger to the quality of human life, and he has done everything within the power of the Word to prevent the degradation of man.

We should have to praise the legendary nobility of such an effort as in itself a proof of that human quality which it hoped to defend. Yet we should have to think it sentimental and more than faintly absurd if this effort were carried on without knowledge of all the forces against it, if human dignity were proclaimed and striven for by men who were ignorant of what seems every day to be nearer the truth: that men are constantly piling up evidence of their depravity and weakness, their inability to rise to the level which the literary optimist says is the true human one. In *The Coming Victory of Democracy* Thomas Mann shows that he is aware of the contradiction between the reality and the assumptions which underlie his own and others' work.

The dignity of man—do we not feel alarmed and somewhat ridiculous at the mention of these words? Do they not savour of optimism grown feeble and stuffy—of after-dinner oratory, which scarcely harmonizes with the bitter, harsh, everyday truth about human beings? . . . The nature of man is transfixed in the sacred words: "The imagination of man's heart is evil from his youth. . . ." Yes, yes, humanity—its injustice, malice, cruelty, its average stupidity and blindness are amply demonstrated, its egoism is crass, its deceitfulness, cowardice, its antisocial instincts, constitute our everyday experience; the iron pressure of disciplinary constraint is necessary to keep it under any reasonable control. Who cannot embroider upon the depravity of this strange creature called man, who does not often despair over his future or sympathize with the contempt felt by the angels of heaven from the day of creation for the incomprehensible interest which the heavenly Father takes in this problematical creature? And yet . . . we cannot allow ourselves, because of such all too well-founded scepticism, to despise humanity. Despite so much ridiculous depravity, we cannot forget the great and the honourable in man, which manifest themselves as art and science, as passion for truth, creation of beauty and the idea of justice; and it is also true that insensitiveness to the great mystery which we touch upon when we say "man" or "humanity" signifies spiritual death.

This same union of knowledge and hope is found in the work of seven men whose age faced a threat to human dignity even as our own has been menaced by the total state. In the nineteenth century in England it seemed as if large numbers of men were being considered as things, means to an end. The aim of civilized activity was apparently to accumulate as much material wealth as possible, regardless of the cost to the beauty of the world and the quality of human lives. English literature, then very prolific and broad in its scope, devoted some of its energy to warning against the consequences of such indifference. The more important figures who devoted themselves to a defense of mankind shared a common belief in human dignity and oneness. In the course of their criticism they denounced the same causes for the evils of their time; in their proposals for reform they became more extreme, until by the end of the nineteenth century nothing would do but a complete break with the existing social order. Their work seems to have been carried on chiefly because of the inspiration which they felt in common; it was more a continuation of the timeless spiritual leadership of mankind than a protest against civilization such as was evinced at the same time by professional sociologists and econ- omists. We shall not now try to exhaust the whole of English hu- manitarian literature in the nineteenth century. We shall study Coleridge, Southey, Carlyle, Kingsley, Arnold, Ruskin, and Mor- ris as the most important figures whose work seems to be unified by a common concern for human dignity and oneness and who show most clearly the literary movement of thought toward the demand for a new society.

We may then summarize our purposes in some such terms as these: to show (1) that an important part of the work of nine- teenth-century English men of letters concerned itself with the degradation of the man who worked with his hands in the society being developed during the industrial revolution; (2) that a com- mon inspiration was shared by the seven writers being studied for their belief that this degradation was a violation of human dignity and the oneness of mankind; (3) that they held in common the opinion that the cause for this evil was the part of classical eco- nomics which emphasized the right of every man to think first of himself and his own welfare, regardless of the fate of others; (4) that the practical remedies offered by these men to improve the conditions caused by such an attitude of selfishness had become more and more extreme, until William Morris asserted that society would have to be completely changed before human dignity and oneness could be restored; (5) that these writers are to be con- sidered less as social reformers than as important followers of the great spiritual leaders of mankind, whose main ideas they perpetu- ated.

I. The Condition of England

> You may breed a pig in a sty . . . and make
> a learned pig of him after all; but you can-
> not breed a man in a sty, and make a learned
> man of him; or indeed in the true sense of
> that great word, a man at all.—Kingsley,
> *Great Cities and Their Influence.*

In the summer of 1843 Carlyle set aside his notes on Cromwell
for two months in order to write *Past and Present.* In this remarkable performance he described the "condition of England"
as "one of the most ominous, and withal one of the strangest
ever seen in this world." The "England" whose "condition" was
under discussion embraced "the working body of this rich English Nation." Carlyle's somber view of human history admitted
that "in all times the lot of the dumb millions born to toil was de-
faced with manifold sufferings, injustices, heavy burdens. . . .
And yet I will venture to believe that in no time since the begin-
nings of Society, was the lot of those same dumb millions of toilers so entirely unbearable as it is even in the days now passing
over us."

We shall now inquire into the actual situation of these "same
dumb millions of toilers" in Carlyle's time. We shall describe the
living and working conditions which brought about their degradation, that affront to human dignity against which the man of
letters felt bound to protest. We shall inquire also into the many
attempts made to improve the "condition of England"; we shall
find that in spite of these efforts the worst evils remained much
the same, until finally William Morris was convinced that the
prevailing social order could not be successfully changed in part,
but would have to be done away with entirely. It will be neither
necessary nor desirable to touch upon every aspect of the English
working man's situation. We shall end with a sufficiently harrow-

ing picture of human wretchedness and degradation if we deal
principally with the aspects of life which were most shocking to
the men of letters who felt obliged to denounce them. To what
level, then, had the dumb toiling millions fallen by Carlyle's time?

One of the chief causes of the plight of many laborers was an
increase in the urban population in the nineteenth century. In the
first twenty years of this period the population of Manchester increased from 94,000 to 160,000, the population of Bolton from
29,000 to 50,000, and that of Liverpool from 77,000 to 118,000.
Between 1801 and 1831 Leeds more than doubled its population,
as did Sheffield and Birmingham. Smaller towns were similarly
flooded, so that the population of the whole of Lancashire, for example, grew in forty years (1801–41) from 672,000 to 1,701,000.
As a rule, population concentrated itself in towns and cities because
industry demanded labor, and labor responded by flocking to
those centers where work was to be had, at what were at first
higher wages than could otherwise be earned. The new industrial
system, besides calling workers into concentrated masses, provided immense scope for the labor of women and children, so that
the workers relied more than ever on the earnings of their children
and considered large families as economically desirable, if not actually necessary.

The problem of housing the new masses became acute. Eager
landlords saw a chance for large profit from small houses which
could be rented to workers making fair wages. People had to live
somewhere, and whole series of houses went up rapidly, the builders offering as little as possible for high rents. Little regard was
shown for the commonest personal or domestic needs of the tenants. The houses were built usually for sixty-five or seventy pounds
each and were often set up back to back to conserve space. When
new, the houses might bring a rent as high as twelve pounds a year,
falling in time, perhaps, to five pounds a year. For this sum the
tenant received less than the elementary decencies; his home was
usually without water supply or adequate provision, if any, for the
disposal of refuse.

The certain result of such accommodations was overcrowding.

A whole family might occupy a single room, which served the purposes of kitchen, bedchamber, scullery, storeroom, and living-room. A doctor once visited a patient and found her at home in one corner of a room. The landlady herself occupied the central part, near the fireplace, and had rented three of the corners to tenants. In one corner was a widow with three or four children; in another was the doctor's patient, who was unable to earn money to pay her rent and had followed the landlady's suggestion to sub-let half her bed to another person. Hundreds of families were found to be living under similar conditions, in one room, containing only one bed, which might be used by three, four, or even five persons. In the notorious cellars of Manchester twenty-seven instances were found in 1845 in which seven people slept in one bed.

Such a concentration of humanity was an obvious danger to public health, and it was investigated by commissioners inquiring into the problem. They found in 1844 that the average density of population in twenty-one principal towns was 5,045 persons to the square mile. But in certain limited areas it was much worse. There was a small section of London where nearly 243,000 persons inhabited a geographical square mile; a district was discovered in Liverpool which if extended to a square mile with the existing density of population would have shown the fantastic ratio of 657,963 persons to the geographical square mile.

It was difficult to prevent such conditions; so, also, it was hard to correct them once they had arisen. Efforts at improvement sometimes defeated their own purposes. When streets were widened and sordid districts demolished to make better thorough-fares, thousands were unhoused and had to crowd into even smaller space than before, because the building of new dwellings failed to keep pace with the rapid growth of population.

Overcrowding would have caused trouble enough even if all other things had been ideal. But many working people lived in courts or small groups of houses, usually in two rows, two or three stories high, with one room in each story. Six or eight houses faced each other, separated by a space seldom more than fifteen feet wide. Most courts were closed at one end or at both ends; at the far end might be the back of an adjoining building, a wall, or occasionally a row of privies. When houses were built back to back all light and air was excluded save from the court itself. What this must have meant to people living in these courts is suggested by a glance at the refuse thrown into the only place available for it. Even when houses each had a privy in the rear, the only means of disposal was an open sewer into which the privies emptied themselves and into which all sorts of additional filth and rubbish were thrown. When privies were provided in the inner courts, they had to serve so many people as to be added causes of unwholesomeness. Nine, twelve, and even twenty to thirty families were found to be using facilities which at best were inadequate. The doors were often torn off to be used as fire wood or kitchen tables, until builders simply took to building them without doors.

The result of such conditions was that people used the open space of the courts as a cesspool or "midden." Here filth of all kinds was allowed to accumulate: ashes, household rubbish, excrement, vegetable waste, night soil, and other waste was indiscriminately thrown into the common heap. Some courts were made worse by the presence within them or nearby of slaughterhouses. These were sometimes operated in cellars; animals were skinned and dismembered, and the entrails and other refuse were thrown into the court to add to the filth already there. Such common dung-heaps were sometimes allowed to accumulate for long periods. In some courts there were found accumulations amounting to from twenty to fifty tons, the result of weeks of indiscriminate dumping. The whole formed a mass of stinking putridity in a state of constant fermentation, often spreading to the doorways of the houses and at times dripping and seeping into the lower rooms of the surrounding apartments. Such conditions were partly the result of the poor facilities for garbage disposal provided by the authorities; more often still, the court inhabitants wanted to keep their refuse to be used as manure in growing their own vegetables on nearby plots of ground or to be sold as fertilizer to help pay the rent. They would then protect their piles of filth and dung against removal by more enlightened neighbors or by the city authorities themselves.

The state of the courts suggests the condition of the surrounding houses. One of the worst scourges of the laboring classes was the foul air they had to breathe, both at work and at home. Even the wealthy classes were ignorant of proper ventilation; the Houses of Parliament were said to be so poorly ventilated that frequent attendance there was harmful. But those who lived on narrow streets and alleys, in houses on courts with no ventilation from the rear or the sides, with two or three families crowded into a few small rooms—these had scarcely any decent air at all. The window tax, which was lowered in 1823, but not repealed until 1851, cut down the number of windows, but in any case the poor were sensitive to cold air. They preferred breathing warm air, however vitiated, to the discomfort of being chilled when they were ill-supplied with clothing and fuel. Certainly those living on courts can hardly be blamed for preferring the air within their homes to what would have come to them through the windows overlooking the court cesspool, to which they themselves made their own daily contribution.

The water problem, described by Kingsley in *The Water Supply of London*, was even more acute. Cleanliness was in direct ratio to the ease of acquiring water; when it was difficult to find water, people gave up ordinary decencies of cleanliness. Only eight of fifty towns examined had even tolerable drainage and water supply; fewer still offered water for nothing; in some places the poor could get water from pumps and springs. Watercocks in the courts were frequent, and a few landlords might pay for the water. Public fountains, rivers, and wells also provided water, but those wishing to obtain it had to stand in line, waiting sometimes from one to three hours. Quarrels arose over the first right to the water, and magistrates tried many cases of assault arising in this way. The laborer suffered greatly from such inefficiency in supplying water. He would return home exhausted after his work, and rather than endure the trouble and fatigue of fetching water, he would let himself and his house go dirty.

One might suppose that the condition of laboring court dwellers was the lowest to which men could sink. Yet it was better than the state of the thousands who lived in cellars. Many of these places were originally weaving shops, chosen for their dampness. When hand-loom weaving declined, the cellars became homes for laborers and factory operatives in immense numbers. Figures for seven towns showed a total of 14,847 cellars housing 67,726 human beings. These dwellings were ten or twelve feet square, extending from three to six feet below street level. As a rule they were flagged, but sometimes the floor was only the bare earth. Many had a back cellar, used as a bedroom, whose light and air came from the front room only. More than two-thirds of the cellars examined had no opening except the single front door. No drainage existed, and all refuse had to be carried up to the nearest place of disposal. Then, too, cellars situated on courts were polluted by the filthy ooze from the dung-heaps, those abominable accumulations that had spread over the entire available surface of ground and had then begun to drip into the neighboring cellars. Some inhabitants dug wells to receive such deposits, lest their homes become flooded. One four-foot well was found in a cellar under the family bed, full of stinking court slime. At Leeds a cellar family kept a pig in the corner as well, as if proclaiming by the animal's companionship the subhuman degradation to which their lives had fallen.

Such were the physical surroundings in which the masses of England's laboring population lived a century ago. The effects were obvious in the state of the public health. Chadwick's famous generalization is appropriate here: "that the annual loss of life from filth and bad ventilation is greater than the loss from death or wounds in any wars in which the country had been engaged in modern times." The most conspicuous disease was fever, diagnosed under the three main forms of typhus, typhoid, and relapsing fever. Many varieties of pulmonary diseases, including tuberculosis, were very common. In Birmingham they made up one-sixth of all illness. Various eruptions, such as scarlet fever, small pox, scrofula, and other skin afflictions, were found, especially where the air was most vitiated. Cholera, on its four major appearances in England in the nineteenth century, claimed its greatest number of victims in the unsanitary districts. Digestive ailments were also common and did much to weaken the bodies of working men and to prepare them for other illnesses.

Under these circumstances the waste of human life was very great. Children born into unwholesome districts were fortunate if they survived infancy. It is true that infant mortality was high for all classes, but it may safely be said that more than half the children who died before the age of five were of the laboring classes. Aside from the natural dangers to life in the worker's districts, the neglect of children did much to lessen their chance of survival. In 1839 nearly a quarter of a million females were at work in factories; most of them had begun work at the age of nine or ten, without learning how to care for a home and children. They would grow up weak and sickly themselves and would give birth to weak and sickly children. Many women, being forced to go on working, would leave their infants to the care of indifferent nurses or older children. These persons would often give opiates to the babies in order to calm them. A whole series of nostrums came into use under such titles as "Infant's Preservative," "Mothers' Blessing," "Quietness," and the popular "Godfrey's Cordial"; the last-mentionad sedative was a mixture of treacle and opium, called by its users with ghastly familiarity, "Godfrey." Such opiates would be certain to keep babies from crying until evening, when the parents were free to look after them. Yet even then some weary mothers might give still another dose so as to insure undisturbed rest for themselves. If the children survived such treatment at all, they grew emaciated and deformed, sometimes degenerating into idiocy. A further evil was the "Burial Clubs," which insured the expenses of burial in return for a small weekly premium. They enrolled twelve to fifteen times as many as the "Sick Clubs," because it was more profitable to parents to let their children die than to spend money to keep them alive. Some parents joined three "Burial Clubs," and on the death of a child they would receive triple payment, leaving them with a nice profit after the funeral. Thus, when an insured child became ill, parents sometimes felt a desire for the burial payment stronger than their normal anxiety for the child's life. Rent collectors testified that they had been told to postpone expectation of the rent, until some member of the family, usually a child, should die and so bring in enough to pay what was owing.

The reader must here be warned lest he blame industrial civilization entirely for the evils under discussion. It should be remembered that while conditions for the poor in English cities in the nineteenth century were very bad, they were, from the point of view of public health, no worse than the conditions prevalent in 1760. Certainly the bad health of the mid-nineteenth century English town was not entirely caused by the industrial revolution, but was partly a relic of the past, doubtless aggravated by the demands of the new era. The rapid crowding into factory towns simply multiplied the defects already present in the eighteenth century, especially for the town worker.

Working conditions for the laborer were in keeping with his home environment. The industrial system, as J. L. and Barbara Hammond have pointed out, encouraged an atmosphere in which the worker was thought of as so much labor power to be used in the service of a master or a system. John Stuart Mill's distinction between ethics and economics was not observed. The fate of the human beings who performed the actual work was of less importance than the work itself, with the result that the nineteenth century was filled with protests against scandalous working conditions. We shall consider three principal elements here: the number of hours of work demanded of the laborer, the exploitation of the labor of children, and the dangers to life and health connected with various occupations.

The working day of a factory laborer too often began with, even if it did not anticipate, the crowing of the cock. Some improvement had been made by 1840 in the hours of work, but in general twelve to thirteen hours were demanded each day, exclusive of time for meals. It was even reported that some employers cheated by moving forward the hands of the clock at meal time. As a rule, however, about an hour and a half was allowed for eating. The regular hours of work were often increased for various reasons. The cleaning of machinery, for example, took additional time, sometimes from meal hours. When work had to be halted because of broken machinery, lack of water, or for occasional holidays, all of the time so lost was made up by adding extra hours to the usual working day; there was rarely any payment for such additional work.

A more notorious evil was the exploitation of child labor. As a rule children were taken into factories at about the age of nine. More than ten thousand under the age of eleven were employed as factory operatives in the British Isles; adding those between the ages of eleven and eighteen, there was a total of 167,144 boys and girls who worked in factories along with adults who numbered 191,671. Even though Chadwick insisted that children who worked in factories were no worse off than those who remained at home, yet the conditions of work were often such as to prevent normal development. Children complained of fatigue caused by their work. Even when the nature of the work, condition of the factory, and treatment by employers were nearly ideal, children became exhausted beyond healthful endurance. Some were so tired they could not take off their clothes at night; one boy said he had once fallen asleep while eating, with food still in his mouth; some could not find strength to get up once they had sat down at the end of day; others would fall asleep at work and would have to be forced into consciousness; others were seen to fall asleep at the end of the day and continue to go through the motions of their labor, for even after the machinery had stopped they were too weary to realize it.

Children and young persons who worked in mines complained even more pitiably. In Derbyshire the hours were often fourteen to sixteen out of twenty-four, and one boy of fifteen testified that he had worked for thirty-six hours running, three times in eleven days. Children were often so tired that they could not get home without their parents' help; one boy would lie down by the roadside until his mother came for him. Others testified that for months on end they had not seen daylight, save on Sunday, when they were too tired to enjoy it. If they lived at a distance of a mile or two from the pits, they had to get up early enough to reach the mines at 6 A.M. and they would remain at work until 8 P.M., taking their meals as best as they could during the day.

In addition, many children said they seldom or never had enough to eat and were without clothing decent enough to permit them to attend Sunday School. They were found to be stunted in growth, pale and sickly in appearance, and so weak as to be easy prey to diseases of the lungs and digestive organs, to distortion of the spine and deformity of the limbs.

The conditions for laborers of all sorts were bad enough to impair their health and shorten their lives. Investigators found that factory employment, in particular, was injurious. Many occupations produced a dust or vapor which the worker could not help inhaling. Corn-millers, paper-makers, and especially maltsters and flax mill workers suffered acutely. The men contracted bronchial inflammation and many became asthmatic for life. The most pernicious branch of manufacture in England, however, was considered by investigators in 1843 to be grinding. Dry-grinding, especially, produced a quantity of iron and grit dust which floated about the rooms until the air was so thick that men entering the door were hardly visible. The effect upon workers was soon apparent. The nostrils and air passages were the first parts affected, followed shortly by digestive disorders, vomiting, and extreme emaciation. A noticeable stoop would appear, then hoarseness, a loud cough, and the spitting of a dusty mucous mixture would follow. Many would linger for months or even years, usually dying between the ages of thirty and thirty-five; very few dry-grinders were known to live more than forty years. Yet these men resisted attempts at improving conditions. Some masters had tried to install flues to carry off the dust and so protect the grinders; the men were afraid that any such precaution, while prolonging life, would also increase the supply of labor and decrease wages. Some refused to use any appliance for safety and would even kick down whatever was supplied and break it under their feet.

The work of coal miners was less destructive of life than was grinding, but the collier too often had the marks of old age upon him before other men had passed their prime. He suffered especially from the bad air deep within the earth. Then, too, work of a most exhausting and enervating kind was demanded throughout a twelve-hour day. Coal had to be not only dug but also drawn or carried to the rails where horsedrawn cars awaited it. Ropes or chains were attached to containers weighing from one to four or five hundredweight when full. Often the heavy loads had to be pulled up steep inclines, through water and mud ankle deep. Many colliers became stunted, bent, and deformed. Sores on the head and back were common because of pressure and friction endured in pushing loads through narrow seams. There was also danger of explosion or other sudden accidents. Although mining was one of the most dangerous of occupations, there was no protective legislation for it whatever until 1842. Not until 1855 were any useful safeguards against injury to life and health prescribed by law. At night men were sometimes left alone in the pits without anyone at the surface with whom they could communicate. Many serious accidents occurred at such times, and commissioners found in 1850 that many men had been wounded or crushed, hours before help was given. A miner's work was therefore such as to render him at best disabled or exhausted by the age of fifty.

The unwholesome conditions of work in the tailoring trades have been described by Kingsley in *Cheap Clothes and Nasty*, a classic of its kind. The plight of these workers and of women who lived by making shirts and dresses was particularly touching to Carlyle. It seems to have inspired also the famous cartoon in *Punch* showing a group of skeletons bending with horrible industry over their sewing. There was a certain ghastly appropriateness in Sir James Graham's description in 1847 of a typical worker's life. It resolved itself, in his opinion, into "eating, drinking, working and dying."

There remains the question of the laborer's remuneration for work which might ruin his health and life. We shall glance first at his actual wages and secondly at the relation of the worker's general wretchedness of condition, aside from his work, to the amount of his wages. Earnings differed greatly for different occupations, but if we accept the testimony of workers reporting to Chadwick in 1842, it was possible for a man, his wife, and three children to live decently on 12 to 14s. a week. Some artisans and workers, having particular skill or training, were very well paid. In 1840 the daily wage in the building trades in London was 5s. for a ten-hour day, making a wage of 30s. a week; "coarse spinners" earned from 14 to 16s. weekly, still a decent wage by the standard of Chadwick's report. In 1842 some colliers were paid 14 to 16s. weekly, a figure regarded as eminently fair at that time. John Bright himself, whose own mill workers praised the justice and humaneness of his dealings, paid in 1844 a wage of 16s. a week to men past twenty-one years of age. Adult women received about 12s. weekly. The lowest wage went to boys between thirteen and sixteen, who were paid 6s. 6d. weekly, and to girls of the same age, who received 6s. 3d. The wages of textile mill workers as a class were apparently large enough to provide decent comfort if economically used. Many families with husband, wife, and children all earning something were able in good times to achieve an income of 30s. to 50s. or more a week. Francis Place was therefore able to assert that wages had consistently improved and were higher than at any previous period. It has, in fact, recently been estimated by C. R. Fay that wages were on the whole 40 percent higher and prices nearly 20 percent lower in 1850 than in 1790, suggesting that if wages alone were considered, the laboring class must have been better situated in the period under discussion than ever before.

But some classes of workers were miserably poor. The handloom weavers in particular had found the transition to a new industrial era painfully slow and destructive. Whereas the hand loom had once been able to bring in more than 15s. a week, by 1844 the weaver had to work fourteen or more hours a day to earn 6s. to 8s. a week. The new machinery had also ruined the business of stocking weavers, who with difficulty earned 7s. a week for a sixteen-hour day. In 1844 the lace industry employed some 21,000 girls and women and about 6,000 men and boys. By 1844 the earnings of these workers had fallen to 3s. 6d. a week for an eleven-hour day. Female workers as a whole were poorly paid for what was often very hard and unpleasant work. Most wretched of all was the lot of those thousands of "distressed needle-women," as Carlyle called them, the makers of dresses, neckties, jackets, and shirts. Their

numbers were swollen by the influx of many women, otherwise unemployed, who took to the almost universal feminine accomplishment of sewing for a livelihood. Women who went out by the day
could earn up to 1s. 6d. daily. These were better paid than girls
making neckties, who might work sixteen hours a day for less than
5s. a week. Some women could produce only one "fancy" shirt in
a day of eighteen hours, for which they were paid 6d. Their difficulties were made worse by the requirement of some employers
that a money deposit be made for materials. Many women could
not do this unless they pawned part of the materials and later redeemed them at a loss. In 1849 there was held a meeting of these
"slop workers," as they were called; more than one thousand
women employed in sewing attended. Of these, only five had
earned 6s. in the previous week. Many could make only 2s. 6d. a
week, and some as little as 1s. From such meager earnings they had
to buy thread and were even fined occasionally for late or defective
work. These were the creatures who achieved immortality through
Thomas Hood's *Song of the Shirt,* a poem which drew wide attention to the shirt-makers' plight.

No discussion of wages can omit mention of the means by which
laborers were often deprived of the full value of their earnings.
Such frauds took the form chiefly of "truck" and of fines. Essentially "truck" meant payment in commodities, a practice which
had been forbidden by law in 1831. But the law was easily evaded,
and "truck" lingered until 1870. Payment was offered in the commodity made by the worker or in articles sold by the employer at
his store; wages were also paid out at public houses in which the
employer or one of his underlings held an interest. Worse still was
the practice of fines and similar frauds, described vividly by Disraeli
in *Sybil.* Miners in particular lost considerable sums in fines which
were arbitrarily imposed by the overseer without informing the
worker until he came for his wages. In some factories fines were
also imposed for tardiness, for leaving the room without permis-
sion, for singing, whistling, or speaking to other workers. Payment was required for all breakage of equipment by the operative;
penalties for bad work were imposed at the discretion of the

overseer, who was often charged with taking in a certain amount each week in fines. With expanding trade, demanding new capital, employers wanted to put every penny back into the business; wages seemed a waste of money and were kept to a minimum whenever possible.

Finally, much hardship was endured because of the poor nourishment which wages could buy. Prices were generally high under protection, and the period came to be called "the hungry forties." Furthermore, as C. R. Fay says, traders seemed bent on treating "the working man's stomach as a sort of wastepaper basket." The adulteration of food was certainly flagrant before 1875, when it was prohibited by law. As if it were not profitable enough to adulterate and cheapen the food itself, false weights and measures were used so widely that many arrests were made on charges of dishonest trading. Stale meat, sometimes taken from diseased animals, wilted vegetables, rancid cheese, watered butter, and chalky flour were frequently all that the laborer's wages would enable him to provide, even when his earnings were otherwise adequate.

We have been discussing the life of the worker who was employed and who tried to provide for himself out of his own wages. But what of those who lost their jobs? The problem of unemployment was certainly grave in the depression years following the boom of 1833–36. At Manchester alone 50,000 workers were idle in the summer of 1837. After 1840 the problem became even worse; more factories were closing down, and industrial laborers by the thousand were left to migrate in search of work. Some wandered about looking for jobs; others begged from door to door for food or picked up a precarious living as best they could. In some places the local authorities forced the idle to move so that poor relief funds would not be burdened. Between 1841 and 1843 more than 15,000 persons were removed from various manufacturing districts to relieve local pressure and to take advantage of better conditions elsewhere.

If all other means failed, one could apply for poor relief. Under the law of 1834 this relief was confined to the workhouse; payments of money to the destitute were no longer made, and the conditions imposed in the workhouse were such as to discourage anyone from giving up his independence to enter it. The very lowest class of laborer was better off than a workhouse inmate. The intentional dreariness of life in these places was openly stated by a guide who was showing visitors through a Liverpool workhouse: "We endeavor to make the life of the pauper a life that no man would submit to, unless under absolute necessity." So for a man suffering under hard conditions of labor the alternatives were for the most part worse than a life of independence, whatever its hardships.

Finally, we must inquire into the connection between poverty and the worker's physical degradation. Certainly hundreds of thousands suffered the direst kind of poverty. Besides the approximately 900,000 who were on relief in 1849, for example, there were thousands living on the fringes of destitution, many of whom would have begged in the streets or even have died rather than enter a workhouse. Not only poor wages but also ill health, especially the fever so common in unsanitary districts, helped to impoverish workers. Such destitute persons were caught between cause and effect. They were so poor that they could occupy only the cheapest lodgings, which were likely to exist only in the most unsanitary areas, where the tenants might contract fever, which in turn made work impossible. So poverty caused physical neglect, which resulted in illness, and this illness then resulted in deeper poverty.

But poverty was not responsible for every hardship. Certainly many persons need not have lived in the subhuman state in which they were found; their wages, if wisely used, would have been adequate for a decent life. Chadwick found that of all the causes leading to pauperism, reckless improvidence, especially drinking, was the most influential. On the other hand, it was found that some very poor workers in point of wages managed to keep their houses at least decently clean and comfortable. Filth and disease sometimes existed along with good wages; cleanliness and fair health was often achieved with comparatively low wages. In the mining districts of South Staffordshire, the wives of colliers said that they were better off in a period of low wages, some of them even dreading the return of high pay for work, because of the drunkenness and extravagance that would ensue. But we must remember that environment did much to make the laborer thoughtless and prodigal. Many who lived sordidly may not have known how to better or improve their condition, simply because of ignorance of any other way of living. Wretched circumstances create the very faults which are responsible for their continuance. The ignorance of the laboring housewife, for example, made her home so inadequate in every way that the husband could not bear to spend an evening there. Since he had little chance for healthful recreation, nothing much remained but the nearest beer-shop. Female children of laborers were removed from school and put to work at such an early age that they had no time to learn to sew or to cook or to acquire even the simplest knowledge of household management or careful.use of money. Coming from ugly and sordid homes, the creatures had no way of knowing what decent living was; they continued the discomfort and wretched food which helped to drive the laborer himself to other sources of consolation.

We now approach the effect of all these conditions upon the laborer's mental and moral state. The training of his mind would have been difficult, even if he had been offered a good education. But the eighteenth century had seldom considered education for the poorer classes. Numerous charitable schools were available, but no general, organized system of popular education existed. Teaching the lower orders was looked upon as a kind of missionary work, a charitable act toward a neglected class concerning whose general intelligence and capacity a low opinion was held. They were not in any case supposed to be well educated. As B. Kirkman Gray points out in his *History of English Philanthropy*, "publicists and religious teachers alike regarded the lower orders . . . as conveniently provided by providence for their support and satisfaction." The oral teaching of the church was thought to be quite enough; more than this would interfere with useful employment, and hence the mass of laborers were to be kept in ignorance. The fear of social unrest was also influential in the late eighteenth century, when the French Revolution and the atmosphere it created prevented many reforms. The fear that educated masses would be discontented, that new knowledge in the spirit of those times would give the people hope and aspiration to rise out of their class perhaps did much to hold back popular education. The desire of those in power was to impress upon the poor the duty of loyalty and contentment, not to educate them so that they would not work hard and submissively for small wages.

Such an attitude could not be carried into the nineteenth century without serious danger. The peasant was gradually lost in the laborer, and no better opinion of his mental powers was held; yet the class to which the laborer belonged became so large, particularly in towns and industrial centers, that popular education had to be thought of as more than a scattered charitable enterprise. The strong religious revival of the late eighteenth century perhaps did something for national education, by insisting that every child should learn to read the Bible.

But the very fact and nature of the changing industrial era emphasized the need for popular instruction. For one thing, the new order challenged a society split up into grades and classes. Individual rights were recognized; the capacities which men have in common regardless of class were stressed, and the possibility of wealth and power offered to those who had natural ability inspired the belief that everyone should have a fair start in life. The center of things moved from country to town, which soon was thought of as the normal environment for the laboring class. Popular instruction now became essential, whereas previously it had been looked upon as needless or undesirable. In the new towns life became much more complicated and crowded with opportunity for good and evil than life in the farm or village had been. A higher social and intellectual level was required in the new era. New difficulties demanded a better mental equipment; new opportunities under freer competition called for better training. New things to use and to consume and new conditions of living demanded more knowledge and self-control. The worker's mental interests had to be enlarged if he were to profit from a wider and more complicated life.

Most important of all was the change in occupation. The problems of the factory system, for example, applied with special force to the young. The influence of home life became much weaker, and the work of children, often exhausting and harmful to health, made proper elementary education impossible, not to mention training for a future career. The evils of child exploitation and the decay of home life certainly existed to some extent before the factories became prominent; yet the old problems were made worse and new ones were created by the employment of women and children away from home in large establishments under the heavy physical strain imposed by machinery. It must be admitted, also, that the work of the country laborer was probably better for his mind than that of the industrial operative. There is no need of glorifying the poor man's chances in the old era, but it is perhaps true that work in the field afforded wider experience and that the normal daily life of the country worker was less stultifying that life under the industrial system of labor. In a sense the farm worker's education sprang from his ordinary life, in which he had fairly certain employment, a measure of independence, and a range of experience which offered some variety and was simple enough so that each man could see the meaning and result of his work and its connection with social and domestic needs. The need of instruction in school was not so pressing in a life which held a certain interest and stimulus for the worker. A good deal of instruction was given at home as well; what a father knew was handed on to his children by the evening fire, and a certain amount of formal learning and oral tradition could be absorbed. These advantages were not enjoyed when life moved into the crowded towns. As Adam Smith himself pointed out, work became far more mechanical for each laborer and less varied. A machine worker might go on for years doing nothing but one simple operation which made no demands whatever upon his mind; as a result, the worker would become as stupid as it was possible for a human being to be.

But England was still inadequately prepared to meet the new task. Even if the children of workers had been able and willing to attend school regularly, they would not have profited greatly from the education then offered to them. The Select Committee on

Education, reporting in 1835, was of the opinion that no class of society in England was really well educated. Children of the lower classes attended chiefly the Dame Schools, as well as the Sunday Schools; the latter did more actual good, perhaps, than any of the others. Dame Schools were the most numerous and the worst of all. They did little save to keep children off the streets and help to get them out of the way of their mothers. Such schools were kept largely by women—a few by old men. In Manchester not a single Dame School teacher was found in 1835 who had been educated for her employment. The schools themselves were usually in unwholesome rooms, some even in cellars or garrets. Usually there were only two or three books to serve all the students, and sometimes there were none at all. The average cost of Dame School instruction was about four pence a week. In Manchester 4,722 children attended such places, and they were very little affected by the instruction received there. Cottage Schools were also numerous in all large towns; these were attended in 1845 by about one-fifth of the children of laborers. They were generally situated in courts or dirty lanes, and surrounded by filth of every description. Some were held in garrets so badly overcrowded that the children could not sit down. Women, again, did most of the teaching, and sometimes carried on other work besides. In one case thirty-six children were "taught" in a small room above the teacher's shop; when customers came in, she would leave the class to its own devices and attend to her second trade. The Common Day Schools were better, but even they gave little in the way of education. Such a high degree of incompetence was disclosed among the teachers that the Select Committee concluded that "the task of education is the only one for which no previous knowledge or qualification" was demanded. A complete lack of order and system usually obtained; the classes were too numerous, books were grossly deficient, and plans of instruction, if any, were usually poor. In one such institution, about one hundred and thirty children created so much noise and confusion that the replies of their teacher to questions of the Select Committee were almost inaudible.

The Sunday Schools were apparently the best means of education available to the lower classes. In Manchester they were attended by half again as many children as attended all the other schools together, eighty-six Sunday Schools accounting for 33,196 pupils. Thirty-nine of these schools also offered evening classes, in which reading and arithmetic were taught in addition to religion.

Most of the children of laborers received no instruction at all outside of brief visits to Sunday School. Sheer weariness kept many away. Long hours and hard work made them unwilling to give up what little leisure they had for a purpose whose importance seemed remote to them. Night school was impossible for most of them, once they had begun to work, usually by the age of ten. Their work as a rule required little thought or intelligence, so that they were willing to fall into an animal routine of work, play, food, and sleep. Illness also kept away many of the children who lived in unsanitary courts and cellars. Parents were sometimes ashamed to send their children to school, especially when they were without decent clothing or were otherwise unfit to be seen. The selfishness of parents was also a factor. A child might earn, perhaps, 3s. a week, and if he were to attend school during the day, the parent would have to pay his tuition rather than receive the child's earnings. Finally, much could have been done and frequently was done by masters to provide for the education of their operatives. But most employers considered themselves free from any moral obligation in the matter. Francis Place suggests that some might even have preferred to keep the lower classes in ignorance and would have resented as presumptuous any effort on the laborer's part to educate himself.

By 1843 an investigator could therefore say of the Birmingham district that children and young persons were "entirely destitute of anything which can be called, even allowing the utmost latitude to the expression, a useful education." Many, especially children employed in mines, were allowed to grow up ignorant and degraded almost to imbecility.

If the laborer's mind suffered, so also did his morality. The evil of overcrowding seems to have had moral consequences as bad as the physical results. The usual separation of the sexes was hardly possible. The sense of decency or shame was lost when families carried on their entire personal lives in a single room. The normal feelings of civilized human beings could not possibly develop under such circumstances. Perhaps the worst results of overcrowding were to be seen in the public lodging houses which had sprung up in most manufacturing towns, partly because of the fluctuating demand for labor, which made for a great deal of migration from place to place. The traveling artisan and his family would often take temporary quarters in such a lodging house, where for two or three pence a night one could obtain all or part of a bed. Here vagrants, thieves, prostitutes, mendicants, and tramps of all sorts might be encountered, indiscriminately thrown together. Every room but the kitchen contained all the beds possible, and each bed took in as many people as it could hold. Ventilation was practically unknown; the constant use of vitiated air by numerous persons, themselves usually filthy and personally offensive, the unclean bedding, and the accumulation of all manner of refuse and filth scattered about the floor created a revolting atmosphere. Many of these lodging houses became receiving houses for stolen goods, schools of juvenile delinquency, and commonly outright brothels, known as such to the police.

Personal morality therefore degenerated under such adverse conditions; the incidence of crime among the laborers in these same surroundings was also very great. Not only did the pickpockets, thieves, and minor pests of society come from the worst districts, but also the most reckless criminals. The effect was, of course, most noticeable in children and young persons, as pointed out in 1853 by the Committee on Criminal and Destitute Children. Chadwick was assured by a Superintendent of Police that there were hundreds of children with no names whatever, "or only nicknames, like dogs." In Edinburgh alone about 2,000 children were vagrant wanderers who refused to go to workhouses and picked up a living as best they could, if they did not actually beg or steal. From such as these the country's criminal population was recruited.

Working conditions also were anything but uplifting. The mere fact that they were obliged to go early to work, the knowledge that they were exploited and obliged to give up their earnings to their parents, deprived children of family loyalties and led them to throw off parental control as soon as possible. In factories their regard for moral values might be lost. They would be thrown in with adults at work and were often misled by dissolute or crude persons before their moral instincts could develop properly. Promiscuity was found to begin very early among factory workers; adolescent youths and girls were associated together indiscriminately at work, and every chance was given them to make assignations. There seems to have been little in the lives of most laborers as we have observed them at home, in school, or at work which would develop in them any sense of moral obligation whatever.

But the most notorious of all the excesses common among the laboring classes was intemperate drinking. The exhausted laborer could most easily forget his miseries and throw off his fatigue in the public house. As Chadwick pointed out, the laboring classes were deprived of places for play or recreation by the stoppage of footpaths and walks and especially by the enclosure of commons. After work the laborer found that every available spot of ground belonged to other people and that he had no place to go for amusement or recreation. He could return to an unpleasant home, or he could find in the beer-shop company and forgetfulness of his hard life. Many also believed that strong drink was necessary in order to perform hard work. In any case, work which was especially exhausting or unpleasant led to drinking, which helped men to go on working. Then, too, liquor was very easily obtained. The number of pubs was estimated by the Committee on Drunkenness in 1834 to be so great that one such place existed for every twenty families in the United Kingdom. Easy access to pawnbrokers also contributed to intemperance. Thousands of articles were pledged, at sums from 3*d*. to 1*s*., seldom more than 1*s*. 6*d*. Most of such pledges were made to buy liquor, largely by women who had pawned personal or household effects, to be redeemed shortly at fantastic rates of interest. Laborers were forced to admit that they spent far more on liquor than on the education of their children or than they deposited in savings banks. In the years when the poor were given relief in money almost one-third of the amount was spent for liquor on the same day that it was received.

A final level of wretchedness has yet to be considered, and we shall have done with this sad picture. Chadwick listed among the conclusions following his report on sanitary conditions "that defective town cleansing fosters habits of the most abject degradation and tends to the demoralization of large numbers of human beings, who subsist by means of what they find amid the noxious filth accumulated in neglected streets and byeplaces." A whole class of such creatures grew up in the larger English towns. They were called "finders," a term embracing the bone-pickers, mud-rakers, rag-gatherers, and dealers in miscellaneous refuse. All led a wandering, unsettled life in search of the articles they dealt in; they spent the night as a rule in "mendicants' " lodging houses. In winter their number was enlarged by "trampers," who came from the country where they had been itinerant laborers during the summer, and who came up to London, for example, to find shelter in the night asylums or refuges for the destitute and to take up "street finding" during the day. The famine in Ireland had sent many of the unfortunates, especially boys and girls, to the ranks of the "finders." Some were old men and women who had been otherwise employed, but because of accident or failure had been reduced to this degraded state. They would pick up almost anything likely to be of use, such as rags, bones, pieces of lead, brass, or other metal, and especially occasional bits of food, which they were sometimes seen to fight for with some equally hungry dog. In London alone, about 1850, there were 800 to 1,000 "finders"; in Manchester 302 were known to the police. They were fortunate to earn 8*d*. a day on their findings, and most of them made from 3 to 4*s*. a week. The most prosperous of them followed the most degraded calling; these were the "pure-finders" or people who collected dogs' dung or "pure" from streets and kennels. They sold it by the bucket to various tanneries in Bermondsey for use in purifying leather. The price was at first high, but competition became so keen that most "pure-finders" felt themselves lucky to earn from 5 to 7*s*. a week. The entire class of "finders" presented a loathsome spectacle of human degradation, some of them apparently little elevated above the animals whose bones they gathered or whose refuse thy collected in their baskets.

At a certain level of misery the mind and spirit of man seem to lose their force, and wretchedness finally destroys the faculties distinctive of human beings. This was seen in the apathetic surrender of many of the lower classes to their lot, which they seemed to accept as inevitable, making no effort to get into happier circumstances. Those living in the most wretched hovels complained the least of their condition. Those working at the most monotonous drudgery developed a certain dull inertness and fell into mental and spiritual apathy. The degeneration of the large majority was only the more obvious against the pitiable aspiration after beauty which somehow lingered in the handful who tried, in the most filthy districts, to grow a few geraniums and roses. It was observed of the working class generally that their lives at home amid squalor and disease and at work, which was, for most, wearisome and cheerless, led to a noticeable sadness of aspect. Their faces and manner became dejected and hopeless, expressing misery in every aspect, the dumbness and bewilderment which moved Carlyle to speak in their behalf.

Such was the lot of the toiling millions. The moral of the various investigations and reports was that abandonment of the lower classes to their own fate was ruinous. Something had to be done by those in authority; there had to be some interference with the course of events which seemed to be forever downward. By the fourth quarter of the nineteenth century much had actually been done to correct the worst evils. There was in the first place, a great deal of personal effort by individuals and charitable organizations to improve the lot of the masses. Many benevolent and generous employers such as Robert Owen established schools and libraries, encouraged musical and choral groups, aided in improving the living conditions of their men, and were eager to promote in every way the good of their employees. More extraordinary still was the immense amount of charitable activity which had always existed in England. Before the passage of the 1834 Poor Law hundreds of legacies were left to overseers of the poor for distribution among those in want. In 1850 there was printed the *Plan for Preventing Destitution and Mendicancy in the British Metropolis,* which listed an immense number of charities and philanthropic enterprises. One "Soup-Kitchen and Hospice" alone had given away since 1847 more than 475,000 warm meals and had accommodated at the hospice more than 5,000 persons in one year. The role of the Church of England in this kind of charitable activity was conspicuous, aside from such larger efforts at reform as Christian Socialism. Among other things it sponsored orders of women, or sisterhoods, who interested themselves in all branches of charitable work. Individual clergymen dispensed charity and made personal visits to their less fortunate parishioners. District visiting societies were formed, so that such personal effort became a regular part of parochial work for all clergymen. The Evangelicals, in particular, were so active that Shaftesbury described them as the greatest philanthropists of the century.

With such aid from the church, the charities in London alone became so great by 1869 that there was not "a want or form of human wretchedness, for which provision is not made. . . . Every malady of the body has its hospital or dispensary; every disorder of the social system some provision for its mitigation. From the cradle to the grave, benevolence steps in to offer aid." [1] One might be born, live, die, and be buried, apparently, all for nothing. Vast sums of money were involved. Including relief of the poor by the state, it was estimated in 1869 that more than eight and one-half million pounds a year were charitably given. By 1890 there were in Great Britain more than 5,000 societies, endowments, charitable and benevolent funds, as well as semi-charitable groups, all of which were to meet the distress of the underprivileged, to prevent or to anticipate it in some way. Yet in the face of this profuse generosity, many of the most deserving cases went unaided because charity was so indiscriminate. The eagerness of benevolent persons to give aid caused a great deal of foolish and even harmful generosity. Overlapping resulted, so that some quarters were richly

[1] J. H. Stallard, *Pauperism, Charity,* London, 1869, p. 15.

aided when others received nothing. Of the 2,000 centers of charity in London in 1869, hardly one was so organized as to give a destitute person all the relief which he required when he required it. Only if he were an old hand at obtaining charity could he be certain of the proper help. The deserving often starved, but the professional beggar lived well. The Charity Organization Society had to be set up to deal with the problem systematically.

In any case, the "condition of England" was not essentially changed by generous gifts, organized or not. The Poor Law of 1834, supplemented by charity, organized or unorganized, had very little effect on the poverty and misery of the poor. Other methods had to be employed; laws had to be passed against existing abuses. There can be no doubt that these laws were more effective than charity. Almost everything that was wrong seems to have had a law passed against it, especially in the realm of public health. Disraeli's famous slogan—"Sanitas sanitatum, omnia sanitas"—suggests the attention which government finally gave to this problem. The principal *Laws concerning Public Health*,[2] when gathered together, made an impressive volume of more than 800 pages. Aside from laws to correct housing conditions, sanitary legislation had begun in earnest in 1846 with a series of Nuisances Removal Acts. The Baths and Washhouses Acts had enabled parishes to build public baths and so to promote personal cleanliness. In 1848 a General Public Health Act was passed, setting up a Board of Health, which, however, soon lost its powers. An effort was made in 1852 to improve water service through the Metropolis Water Act. There followed shortly a law requiring compulsory vaccination and, in 1855, the Diseases Prevention Act, which consolidated several previous laws. Another Public Health Act was passed in 1856, and a Sanitary Act followed eight years later. In 1871 establishment of the Local Government Board helped to insure that local sanitary work should be properly done. But the great Public Health Act of 1875 consolidated the entire system of sanitary law and superseded almost all previous acts.

The reforms of housing began chiefly with Lord Shaftesbury's

[2] Edited by W. R. Smith and Henry Smith, London, 1883.

two measures, the Common Lodging Houses Act and The Labouring Classes Lodging Houses Act, which became law in 1851. The latter was scarcely enforced at all, and in 1855 Sir Benjamin Hall's Metropolis Local Management Act again touched the housing problem, as did the Diseases Prevention Act of the same year. A mild law was passed in 1866, called the Labouring Classes Dwelling Houses Bill, to be followed by the more important measure of 1868 which is usually called "Mr. Torrens' Act," after its sponsor. By this time interest in housing was so great that eight Metropolitan Dwellings Improvement Associations had sprung up in London alone. There followed the laws passed in 1875 and 1879, called the Artizans Dwellings Improvement Acts, or simply "Mr. Cross's Acts." These measures provided for gradual removal of unhealthful dwellings and for building and maintaining new houses instead. Local authorities were empowered to demolish and to reconstruct whole areas. The most important of these many laws was that of 1875, the *annus mirabilis* of Disraeli's social legislation, when the great Public Health Act, as well as A Sale of Food and Drugs Act, condemning adulteration, was made into law. All these measures of the central government were supplemented by municipal effort. Birmingham, under Joseph Chamberlain, put through extensive reforms, including a housing project that covered more than 40 acres. Manchester, Liverpool, and Glasgow also pressed the clearance of slums and became more careful of public health, especially by making the supply of water a municipal activity.

A great deal was therefore done to improve the health and homes of laborers. The same is true of their working conditions. It is simplest for us to glance at the series of laws concerning factories. At least ten principal acts, as well as less important measures, were passed before 1880 to regulate work in factories. These laws began as early as 1802 with the Health and Morals of Apprentices Act, which, like that of 1819, dealt chiefly with child labor in cotton mills. The act of 1833 called for new regulation of children's work and established a group of inspectors who were to see that the law was obeyed. In 1844 the working day for women and others under eighteen was cut to twelve hours, and in 1847, after tremendous agitation, it was reduced to ten. These acts applied largely to textile factories, but the Extension Acts of 1864 and 1867 brought a large number of new industries under control. The Act of 1878 consolidated and amended previous laws and set up new regulations as to hours, sanitation, and prevention of accidents due to dangerous machinery. So much progress had been made in removing former abuses that even Karl Marx was able to praise the benefits which labor had derived from the Factory Acts.

Great strides had also been made in providing elementary education, which was at first conducted by private persons and by the two chief educational societies, The British and Foreign School Society and the Church of England's National Society for the Education . . . of the Poor. In 1832 an annual grant of £20,000 was made to these groups, which was increased to £30,000 in 1839. School inspectors were appointed, and schools for training teachers were established. The annual grants increased, until in 1860 the state was giving £800,000 a year for elementary education, but results were still unsatisfactory. Hence Forster's Act in 1870, which recognized that voluntary schools aided by government grants could not cover the field. The act provided for local boards of education, which were to build public elementary schools where needed. These board schools were to receive aid just as the voluntary schools did, but the local rates had to supplement the annual grant. The local taxpayer was now obliged to contribute to public education, and from 1870 steady progress was made in accommodation for students and in attendance. In 1876 and 1880 other laws were passed to make attendance compulsory, so that by 1880 more than 2,500,000 pupils were receiving elementary education. In 1891 education finally became free, so that everyone had to get at least an elementary education and could do so free of charge.

All these reforms would have done much to improve the "condition of England" without the "golden age" of British capitalism, which followed repeal of the Corn Laws in 1846. For twenty-five years economic expansion was almost uninterrupted, save for brief and minor recessions. New discoveries of gold stimulated industry and commerce the world over, and prices rose as money became more plentiful. Tremendous development of steamships and railways helped to distribute British goods, so that exports more than tripled in value between 1848 and 1872. The iron and steel, chemical, and textile industries expanded enormously. Employment in various branches of trade increased rapidly; the number of clerks, for example, was at least doubled by the volume and complexity of business.

Such a boom in production was profitable to all classes, and labor, especially skilled labor, enjoyed a large increase in wages. Estimates vary as to the size of this increase, but money wages in the chief occupations certainly rose by almost 50 percent between 1850 and 1875. It is true that many trades and individual unskilled workers did not share the general prosperity, but even when the entire mass of labor is considered, an average rise of approximately a third in money wages was enjoyed. Prices also went up, yet there was a general improvement of perhaps 30 percent in the standard of living for all workers taken together. The increase in real and money wages was accompanied by a reduction in hours of labor, and even the Saturday half-holiday became more general. The laborer must therefore have found himself on a rising plane of prosperity and comfort. His position in 1870 was on the whole much happier than it had been a generation earlier.

Yet many of the old abuses lingered, so that once more commissions had "to inquire." The Commission on Housing of the Working Classes (1884–85) found that improvement in housing had been "enormous," as Lord Shaftesbury said, but that overcrowding was still bad, in some places worse than ever. It was aggravated by the demolition of many buildings for the sake of public health, for street improvements, and for railway construction. Over a period of ten years, at least a million persons had been forced to move because of railways and improvement schemes, but new housing had been provided for only 20,000. Although sanitation had also improved, investigation showed the continued existence of bad drainage, insufficient, contaminated water, and damp, ill-ventilated houses, filthy with vermin. People were still living miserably in cellars in spite of laws against the worst of such places. The truth was that some of the laws designed to improve sanitation had remained a dead letter from the moment of their passage. Even when action of some kind was taken, delays would occur and administrative complications would prevent any real progress. The usual efforts of timid officials to shift responsibility were common; enforcement of the law was often lax, partly because the number of building inspectors was too small and partly because members of boards who were supposed to correct sanitary conditions were owners or agents of the very properties they should have condemned.

The laborer's working conditions were also found to be as bad as or worse than ever in many trades. Unskilled workers not yet organized into unions or those working outside the influence of factory acts were found to be victims of "sweating." The House of Lords' Select Committee on the Sweating System (1889–90) applied this term to all unskilled or partly skilled labor whose wages would barely sustain life, whose hours were unreasonably long, and whose surroundings were injurious to health. Sweated work was carried on by small masters in obscure shops or by workers at home, so that no large employer could be held responsible for the conditions under which the work was done. Hours might be anything a sweater chose to make them, and wages no better than those which had aroused the anger of Kingsley in 1850.

The very nature of English reform was chiefly to blame for all these continued evils. The English mind moves slowly and unwillingly against what is ancient and established. Its tendency in the nineteenth century was to remedy evils only when they had been proved harmful. As Macaulay said, Parliament had always determined "never to innovate except when some grievance is felt; never to innovate except so far as to get rid of the grievance; never to lay down any proposition of wider extent than the particular case for which it is necessary to provide." There was little effort to anticipate or to prevent the growth of a problem. Legislation followed the line of least resistance, so that in some respects labor had been well protected and in others conditions were unchanged until they became so bad that action to improve them was forced.

But continued trouble was not all due to negligence or inadequate laws. After the period of prosperity which had reached its height in 1873, there occurred the so-called "Great Depression," which continued, with periods of alternate recovery and recession, for some twenty years. English agriculture suffered a long slump, which grew steadily worse after 1878 in the face of American competition. The virtual abandonment of farming as one of England's major activities affected the nation's prosperity as a whole. England had to become the world's workshop more completely than ever; yet even here, the commercial rivalry of France, Germany, and America, not to mention the tariff walls erected by these nations, caused England to lose ground. How this decline in prosperity affected the worker is clear from the Royal Commission's Report on the Depression of Trade and Industry (1886), and from the report of the Industrial Remuneration Conference (1885). The problem of unemployment in particular seems to have become so acute that riots, meetings, and marches of the unemployed took place. In 1885–86 even the unions reported an unemployment of 8 to 11 percent. Reliable figures for the mass of English labor are difficult to obtain; some estimates hold conservatively that 15 percent of all English labor was continually unemployed. Others assert that from 20 to 30 percent of all workers were at one time or another out of employment. Impoverished thousands of dock-workers stood at the gates clamoring for work, which was at all times irregular and brief. Full employment in the iron, coal, earthenware, and other trades became rare. Men were being hired for shorter periods in 1885; engagements were made by the quarter, the month, or the week. Some were even hired by the day or the hour, thus making work extremely irregular and offsetting any increase in wages.[3]

Thus, when prosperity was not at a high level, a large portion of the English people were destitute. The monumental study of

[3] Some writers feel that the term "Great Depression" is a misnomer and that conditions were on the whole not as bad as people thought they were. See especially W. W. Rostow, "Investment and the Great Depression," *The Economic History Review*, VIII (1938), 136–58; H. L. Beales, "The Great Depression in Industry and Trade," *ibid.*, V (1934–35), 65–75; G. D. H. Cole, *British Trade and Industry*, London, 1932, pp. 77–97.

Charles Booth, *Labour and Life of the People*, carried on over many years showed that in London alone 30 percent of the inhabitants lived at or below the level of bare subsistence. A million persons in London tried to exist on a family income of 20s. a week at best, and at worst lived in a state of actual want.

Under these circumstances it is not strange that a revival of socialism occurred after 1880, a revival in which William Morris played a conspicuous role. During the economic boom there was little interest in radical working-class movements. Even though Karl Marx lived and wrote in England, no real challenge was made to the existing order in a time when everyone was eager to get his share of prosperity and to enjoy the world's good things. Ruskin raised his voice in this period, but was not widely heard. A successful movement for political reform gave the working class new voting strength in 1867, which was further increased by the Act of 1884. This new political power did much to force both parties into social legislation and reform and to make concessions to popular demand.

But the requirements of William Morris went beyond all such changes within the existing scheme of things. The economic slump aroused great interest in the "condition of England" once more, and many publications went in for detailed descriptions of the life and work of the people. Along with the government reports already referred to, books and articles appeared dealing with the poor, the slums, and various social questions. One of the most sensational in its effect was *The Bitter Cry of Outcast London*, which outlined a lurid picture of the miseries of poverty and aroused great public excitement. Another best-seller was Henry George's *Progress and Poverty*, which saw ten London editions between 1881 and 1884; the author lectured in an atmosphere of religious revival. Before his doctrine of a single tax on land had been exploded, he was able to stir up new thoughts on inequality and socialism. In this atmosphere socialism became an important movement. There had been an effort in 1877 to identify socialism and Christianity once more; a group of churchmen set up the Guild of St. Matthew, which was not, however, a political movement. In 1881, under the leadership of H. M. Hyndman, the Democratic Federation was founded. Favoring land nationalization at first, this group became in 1884 an outright socialist body, calling itself the Social Democratic Federation. The Fabian Society had also arisen in 1884, for the purpose of spreading socialist ideas among existing political parties.

Meanwhile William Morris had joined the Democratic Federation in 1883, after having spoken and written from a humanitarian and aesthetic point of view for several years. In December, 1884, after much internal dissension, Morris and his friends left the then Social Democratic Federation and set up the Socialist League. Morris became treasurer of this group and editor of its organ, *The Commonweal*, in which he advocated a complete break with the social order of his time. Seeing the evils which still remained after all the efforts which had been made to remove them, Morris went beyond the remedies and even the hopes of any of the humanitarian men of letters preceding him. He became convinced that true human dignity could not be realized under the prevailing system, even though more was being done to improve the "condition of England" than ever before.

II. The Alleged Cause

I$_F$ THIS PICTURE of the "dumb toiling millions" is a fair one, the humanitarian poets were justified in turning aside from their own labors to denounce so great an affront to the dignity of man. Their analysis of the cause for this prevailing evil condemns especially certain economic and social theories called variously "laissez-faire," "supply and demand," "mammon worship," "the anarchy of competition," or as Carlyle and Morris were fond of calling it, "Devil take the hindmost." These are names for the single great failure of men to recognize their unity with all other men. Denial of this human oneness resulted practically in all the evils summarized under the "condition of England," itself a denial of the individual man.

We must again be on our guard lest we lose historical perspective. Long before English economists and social thinkers had built up "the dismal science," the eighteenth century was carrying out in actual practice much of what was later described in theory. Laissez-faire, supply and demand, freedom of contract, and individual competition were being practiced in anticipation of the works of Smith, Ricardo, and Malthus, which announced the theories that lay behind existing practice. It would be wrong therefore to assume that the nineteenth-century "condition of England" was caused by practices which followed from the writing of certain economic and social theorists. Rather, the theorists wrote to justify or to show the virtue of what was already being done.

Several things clarify this anticipation of theory by practice. The nature of eighteenth-century government in England emphasized the liberties of the subject. The courts laid great stress on protection of the special rights and freedom of the private citizen. A spirit of independence was fostered also in the separate units of local government. Very little central control was exercised over these smaller units. Men were not willing to entrust great power to the central government; in the century following Locke the powers of the state were so divided that the separate branches checked and balanced one another. A larger freedom of action resulted from such a diffusion of power. In matters of commerce and trade, in the relationship between worker and employer and their contracts, the tendency was toward laissez-faire long before Adam Smith arose to tell everyone that the let-alone principle was best. The system of independent local government was cheap, and cheap government was an aid to economic expansion. Control over commerce and industry gradually ceased, and little was done to prevent traders from conducting business as they pleased. Previous laws as to wages and other restrictive acts were not enforced. Professor Conyers Read has said that "probably at no time in the whole history of England was the national attitude toward the laboring class so heartless and inhuman as it was in the first half of the eighteenth century; at no time were the interests engaged in exploiting him so completely in control of every possible avenue of escape for him." [1] The ruling classes were doing nothing about the problems of the new economic expansion, when along came the theoretical economists to announce that doing nothing was after all the best thing to do. They defined and justified policies which had been in the air for almost a century. The evils against which humanitarians protested in the nineteenth century would therefore have arisen as a result of long-established or growing practice, even though the "dismal science" had never been devised. Humanitarian literature would have been written just the same, so long as there was evil in the state. Yet, since social and economic thinkers did spin their theories and men of letters did blame the attitudes fostered by these theories for the "condition of England," we shall examine briefly what these ideas were. There can be no pretense of a complete analysis of classical economics. We shall deal only with those principles directly touching the laborer and his personal fate, which were, after all, the main concerns of the humanitarian.

[1] Conyers Read, "Mercantilism: the Old English Pattern of a Controlled Economy," in *The Constitution Reconsidered*, New York, 1938, pp. 72–73.

A last word of caution so that we may avoid one more, perhaps minor, error. It must not be assumed that the classical economists were as arbitrary in their preaching as they were understood to be. Many of the qualifications and exceptions which they originally insisted on were ignored by persons who found it useful to believe in a ruthless economy. The following analysis should therefore be thought of as the special interpretation of economics by certain powerful classes who profited from it. As Mr. and Mrs. Hammond have pointed out, "Neither Malthus nor Ricardo really taught the dogmatic despair which was generally received as the lesson of their philosophies . . . their ideas when adopted by other minds, hardened into a rigid and inexorable theory from which both of them would have shrunk." [2] With these reservations in mind, we may inquire what the ideas were whose application was alleged to have caused the hardships of the laboring classes. It will be convenient to speak of these principles as the "laws" of self-interest, of free competition, of supply and demand as applied to labor, of wages, and of population.

The law of self-interest assumes that selfishness is the basic motive in all human action. It is the nature of man to think first of himself, of his own profit, security, and preservation. This natural instinct teaches every person what is best for his own welfare. If allowed to pursue his own personal ends and satisfactions, he will, as a rational being, do what is best for his own welfare. Now the community or society is composed of individual members, and the interest of the community as a whole is simply the sum of the interests of all the members who compose it. One cannot talk of the welfare of the community apart from the welfare of its individual members. Therefore if individuals are left alone to seek their own interest, they will inevitably preserve not only their own welfare but that of the whole community as well. The miraculous operation of this law of self-interest is such that although each

[2] J. L. Hammond and Barbara Hammond, *The Town Labourer*, London, 1920, p. 204. For the opinion that the importance and influence of laissez-faire has been exaggerated and that its chief theorists were not as doctrinaire as some believed, see E. L. Woodward, *The Age of Reform*, Oxford, 1938, pp. 14-15, 427-28.

person thinks only of his own gain, he actually promotes the good of society as a whole. As Adam Smith pointed out, each person in pursuing his own aims is "led by an invisible hand to promote an end which was no part of his intention." So long as he does not interfere with the right of other men to seek their own interest in their own way, he is free to think and act solely for his own benefit.

The law of free competition naturally follows from this. If when pursuing their own interest, men inevitably contribute to the good of society, whether they intend to do so or not, they should be left alone by their governments. As Macaulay insisted, there is no reason for believing that governments are better able to lead people in the right way than the people are to fall into the right way by themselves. As a rule, most things are done worse by the interference of government than by the persons most interested when left to themselves. Every coercive law, as Bentham declared, has one reason against it which alone is sufficient to render it suspect, namely, restriction of liberty. Let those who propose coercive laws therefore have very cogent and specific reasons for them—reasons stronger than the evil that is inherent in every law.

The government then should mind its own business, which is principally to protect society from violence and invasion, to administer justice to each individual, to preserve law and order, to maintain the rights and security of property. Adam Smith includes popular education as well as the erection and maintenance of certain public works.

The law of competition among individuals should therefore have complete sway. Each person must have freedom to use his powers up to the limits fixed by a similar freedom for others. Every restriction of this liberty is an evil and every extension of it operates for the ultimate good of the community. As John Stuart Mill observed, "to be protected against competition is to be protected in idleness, in mental dullness; to be saved the necessity of being as active and as intelligent as other people." If one is less energetic, less active and less intelligent than other people, it follows from the demands of the competitive struggle that one will go down to defeat, because one is essentially faulty. According to Herbert

Spencer, the stern discipline of nature operates also in the life of man. The warfare is pitiless for the individual in order that it may be kind to society as a whole. It seems hard that in spite of intense labor the poor artisan should starve; it seems hard that when he is incapacitated by illness and cannot compete with his stronger fellows, he must endure privation and death; it seems hard that his widow and orphans should be left alone to struggle for their lives. "The poverty of the incapable, the distresses that come upon the imprudent, the starvation of the idle, and those shoulderings aside of the weak by the strong, which leave so many 'in shallows and in miseries,' are the decrees of a large far-seeing benevolence." Spencer admits social evils, yet he insists that "the process *must* be undergone, and the sufferings *must* be endured. No power on earth, no cunningly devised laws of statesmen, no world-rectifying schemes of the humane, no communist panaceas, no reforms that men ever did broach or ever will broach, can diminish them one jot."

This is the law by which the fittest only survive; it follows from this that indiscriminate charity from one individual to another, as well as a too-generous state distribution of relief to the weak and the unfit will eventually harm society. Superior individuals may give help to the worthy who have, perhaps, been unlucky, but such individual assistance should not go so far as to aid the multiplication of the unfit. Not only will indiscriminate kindness cause the spread of organized professional beggary but it will actually increase suffering rather than diminish it. Those worst fitted for life will be able to increase their numbers; the reckless and incompetent will be encouraged, but able, provident individuals will be discouraged because of the added difficulty of keeping their families. Persons who are thus foolishly kind to the weak and unhealthy are "sigh-wise and groan-foolish"; they simply prevent the purification of society which would normally go on, and they allow mankind to be vitiated by the stupid and incompetent.

Much the same result follows from too much benevolence by the state itself. The state as a whole is not a family, and that society which interferes with the operation of natural laws is facing disaster. It is essentially wrong to tax the property of one man in order to give benefits for nothing to another man, thus depriving the better and stronger of what is rightfully his. Malthus was among the first to say that poor laws weaken the spirit of independence in men. Although it may seem hard in special cases, he insisted that nonetheless "dependent poverty ought to be held disgraceful." The poor should not be encouraged to suppose that no matter what their improvidence or weakness may be, a parish provision will be in store for them. If they are always certain of assistance, they will marry and reproduce themselves and so increase the number of the poor who will eventually need help, not to mention those who will add to competition in the labor market. Relief should therefore be made as difficult and as unpleasant as possible, so that the poor will ask for it only as a final alternative to starvation.

If there is to be a minimum of charity by well-meaning persons and by the state, it follows that the only help for the impoverished worker must come from himself. Richard Cobden bluntly announced that the people should trust to themselves alone for working out their own happiness. "Look not to Parliament, look only to yourselves," was Cobden's simple advice. If anyone wishes to aid another man, therefore, the only salutary aids must be those to self-help; that charity is best which helps men to help themselves.

It is difficult to separate the law of supply and demand in the case of the laborer from the laws of wages and of population, since all three are a part of the same problem which faces the worker in his struggle for existence. He must sell his labor just as if it were any other commodity, and its price, or his wages, must be determined by the relation between the supply of persons offering to work and the amount of work to be done. The supply of persons offering themselves in the market in turn is related to the law of population, which contains within itself a warning to the laboring classes that they must keep down their numbers. We may, however, examine the law of supply and demand to show the special difficulties which handicap the laborer in selling his commodity, which is himself.

According to this law, the supply of a given commodity and the demand for it tend to seek an equilibrium. If producers of a cer-

tain thing have underestimated the required supply, they will begin
to receive a higher price for it than is necessary to repay them adequately; that is, than is necessary to cover the cost of its production
and to insure a fair profit. The rising price encourages the production of a larger supply, which supply will increase until there is
enough to meet the demand. When this is true, the price will fall.
On the other hand, if producers have overestimated the required
supply, the price will begin to fall, because there is more than
enough of the commodity to meet the demand. This will discourage production until the supply falls so low that its price rises
once more. Thus, the relationship between the supply of a given
thing and the demand for it will always move toward a point
where the supply is just enough to equal the demand.

This same rule seemed to apply to human beings as well. "The
demand for men," says Adam Smith, "necessarily regulates the production of men; quickens it when it goes on too slowly, and stops
it when it advances too far." This rule is applied with special force
to the laborer, who, like other men entering the market, has a certain thing to sell. But what the laborer sells is unlike what any other
dealer in commodities has to offer. He sells his own power to work,
which is inseparable from his own person; in short, he sells himself.
He and his power to work are commodities whose price is governed by the law of supply and demand. The price obtained by the
single worker falls or rises according to the ratio between the
number of laborers and the number of jobs that are open. The relationship between the employer and the worker then becomes
much the same as that between the buyer and the seller of any
other commodity.

Such was the theory, but the laborer found that in selling his
special commodity, he faced certain handicaps. For one thing he
found that in order to live he had to sell his labor at any price;
it was all he had to sell, and so while isolated and unorganized he
had to be satisfied with any labor stipulations which the man buying his labor cared to impose. His employer then decided where
the laborer should work, what he should do, and how much he
was to be paid for it. Further, unlike the seller of other commodi-

ties, isolated laborers could not diminish the supply of labor quickly when the demand for labor fell. If at any time the demand for labor sinks, more laborers instead of fewer become available for work, because many lose their places. A smaller number than ever can find work, and in order to belong to this small number a single worker must work for less than the others and for longer hours. Hence the indignation which the law of supply and demand aroused among the humanitarians of the nineteenth century. The price of labor, that is wages, fell as those being thrown out of work constantly offered more and more labor for less and less. The employer of labor therefore obtained great control over the lives of those working for him. They were dependent upon him, since they were inseparable from the thing they sold; their entire existence in all of its aspects was regulated by their employer, for when they sold their labor into his hands, they sold themselves.

We are led now to the law of wages, containing further gloomy implications of the law of supply and demand. "Like all other contracts," Ricardo insisted, "wages should be left to the fair and free competition of the market, and should never be controlled by the interference of the legislature." If this rule obtains, then wages are governed by the ratio of the supply of laborers to the demand for them. As Ricardo simply states, "Labour is dear when it is scarce, and cheap when it is plentiful." To decide the effect of this upon the condition of the laborer, we must glance at the theory of the wages fund and at the "iron law" of wages.

The concept of a wages fund was widely held between 1820 and 1870. The belief was that at any given time only a certain fixed proportion of a nation's capital can be available for wages. Each capitalist has a definite sum which he invests in the purchase of labor, a sum which is the nation's circulating wealth as distinguished from what is fixed. Thus, the amount that all the laborers of the nation could earn at any time was stationary and confined to definite limits. The conclusion was held to be obvious: under competition, wages cannot possibly be affected by anything except the relation between the number of workers and the amount of the wages fund. Since this is true, any efforts by the working class to gain better terms from their employers through trade unions or other means, were certain to fail in themselves, or if successful, would only benefit one class of workers at the expense of all the rest. In order to arrive at the wages of each laborer, one simply divided the amount of the wages fund by the number of workers among whom it was distributed. If the number fell, each man's wage rose. If the number increased, each man's wages fell. But how low did they fall? What was the point below which the laborer's wages could not go?

This question is answered by the "iron law" of wages. Ricardo said that the price of a thing tends always to hover around the cost of its production. Since labor is also a commodity, it, too, is subject to the laws of price and cost of production. The price of labor will also tend to hover around the cost of its production, which is simply the amount needed to keep the laborer and his family alive and to insure the propagation of the species. Wages cannot permanently rise above this average, because if they do, the easier and better condition of the worker will cause an increase in the laboring population and in the supply of labor. This would again lower wages, which in turn cannot permanently fall below what is needed to keep the laborer and his family alive, because if they do, starvation and disease would so diminish the number of laborers that wages would rise once more as the supply of workers fell.

The moral of these doctrines for the laborer was held to be inescapable. He alone could do anything permanently to help himself, by facing the implications of supply and demand and by confessing finally the truth of the law of population. This law held, as Malthus put it, "the constant tendency of all animated life to increase beyond the nourishment prepared for it." Malthus saw perpetual effort in the population of most states to increase beyond the means of subsistence, with the result that the lower classes of society were subjected to distress with little hope of any permanent improvement in their condition. While it was true that population was somewhat retarded by "vice and misery," the only permanently effectual check on population must come through prudence and restraint on the part of the laborers themselves. Early and improvident marriages must be discouraged. There must be fewer laborers and fewer, smaller families. The worker must be made to understand that his class depends for well-being upon its own common sense. The famous analogy of Malthus makes this clear. At the mighty feast of nature there are only a certain number of places. If a man comes into the world and finds that his parents can't support him and learns that society has no work for him, he is simply one too many at the table; there is no room for him and he has no right to expect any food. If some of the other guests at nature's table get up to make room for him, others will intrude, demanding the same favor. Soon there will be many more asking admission than nature can possibly feed; scarcity and hunger result for those who are superfluous. Therefore it is best for men to obey the orders of nature, mistress of the feast, who wishes that all her guests should have plenty and therefore humanely refuses to admit new visitors when her table is already full.

Thus, all indications of the unvarying laws governing the worker's condition are that outside of himself he can find no permanent help. It is this dismal picture of the fate of the common man which inspired the humanitarians to denounce these doctrines as the cause of the "condition of England." Indeed, many who held these notions did not deny the "condition of England," but they asserted that the evils could not be helped. There was no escape from the law of supply and demand; the poor must do as all other sellers of a commodity must do, adapt the supply of what they have to sell to the demand for it; in short, they must control their numbers. But such a solution was not satisfactory to the humanitarians. It ignored the value of the individual man as an end in himself; it denied the entire concept of the oneness of mankind. We have now to read their criticism based upon these two principles.

We should pause here a moment for a clearer definition of terms. "Humanitarian" is, perhaps, misleading when applied to the writers under discussion, because as a group they did not actually lead movements for the suppression of cruelty, nor did they campaign in any organized way for humane behavior. Matthew Arnold, for instance, the most intelligent and useful of them all, is not a "human-itarian" in the sense of working publicly for social improvement after the manner of Lord Shaftesbury or Octavia Hill. Nonetheless he, along with those who shared his general attitude, was humani-tarian in aim, since he was deeply moved by the miseries of the people and did his best to explain how to relieve them. If the term "humanitarian" can apply to men who were angry and sorrowful over human suffering and tried to show how life could be improved if men would elevate themselves, then Arnold and his fellows are humanitarians. It is true that they offered many practical schemes, but this is not why it is useful for us to study them. We do not need to have them tell us how to improve sanitation among the poor. Our plumbing is by now superb. But we do need to be told by them how important it is to improve ourselves.

We ought also to decide at this point what these men believed about human nature, since they are so much concerned with the "dignity of man." Their final optimism and their enthusiastic praise of human possibilities may sound like a sentimental Rousseauism. But if they believe in human goodness and in the coming of better things for men, they are not so sentimental as to say without quali-fication that man is good and that his corruption is due only to his environment. They recognize that man is a mixture of good and bad. If they think that good has a chance to conquer, it is not be-cause they are blind to the opposition. In fact, they are so conscious of both good and evil in human nature, that they seem to believe in two separate natures or selves, as if man were divided really into halves and were a kind of stage on which these two selves fought a perpetual conflict. It would be a mistake to read this literally. Rather, this should be considered literary language used in order to clarify or to dramatize man's effort to become better than he is. Actually, the view of human nature adapted by these men re-sembles that of Kant in the *Philosophical Theory of Religion*. Kant would not trouble himself to prove anything so obvious as the cor-rupt propensity in man; there it is before us: "the multitude of crying examples . . . a long melancholy litany of complaints of humanity," of falsehood, hatred, malice, hypocrisy, selfish materi-

alism, and meanness. Yet when every admission is made, Kant believes that man is not so much naturally bad as perverse in his
disposition. Human nature is weak; it does not follow the right
principles because of this weakness, not because it prefers what
is bad for the sake of badness. On the contrary, "there is . . . one
thing in our soul which . . . we cannot cease to regard with the
highest astonishment . . . and that is the original moral capacity
in us generally." We may even say that man is created good. This
means, however, that man is created for good, that his original
constitution is good, that he is intended for and has a capacity to
achieve, goodness. Kant warns, nonetheless, that "this does not
make the man himself good, but according as he does or does not
adopt into his maxim the springs which the constitution contains
(which must be left altogether to his own free choice), he makes
himself become good or bad." Kant is certain that "a germ of good
has remained in its complete purity which could not be destroyed
or corrupted." It is within every man's power to nourish and to
develop this germ until he achieves goodness and rejects badness.
Kant insists that this must be done within every man by every man
himself; like St. Paul and his disciple Arnold, Kant requires an
inner revolution, "a kind of new birth, as it were by a new creation . . . and a change of heart." Yet how can this restoration by
a man's own strength be achieved in view of the corruption of
man for everything good? Kant admits that we cannot discern
how this paradox is to be resolved, but that its resolution must be
possible because of the voice of duty within us. In spite of all that
man is guilty of, "the command 'we *ought* to become better men,'
resounds with undiminished force in our soul." If the moral law
commands that we must be better, it follows that we can be better.
From this results the struggle between our " 'two selves,' " as the
humanitarians phrased it. Kant explained the struggle by saying
"that in the moral cultivation of the moral capacity for good created in us, we cannot begin from a natural state of innocence, but
must start from the supposition of a depravity of the elective will
in assuming maxims that are contrary to the original moral capacity, and, since the propensity thereto is ineradicable, with an

unceasing effort against it." This effort can be successful; a man is able to arrive by his own strength at goodness, simply because he commands himself to do so. Duty commands it, says Kant, "and duty commands nothing that is not practicable for us." The fact that men are forever telling themselves that they must be good shows that they have the capacity to be good. Otherwise why should they feel guilty when they behave badly? It is not to be supposed that men set themselves an impossible task of virtue in violation of their own nature and then accuse themselves for not having performed what was never possible to begin with.

The writers now to be studied have taken a similar view of human nature. They believe that men can improve the world in which they live, if they first improve themselves. They see that men's actions are often bad, yet they see also that men are able to elevate themselves, to become better than they have been; all is not lost if men will respond to the voice within their souls and will struggle to obey it. Since this voice is the same for all men because they are men, every single individual has it in him to become better than he is; he must be recognized then as precious and dignified.

III. Coleridge

> Men . . . ought to be weighed not counted.
> Their worth ought to be the final estimate
> of their value.—Coleridge, *Second Lay Ser-*
> *mon.*

It is hard for a modern reader to understand how J. S. Mill could open his essay on Coleridge as follows: "The name of Coleridge is one of the few English names of our time which are likely to be oftener pronounced, and to become symbolical of more important things, in proportion as the inward workings of the age manifest themselves more and more in outward facts. . . . No one has contributed more to shape the opinions of those among its younger men, who can be said to have opinions at all." The only comparable influence is that of Bentham, and in writing of the great utilitarian in 1838, Mill also praises Coleridge as a teacher of teachers. Most Englishmen of any intellectual importance are held to have learned how to think from either Bentham or Coleridge. "There is already scarcely a publication of any consequence, addressed to the educated classes, which, if these persons had not existed, would not have been different from what it is." In short, these are "the two great seminal minds of England in their age," and every Englishman is by implication either a Coleridgian or a Benthamite.

Coleridge has long ago ceased to be so influential, yet for the purposes of this history Mill's estimate may be allowed to stand. If we accept his twofold division of thinking men, the writers under consideration here are Coleridgians. Coleridge was conservative and religious, as William Morris could never be, yet Morris is his remote but unmistakable descendant. Though Coleridge merely hinted at what was more fully developed by those who came after him, he stands appropriately at our beginning.

Writing to Thomas Poole in 1801, Coleridge expresses his humane sympathy:

Oh, for a Lodge in a land where human life was an end to which labor was only a means, instead of being, as it is here, a mere means of carrying on labour. I am oppressed at times with a true heart-gnawing melancholy when I contemplate the state of my poor oppressed country. God knows, it is as much as I can do to put meat and bread on my own table, and hourly some poor starving wretch comes to my door to put in his claim for part of it.

Coleridge was touched by sight of "the wretched Many," removed from all that "softens or ennobles Man," deprived of knowledge and of the plenty of life. He was among the first to point out the sad condition of children working in factories and to insist that their labor would result in diminished vigor and future ill-health. To him their "condition is an abomination which has weighed upon my feelings from earliest manhood, I having been indeed an eye-witness of the direful effects." It seemed grotesque that such children should be called "free," when their labor was extorted from the poverty of parents. If the labor were indeed free, such a contract would amount to near suicide by the poor and to manslaughter, or as Coleridge termed it in a letter to Crabb Robinson, "*soul-murder* on the part of the rich." Coleridge's appeal for these "poor little children" is fine and moving; it is an appeal made to "conscience and to common sense," to the sympathy which men must have for a child forced, against all its natural instincts, to continue in a stifling atmosphere where it might be found, long after the tenth hour, still at work.

But the parents were to be pitied equally with the children. They suffered under a designation which seems greatly to have irritated Coleridge; he wonders whether despite the tremendous increase in English commerce, the nation as a whole is any happier, whether the condition of the lower classes has not actually deteriorated and whether a prosperity is genuine "in which healthy labourers are commonly styled 'the labouring poor.'" The wealth of England may have trebled, but what of the quality of human life? Coleridge finds that too high a price has been paid and that "the machinery of the wealth of the nation" is made up "of the wretchedness, disease, and depravity of those who should constitute the wealth of the nation!" In the country, England's peasantry sinks into pauperism as the land itself falls subject to commercial exploitation. The peasant becomes a dependent laborer at the mercy of his landlord, who operates tremendous farms on a business basis. There results the extinction of the one thing which in Coleridge's opinion distinguishes the free man from the slave, that is, hope. In order to increase their pittances, parents let their children out to factories, and at the earliest opportunity the young escape into towns and cities. Here they are likely to become the victims of an exploitation which is in many ways similar to the hated slave trade itself. They must labor to produce and then to send away the comforts which they themselves want in order "to procure idle superfluities for their masters." They are fortunate to have this privilege, for even in the best of times there is fluctuation in trade causing great individual distress, unemployment, and pauperism made worse by the dissipation and improvidence of a weak, demoralized human nature.

Coleridge finds, then, that the lower classes of men are "brutalized by ignorance and rendered desperate by want," with the government strangely indifferent to their welfare. A dangerously bitter resentment has arisen.

The poor infant born in an English or Irish hovel breathes indeed the air and partakes of the light of Heaven; but of its other bounties he is disinherited. The powers of intellect are given him in vain: to make him work like a brute beast he is kept as ignorant as a brute beast. It is not possible that this despised and oppressed man should behold the rich and idle without malignant envy. And if in the bitter cravings of hunger . . . the poor wretch rush from despair into guilt, then the government indeed assumes the right of punishment though it had neglected the duty of instruction, and hangs the victim for crimes, to which its own wide-wasting follies and its own most sinful omissions had supplied the cause and the temptation.

Coleridge here emphasizes what to him was the most tragic element in the sad condition of the people—their ignorance and "general want of intellect." A society based upon an ignorant populace is nothing but a house of cards, and Coleridge lived in constant fear of a social revolution.

The poet's true sense of the value of every human life becomes more clear when he analyzes the cause of existing evils. We find him denouncing violently the dominant system of political economy and its practical result, the spirit of trade and commerce. Like most of the humanitarian men of letters who followed him and shared his point of view, Coleridge did not know much about economics except that he did not like what was accepted under that heading in his time. In fairness to Mill's critical powers, his opinion of Coleridge as an economist should be included here. Later in the essay on Coleridge, Mill says that in "political economy . . . he writes like an arrant driveller; and it would have been well for his reputation, had he never meddled with the subject." Coleridge admits that he knows only "too well the complexity of all questions relative to political economy." No two professors of this science seem able to understand each other. Coleridge has often been present among merchants and manufacturers who finally had to confess "that the matter was beyond their comprehension. . . . It was avowed that to arrive at any understanding of these matters requires a mind gigantic in its comprehension, and microscopic in its accuracy of detail." Actually the man of letters did not ignore economics because it was too deep for him, but rather because it seemed pointless. What mattered was that men should realize fully their highest human powers and should be happy as men. Abstract economics was relevant only in so far as it affected, for good or evil, this desirable end. Coleridge and those who came after him denounced political economy because it seemed to influence the happiness of men for evil and because it seemed to lack what men of humane feeling insisted that it should possess—some ethical or moral sense and concern for the quality of human life. And so Coleridge inveighs against "the new blasphemy," the "presumption, temerity, and hardness of heart in political economy." It is largely "solemn humbug." What there is of truth in it can be found in the moral and religious principles of any good man, and is constantly being acted upon anyway by everyone with common sense. Among the individual economists against whom Coleridge speaks was Adam Smith, but he was even more violently opposed to Malthus. The doctrine of population is a "monstrous practical sophism," whose influence Coleridge deplores.

I do not believe that all the heresies and sects and factions which the ignorance and the weakness and the wickedness of man have ever given birth to, were altogther so disgraceful to man as a Christian, a philosopher, a statesman, or citizen, as this abominable tenet . . . it is so vicious a tenet, so flattering to the cruelty, the avarice, and sordid selfishness of most men, that I hardly know what to think of the result.

It was this seeming appeal to the lowest, not the highest, powers of man that made the prevailing economy unacceptable to Coleridge. There was a tendency to think only of what was immediately expedient, to suppress the better nature of man. There was talk of making articles cheaper and selling more of them in the market, yet no one inquired as to the human consequences involved. Coleridge wonders whether the cheapened article is not "tolerably dear" after all. If "you have demoralized thousands of your fellow countrymen, and have sown discontent between one class of society and another . . . is not its real price enhanced to every Christian and patriot a hundred-fold?"

Now the practical result of this political economy was to make England an enterprising commercial nation. Coleridge was willing to admit that such enterprise had many valuable purposes; yet it had flourished too long without discipline. Men of trade wanted to levy duties and "then grant their only request—'Let us alone!'" In time this led to a dominance of the spirit of trade, which simply meant that Englishmen began to look at everything through the market. What should have been only a means to an end, subservient to "nobler and more inherent blessings," was permitted to become an end in itself, until England began to barter freedom "and the poor man's life for gold, as at a market!" The consequences were not far to seek. There was lost a law of God which held that cultivation of the earth must be connected indissolubly "with the maintenance and watchful labor of man." The possession of land had meant commensurate duties to those who tilled it. But the need for profit recognized no such duties and so the land was absorbed into large holdings, the small holder was forced into dependence, the lowest practicable wages were paid, and machinery was substituted for human labor whenever it was cheaper to do so. For Coleridge, this was "the groundwork of our calamity." He was among the first to see the paradox of want in the midst of plenty. He saw England fallen into a state so remote from the simplicity of nature as almost to have "deprived Heaven itself of the power of blessing us," a condition in which "without absurdity, a superabundant harvest can be complained of as an evil, and the recurrence of the same a ruinous calamity." To care for those in need, a system of poor laws was set up whose pernicious tendency Coleridge held it impossible to exaggerate. In the agricultural districts three-fourths of the poor rates were paid to "healthy, robust, and (O sorrow and shame!) industrious, hard-working paupers. This enormous mischief is undeniably the offspring of the commercial system," a system which was willing to pay poor-rates as the price of having enough people always at hand for labor. Ideally the doctrine held that population should be curbed by an appeal to men's prudence, their desire for independence and security. Yet it became possible to increase enormously the national wealth and to make many men rich if vast crowds of people could be brought into being who would be concentrated in great masses and employed in direct violation of their human dignity "as parts of a mighty system of machinery." In prosperous times these people could be maintained. But if something should go wrong—and this was likely to occur at any time, says Coleridge—then "the principals are to shift for themselves, and leave the disposal of the . . . multitude, now unemployed and useless, to the mercy of the community, and the solicitude of the State; or else to famine, violence, and the vengeance of the laws!" Coleridge was willing to admit all the ostensible good that commerce had done for England.

[But, has it] given us a truer insight into our duties, or tended to revive and sustain in us the better feelings of our nature? No! no! when I consider what the consequences have been, when I consider that whole districts of men . . . are now little less than brutes in their lives, and something worse than brutes in their instincts, I could almost wish that the manufacturing districts were swallowed up as Sodom and Gomorrah.

The essential error of the spirit of commerce lay, therefore, in its misconception of the value of man. It confused men with things and treated them as if they were a commodity. "Men, I still think, ought to be weighed not counted. Their worth ought to be the final estimate of their value." But the tradesman says:

Am I disposing of a bale of goods? The man whom I most love and esteem must yield to the stranger that outbids him. . . . I seek wealth for the sake of freeing myself more and more from the necessity of taking trouble in order to attain it. The personal worth of those, whom I benefit in the course of the process, or whether the persons are really benefited or no, is no concern of mine. The market and the shop are open to all.

Thus, the failure of the spirit of trade to be concerned over the worth of men or to distinguish between men and things shows its essential fallacy as a national force. Coleridge solemnly insists that "on the distinction between things and persons all law human and divine is grounded. It consists in this: that the former may be used as mere means; but the latter must not be employed as the means to an end without directly or indirectly sharing in that end." This definition of the meaning of human dignity has yet to be improved upon. Coleridge's point may be illustrated by his objection to the famous economic adage that things tend to find their level in spite of occasional fluctuations. Coleridge agrees that things find their level, but human beings do not, because they are not things, but creatures of body, mind, and spirit. Man does not find his level, either in body or in soul. Coleridge speaks with sympathy of the children he has seen "during the heat of the dog days, each with its little shoulders up to its ears, and its chest pinched inward, the very habit and fixtures, as it were, that had been impressed on their frames by the former ill-fed, ill-clothed, and unfuelled winters." Even granting that plenty has returned after a calamitous season of unemployment and want, Coleridge is certain that health and temperance and habits of decent industry or self-respect and good manners are not so easily recovered.

"Alas!" the poet mourns, "it is easy to see the evil; but to imagine a remedy is difficult in exact proportion to the experience and good sense of the seeker." Coleridge believed that England could not go on so strangely indifferent to the human consequences of its way of life. There must be a concern for the welfare of men both by the government itself and by those individuals or classes best able to improve the quality of the life of the common man. In his early maturity, Coleridge had no illusions as to the "talismanic influence" of governments over the virtue and happiness of man, since governments were in a sense "more the effect than the cause of what we are." He tells his brother George that no matter what the form of government, rulers have always shown that "they are as bad as they dare to be." Nonetheless, if those who govern will think first of the well-being of the people and only then of wealth and revenue, immense improvement will follow. Coleridge is not afraid lest interference with the economic doctrine of free labor should ruin the nation's commerce or violate its constitution. On the contrary, the most prosperous countries are those which govern themselves in clear opposition to the doctrines of classical economy, and English law itself recognizes that the welfare of the whole is paramount and that the rights of individuals must be curbed when they are injurious to the community.

The state should therefore have certain clearly defined ends. Here Coleridge shows again his deeply rooted concern for the happiness of man and the preciousness of his human powers. He considers that the state has an essential property which it must protect from injury and trespass. This property is "the health, strength, honesty and filial love of its children." Negatively, of course, the state must maintain its own safety and must protect the persons, property, and freedom of all its members. Assuming that these ends have been attained, the state should first of all make it more easy for each individual to get the means of subsistence. The state should then see to it that beyond these mere necessaries of life, every person receives "a share of the comforts and conveniences which humanize and ennoble his nature." Every person should likewise be assured of "the power of perfecting himself in his own branch of industry by having those things which he needs provided for him by others . . . the tools and raw or manufactured materials necessary for his own employment being included."

More important still the state must secure to each of its members the hope of bettering his own condition and that of his children. Coleridge was most emphatic on this point, because God had distinguished man "from the brute that perishes by making hope an instinct of his nature, and an indispensable condition of his moral and intellectual progression." Since a natural instinct is actually a right, so long as it can be gratified without interfering with the equal rights of others, the lower ranks of society must be encouraged to hope that the worthiest among them will be drawn up into the higher classes. The humblest cottage mother may dream of her child's future and may think to herself that he will become a rich merchant or a bishop or a judge. Coleridge admits that the prizes are few and rare, but "the hope is universal, and perhaps occasions more happiness than even its fulfilment." Lastly, Coleridge insists, in a striking anticipation of the very words of Matthew Arnold, that the state must secure to every subject "the harmonious development of those qualities and faculties that characterize our humanity." These are the faculties of man's rational and moral being, the things which raise the civilized human being above the savage and the brute. The state must therefore insure instruction to all; men must be given knowledge to increase their intellectual powers; they must learn their essential duties and dignities as free men. Under no circumstances may the state permit "the debasement and mutual disfranchisement of any class of the community," but every person must have a chance for knowledge and improvement. Most important of all, there must be instruction in morality and religion. Coleridge was enthusiastic over the educational system of the Reverend Andrew Bell, who had devised a scheme of having the younger children taught by the more advanced students. Coleridge considered this plan as "an especial gift of Providence to the human race," which he could never be weary of praising "while my heart retains any spark of regard for human nature, or of reverence for human virtue." When knowledge had thus overcome the ignorance of all, and religion had made vice impossible, every desirable end would stand accomplished and the state might rest after the performance of its entire duty.

Meanwhile, the common welfare may be advanced by non-governmental agencies. What of the aristocracy and the gentry, those who, because of superior rank and wealth, are best able to help others and to raise the level of human life? Coleridge thought of these classes as bearing a kind of feudal obligation toward the less fortunate. One of his principles was that "there are no rights whatever without corresponding duties." No man has a right to think only of himself, to expect benefits from society without assuming duties as well. The landowner, for example, should subordinate the marketable produce of his estate to a prosperous and healthy peasantry which will be loyal and cheerfully industrious. Let the estate be looked upon as an office of trust, with the tenants as natural clients and dependents. So also, the master manufacturer should think of his laborers as part of his family. He should make certain that they are never without the chief articles of consumption in return for their labor, rather than make a mere payment of money which may or may not be adequate. But if, on the other hand, the powerful classes are indifferent to their duties of guidance and care, they must not expect loyalty in return. If they ignore the claims of the common man, he is then free to say that he has no duties toward them; he may even cry out one day, in his consequent desperation, "this pistol shall put me in possession of your wealth."

It is obvious that in his maturity Coleridge was anti-democratic. He believed in an aristocracy, in respect for rank and ancestry and the maintenance of certain fixed gradations of society. He was able in the course of time to look back upon his early communistic scheme of pantisocracy, which was to end selfishness by abolishing property, as an emotional outburst, a harmless means of working off young energy, after which he and Southey "alighted on the firm ground of common sense from the gradually exhausted balloon of youthful enthusiasm." Of Southey's fervent play *Wat Tyler* Coleridge could say when it was pirated in 1817, that it was "a schoolboy's arrow," yet of possible danger, for all its absurdities.

His mature conviction was that unequal distribution of property was inevitable and that all human laws were somehow related to such inequality. He came to believe "that that government was the best, in which the power or political influence of the individual was in proportion to his property," although he desired a free circulation of property, not an accumulation of it in great masses. In any event, property and the privileges it bestowed were to be used conscientiously, and every effort was to be made to alleviate the evils which Coleridge admitted were inseparable from the class system. He was too close to the French Revolution not to be impatient with "the rage of innovation, and the scorn and hatred of all ancient establishments." He was certain that the overbalance of trade and of the commercial spirit should be counteracted not only by the progress of intellect and religion but also by a renewal of the ancient feeling or rank and ancestry. Thus, the middle classes, important and respectable as they were, might have their mere wealth balanced in society by reverence for ancient families. Yet Coleridge was not satisfied with the behavior of the existing aristocracy. The deterioration of the lower classes must be charged in large part to an indifferent gentry, who must themselves undergo an extreme intellectual and moral improvement if they are to lead their social inferiors toward a better life.

But Coleridge expected fully as much from human kindness. A government has its special ends and duties; the privileged classes have their obligations to society; but men have a duty toward other men which proceeds from their common humanity. Coleridge believed that for anyone who desired to solve existing social problems, "benevolence and kindly feelings towards all that has life, must precede intelligence and mental activity." Two years before his death, when so much was expected from the changes in Parliament, Coleridge could remark that he had no faith in "Act of Parliament reform. All the great . . . things that have been achieved in the world have been so achieved by individuals, working from the instinct of genius or of goodness."

Coleridge was not satisfied with the mere machinery of charity, the giving of a few pounds which might actually do harm if, as was often the case, it made the poor improvident. Some persons bestirred themselves, only to remove those evils which were a personal annoyance. These philanthropists cared nothing for any dunghill which was not directly beneath their parlor windows. Others were denounced by Coleridge as "self elected protectors of the poor," who sought "the delight of beholding in printed reports and circular letters their own names and busy doings, their orations and donations, motions and emotions" so that they might enjoy the moral titillations of self-conscious virtue. Such activity had nothing to do with real benevolence, which Coleridge defined as a natural sympathy made stronger by believing that the interests of each individual are the same as those of all men. It was the intention of God that mankind should be a mighty family, acknowledging Him as father and inhabiting the world as its home. Men were to find their happiness and peace in forgetfulness of themselves, in an acceptance of their relationship to other men simply because they are men.

Again, Coleridge's statement of the oneness of mankind remains fundamentally unaltered. Yet we must remember that in all the proposals which Coleridge has brought forward to improve the condition of "the labouring poor," there has been no suggestion that the poor should independently solve their own problems. All good things were to come to them from above. Coleridge shows in this opinion the almost reactionary conservatism of his later years, a conservatism which was characteristic of the humanitarian man of letters until the Victorian age had reached its climax. Coleridge was unfriendly to unions and combinations of laborers, brought together "for the sworn purpose of lording it over their employers and the public." In his opinion these associations had a revolutionary tendency, because they dislocated "the ordained and beneficient interdependence of the higher, middle, and lower ranks" of society upon which the greatness of England had been established. No, the uninstructed man was not to obtain the good things of this life save by remaining an industrious laborer. The enlightened philanthropist, moreover, must see it as his duty "to plead for the poor and ignorant, not to them." Meanwhile, the lower classes would find everything needed for the right per-

formance of their duty in the Bible. The laboring classes as such—
aside from exceptional individuals—"are *not sought for in public
counsel*, nor need they be found where politic sentences are spoken.
It is enough if every one is wise in the working of his own craft:
so best *will they maintain the state of the world.*"

Coleridge, like Matthew Arnold, found that all questions finally
raised the question of religion. Even if all his suggested remedies
were to be realized in action, they would still be less than ideal if
some form of religion were not generally accepted. "In fine, religion, true or false, is and ever has been the centre of gravity in
a realm, to which all other things must and will accommodate
themselves." Coleridge would have been far more radical in the
absence of his religious beliefs. He was deeply impressed by the
Socialist Robert Owen and bestowed the highest praise upon
Owen's unselfish benevolence. Coleridge regretted only that Owen
had "wilfully stumbled over religion." He speaks of having written
"a long letter to Mr. Owen, and conjuring him, with tears in my
eyes, to avoid this rock," suggesting how seriously Owen had set
back the cause of social reform in his time by building up the
association which still lingers between radicalism and irreligion.

For Coleridge himself the ideal belief was Christianity, in whose
teachings he found everything men needed to insure ideal conduct.
For statesmen the Bible was a sufficient guide through all difficulties of political science. Besides being an immense comfort to the
poor, the Bible was a help to the clergy in training obedient, free,
and useful citizens. The people's situation is a sad and perilous one,
full of hardship and temptation. They tend to think with bitterness
of their present troubles, whereas religion will cheer them with
promises of a happier life in another world and may prepare them
"for the sudden reception of a less degree of melioration in this
world." To every man, finally, regardless of station, the apostle
teaches beneficence—to love his fellow man as himself. The English
as a nation should act nationally as well as individually as Christians
and lead the way for all nations to adopt the principles taught by
God's law and so end social evils.

Coleridge remained thus optimistic and humane to the end of

his life. He believed more fully than his followers that man was good by nature and became evil through temptation and adverse circumstances. He was certain that man would become better and that from this improvement there would follow reform of all public grievances. When Coleridge had less than a year to live, he could still write that he had hope "in *Humanity*, in despite of *men*." In the face of many disappointments, he looked to individual action and urged every man to do all within his power for the common good. "Let us palliate where we can not cure, comfort where we can not relieve," and for the rest, rely upon God. His belief in human dignity and oneness was nobly expressed and remained the unifying principle of a large body of work throughout the next three generations.

IV. Southey

> . . . with what feelings will a good man
> contemplate these wretched beings in their
> every-day state, when he thinks of the maj-
> esty of human nature, the capacities with
> which it is endowed, and the immortality
> for which it is created?—Southey, *State of*
> *the Poor*, 1816.

Southey differs from Coleridge just as we should expect him
to differ. He has less power of thought and feeling and of abstract
analysis. A. V. Dicey says of Southey that "even his friends could
not have thought him a powerful reasoner." [1] Yet he is no less sincere, and we welcome his greater clarity. Southey proposes an
abundance of remedies, many of which advance little, if at all,
beyond the conservatism of Coleridge, yet they show a marked
purpose and are impressive because of their mere number and variety. Also he has an even greater feeling for the preciousnss of
human life.

In the year after Waterloo, England was already suffering the
usual dislocation which follows a long war. The condition of the
people grew steadily worse. It seemed to Southey that "the sum
of existing wretchedness is not to be numbered; its intensity every
man may estimate by what has fallen under his own notice, if he
be not one of those who keep aloof from the contemplations of
human misery; but its extent is known only to Him unto whom
the prayers and the groans of the miserable ascend." Southey was
appalled at the mass of ignorance, vice, and wretchedness which
existed in England alongside the great advantages enjoyed by the
favored classes.

Like Coleridge, he was moved to sympathy for the laboring
children. In a burst of indignation over conditions in a cotton-

[1] *Law and Public Opinion*, London, 1905, p. 224.

mill, he thought "that if Dante had peopled one of his hells with children, here was a scene worthy to have supplied him with new images of torment." Southey wondered "that the very pavement of the streets has not risen up and stoned" those responsible for this "abominable inhumanity." The working children got no education to speak of, their health was seriously undermined, and they were faced by such temptations that they soon lost all sense of morality. Since they were able to rely on themselves when very young, they tended to cast off parental restraints and to go the way of improvidence.

Furthermore, Southey found that the general physical condition of those who worked with their hands by the day was worse than it had been for two centuries. He was the first of the literary humanitarians to complain of the industrial era on aesthetic grounds, as well as to emphasize the squalor and filth in which men lived, with its accompaniment of disease and early death. The old towns had plenty of dirt, but it was inoffensive compared, for example, with the state of things in Birmingham. Here the dirt was "active and moving, a living principle of mischief, which fills the whole atmosphere and penetrates everywhere, spotting and staining every thing." Instead of the church steeple, which used to adorn the landscape, one saw the tower of some factory "vomiting up flames and smoke, and blasting everything around with its metallic vapours," making the face of the country hideous, "uncultivated, black and smoking." It was not only that things became physically dirty and therefore ugly.

Southey anticipates Morris when he asks,

How is it . . . that every thing which is connected with manufactures, presents such features of unqualified deformity? From the largest of Mammon's temples down to the poorest hovel in which his helotry are stalled, the edifices have all one character. Time cannot mellow them; Nature will neither clothe nor conceal them; and they remain always as offensive to the eye as to the mind!

Southey anticipated Kingsley, too, and his lifelong crusade for sanitary reform; he described the living quarters of the poor and their overcrowding in narrow streets and cellars shut away from

light and air. Inevitably disease followed from these conditions,
so that the poor in large towns were rarely without some infectious
fever. In 1832 Southey was actually able to see some good in the
visitation of cholera, because it "made the squalid misery of the
lower orders matter of public notoriety." It was notorious, also,
that the poor simply did not have enough to eat, even of their
indispensable, but comfortless, potatoes, and except in the vicinity
of coal mines they suffered bitterly from the cold.

Southey adds a gloomy picture of the poor man at work, if, indeed, he could find work at all. Again the poet was among the first
to sympathize with the lot of men who could derive no happiness
from their labor, another of the obsessions of William Morris.
When Southey looked at Birmingham his heart ached "at the sight
of so many human beings employed in infernal occupations, and
looking as if they were never destined for anything better!"
Southey could never think of England's wealth without remember-
ing what he had seen in the mines. "I cannot pretend to say, what
is the consumption here of the two-legged beasts of labour; commerce sends in no returns of its killed and wounded." Yet those
who had work, such as it was, were fortunate; greater evils came
with periodical unemployment. To Southey occasional periods of
prosperity seemed like mere intervals in the disease. He could only
wonder "where the misery, and the danger, and the ruin, are to
end."

The cost of the new era to those who became manufacturing
laborers seemed even worse when Southey thought of the country
worker. The poet had a romantic love for the country, where he
found everything beautiful. But the rural worker once enjoyed advantages other than the charm and peace of his surroundings. He
had the softening influence of religion and family connections.
He felt the security of mutual affection between his master and
himself, built up by generations of service, on the one side, and of
guidance and care, on the other. Southey felt that the worker of
his time had paid dearly for his independence through the loss of
these feudal attachments. These were obviously no longer possible
for the manufacturing laborer; but even the peasant who remained

on the land found his status changed when the commercial principle was applied to farming. "A link in the social chain" was lost
when a useful and respectable class was degraded from the rank
of small farmers to that of day laborers. Here the humanitarian
wonders again at the human cost, the deterioration of pride and
selfrespect, and the death of hope.

Thus, the impoverished English laborer is presented as a special
victim of modern civilization, but a victim rapidly becoming em-
bittered. For every rich and successful man in England there were
"a hundred human beings like himself, as wonderfully fashioned
by Nature, gifted with the like capacities, and equally made for
immortality," who were nonetheless sacrificed in body and soul.
"They live to grow up without decency, without comfort, and
without hope, without morals, without religion, and without
shame, and bring forth slaves like themselves to tread in the same
path of misery." Southey constantly repeated his warning that
rebellion was inevitable unless the "condition of England" was improved. Like Carlyle, he feared the despair of a brutalized populace
which could not help feeling "a dreadful reality of oppression, a
dreadful sense of injustice, of intolerable misery, of intolerable
wrongs, more formidable than any causes which have ever moved
a people to insurrection."

In 1828 Southey wrote to his friend Rickman and with characteristic openness denounced what he thought was the cause of
the "condition of England."

When will you pounce upon the political economists? The more I
know of them the more I perceive that they are radically wrong in
everything, for they always disregard moral considerations; dealing
thus with the interests of a community as the surgeon would with a
living patient if he treated him like a corpse—leaving life and feeling
out of his thoughts. No greater good could be done than by exposing
this very mischievous quackery.

To this exposure Southey devoted much of his effort, arguing
once more on humanitarian grounds. He, too, professed to know
almost nothing about economics. But he knew enough to be sure
that no words could express "the thorough contempt" which he

felt for economists. They missed the point entirely when they ignored all morality and compassion for flesh and blood. Their philosophy was a thing of the earth, earthy, completely materialistic.
Specifically Southey denounced Adam Smith for his concept of
man, "the manufacturing animal," but Malthus suffered the worst
at his hands. This man should have done "justice upon himself with
a rope." Southey was convinced that Malthus had been wrong in
his facts and deductions, but most dangerous in the practical results of his ideas.

These ideas and those of the whole school of economic thought
then dominant were held responsible for the growth of the manufacturing system which in turn had caused the "condition of England." The inevitable tendency of the system which Adam Smith
has inspired is "to multiply the number of the poor, and to make
them vicious, diseased, and miserable." In the first place, the system
encourages a grasping spirit of ambition and a selfish desire for
gain. Southey is not averse to the common acquisitive instinct for
property which seeks the comforts and respectabilities of life and
has a normal, beneficial outlet in commerce of "the mercantile profession."

This is quite different from the basis of the manufacturing system, which has no other god but gold and cares nothing for the
human consequences of its operations. Southey finds cannibalism
itself no worse than every man trying to oppress his neighbor and
to gain more for himself, endeavoring only to buy at the lowest
price and sell at the highest. Competition demands a large sale at
a small profit, which in turn makes for low wages. In prosperous
times a shortsighted and rapacious effort is made to produce quantities of goods, the market is overstocked, men are thrown out of
work, and every new visitation of this cold fit is worse than the last.
So long as men are moved only by selfishness, so long will the distress of the poor go on and they themselves "become year after
year more numerous, more miserable, and more depraved."
Southey would almost prefer the slavery of a West Indian plantation to the calculated inhumanity of an English cotton mill. "I
can imagine a plantation which should be as happy as a patriarchal

family; but I cannot conceive of a great cotton manufactory as anything but an abomination both to God and man."

Once more it is the human cost that moves Southey, the loss of kindly and generous feeling, of honor and integrity, the decay of the highest powers of man. He sees the spirit of selfish gain causing a degeneration in the quality of English goods, which are flimsy and adulterated for rapid sale and profit. He is concerned over the loss of old feudal distinctions, the decline in family pride as the spirit of ambition enables the newly rich to buy titles and so to cheapen the nobility of England. But the greatest tragedy of all is the degeneration of human life under the system which denies the oneness of mankind and abandons every man to his own resources. The result is the more deplorable when one thinks of "the majesty of human nature, the capacities with which it is endowed, and the immortality for which it is created." The manufacturing system and the philosophy underlying it were therefore evil, because they were not concerned with the dignity of man. "Scarce lower than the angels in the capacity of his nature, man is yet, when left to himself, scarcely above the brutes." All things should be therefore subordinated to man's fulfillment of his specifically human destiny. And because it ignored, to a degree never before known to England, the proper end of human life, Southey held the competitive system to be the cause of the worst thing that had ever happened to the nation.

Southey called it "one of the worthiest employments of enlightened man" to inquire what has been done and what remains to do in diminishing human misery. He doubted the possibility of a new utopia, but he urged men "to look on in hope and in faith to the gradual and possible amelioration of society." Southey's radicalism, although fruitful, was never subversive; his mind looked backward into the past as often as forward for its inspiration. He avoided sudden and rapid change, especially any variation from long-established institutions. In his maturity he too, like Coleridge, disclaimed the "crude and misdirected" efforts of his early years and acknowledged what had been "erroneous and intemperate" in his former opinions. Yet he insisted that the real intention of his work never varied, even though in his maturity he grew more conservative. "The one object to which I have ever been desirous of contributing according to my power is the removal of those obstacles by which the improvement of mankind is impeded; and to this the whole tenour of my writings . . . bears witness." Southey considered it his business to "effect the greatest alleviation of human misery, to mitigate the sufferings of the poor, to amend their morals, and to redress their wrongs." Yet this was all to be done while preserving the established classes of society and the institutions founded upon them.

Southey would require, to begin with, a new attitude of mind on the part of government. Those who govern must think more favorably of human nature and must then act in response to the infinite possibilities of man. "The better they think of mankind the better they will find them, and the better they will make them." They must act and conceive plans for the improvement of society as if they thought that man was capable of anything. They must expect only the best to issue from the effort of man. They must not be deterred by the immense difficulties in the way of betterment; they must believe in the miracles that can be wrought by benevolence and zeal. They must have a religious sense of duty toward God and man in conformity with the gospel itself. They must cease to think of men as machines or animals, but must care for them as human beings and bear to them a parental sense of obligation.

Now this optimistic and humane attitude of mind will show itself in many practical ways. In Southey's time the chief evidence of the government's interest in popular welfare was the poor laws. Southey favored a system of poor relief as "humane, just, necessary, befitting a Christian state, and honourable to the English nation," but the existing laws, especially after 1834, were held to be cruel, poorly administered, and perverted. The poor received scanty relief ungraciously bestowed, with nothing to look forward to in their helplessness but the workhouse as an alternative to death itself. Southey wanted a reform of the poor laws based on the personal merit of the recipient; he would help the worthless pauper only to keep him from famishing, but he would be liberal to the deserving poor, thus encouraging the industrious laborer.

Yet better still would be such an improvement in the "condition of England" that poor laws and rates would no longer be necessary. If the poor could be elevated from their poverty, a new home market would be created. People could be made to pay taxes instead of claiming poor relief, thus increasing the wealth and security of the state. Obviously the problem of unemployment would have to be solved before the poor could be given new wants and the means of gratifying them. The right attitude of paternal concern by the government would demand that work be created for those who could not find it themselves. Southey anticipated Carlyle's horror of idleness among men, as much for its human as for its economic consequences. He could even say that any work, no matter how futile its results, was better than none.

Public works were among Southey's favored schemes for improvement of the poor, since wages were better than direct relief. He proposed the reclamation of waste land, which was related to another pet scheme, the distribution of small plots of arable land. Along with building roads and footpaths, setting up monuments and memorials, erecting new naval stations, churches, schools, and colleges, and other forms of public spending, Southey desired that waste lands, marshes, and lonely heaths and moors should be purchased and offered to disbanded service men and other unemployed workers for cultivation. He deplored the concentration of many small farms into larger holdings and hoped that as many laborers as possible could be given a grass plot or a garden. All laborers of good character who desired it should be given some area now being wasted, to cultivate and to provide food independently for themselves. Southey's desire to give independent security and self-respect to the poor man inspired his interest in savings banks. His ideally paternal government should establish county banks so that there would be no fear of bank failure, thus encouraging thrift and foresight among the poor.

Southey felt, too, that the morale of the people would be improved and their own struggle upward made to seem worth while if the government would force changes in working conditions in favor of workers, especially children. Those in authority should interfere still more in the daytime labor, as well as the night work, of factories. In his endless concern over those whom normal industry could not absorb, Southey recommended making the army and the navy more attractive and even training children who needed asylum for the nation's service, paying enough so that men could retire after twenty-one years of service. In addition to these larger suggestions Southey advocated numerous minor reforms, some of them to be applied locally. The government ought to reform the game laws so that the poor would no longer be tempted to steal game; the number of public houses should be greatly reduced because of the misery and pauperism brought on by drinking. Southey also favored taxes to break down great accumulations of wealth and restore a more proper balance between wealth and poverty.

All these reforms were temporary makeshifts compared with the two main obsessions of Southey's mind—emigration and education, which was for him inseparable from religion. Southey professed to have outgrown his pantisocratic enthusiasm in later life, but he never forgot its basic command: leave the evils at home and go somewhere else to make things better. Probably not realizing how much of Malthus he really believed, Southey was sure that population would go on increasing and that the poor would multiply with time. Therefore a regular system of emigration was "as necessary in the economy of a state as of an ant-hill, or a bee hive." Southey quoted the Biblical admonition to be fruitful, to replenish and subdue the earth. For the swarms of Englishmen and their increase there was plenty of room in the colonies and other rich, unexploited regions of the earth. The money needed to send emigrants away could be paid back in a series of installments if need be, but go they must if their problem of unemployment was ever to be solved.

Yet for a properly solicitous government nothing was so important as national education. As no one should be allowed to die for want of food, so also no one should perish for lack of knowledge. It must be said to the credit of Southey that he never ceased to plead for the moral and intellectual improvement of the people and to denounce the human consequences of a system which he charged with degrading and brutalizing men. He wanted men to have a high opinion of themselves because they were men, to look above and beyond themselves for high standards of behavior, honor, and justice. He believed that education and religion were the answer to the deepest needs of the common man. He felt that under any system of society some members would be lost, but that "if any be lost for want of competent instruction, the fault is in the Society more than in the individual." At the very least, public education should enable the people to "read, write, cypher, and understand their moral and religious duties." Southey was not afraid that such training would dissatisfy the people or make them aspire above their proper station; if it were general enough, it would, on the contrary, be a kind of outwork to preserve established institutions and gradations. Along with Church of England parochial schools, he, too, advocated Dr. Bell's Madras System, in which one master could, by deputing his authority and function to the advanced students, superintend hundreds of children.

Southey would have the established English religion taught as part of the basic function of popular schools, since no effort to elevate the quality of human life could possibly succeed without religion.

. . . religion is the one thing needful for young and old, and all intermediate ages, for individuals and for communities . . . neither the virtue nor the happiness of individuals can rest upon any other sure foundation. . . . This is the only permanent good. . . . This it is which should be the Alpha and Omega of our existence. Here is the right basis of education . . . and not only the welfare, but the very existence of the state depends upon the same cause.

Again, the poet's religion tended to make him conservative and at times even reactionary. He was sincere in trying to improve the quality of English common life; he believed in education and religion for the people, because he honestly thought that these would elevate and dignify their lives as human beings. Yet he thought of these forces also as means to keep things as they were, to prevent radical change by the people. "Give us an educated population," he says, "bred from their childhood with the milk of sound doctrine, not dry-nursed in dissent . . . taught to fear God and honour the King, to know their duty toward their fellow-creatures and their Creator . . . the more there are of such a people, the greater will be the wealth and power and prosperity of a state."

Southey, too, desired a return to something nearer the feudal system. He found in fact a great deal to be said for feudal slavery itself, in which a man might belong, like one of the cattle, to a certain estate, but at least he was sure of a livelihood and could be free from the insecurity of the modern worker. Southey was probably not aware that this position seemed to contradict his belief, so often repeated, in the dignity and possibilities of man. Unlike conditions in the new industrial era, in feudal times every man had his place.

There was a system of superintendence everywhere, civil as well as religious. They who were born in villenage, were born to an inheritance of labour, but not of inevitable depravity and wretchedness. If one class were regarded in some respects as cattle, they were at least taken care of; they were trained, fed, sheltered and protected; and there was an eye upon them when they strayed. . . . None were beneath the notice of the priest, nor placed out of the possible reach of his instruction and his care. But how large a part of your population are like the dogs at Lisbon and Constantinople, unowned, unbroken to any useful purpose, subsisting by chance or by prey, living in filth, mischief and wretchedness; a nuisance to the community while they live, and dying miserably at last!

Obviously, then, the people could not be left alone to fashion their own destinies. It is here, again, that Southey's religion tended to fix his conservatism. His religion did not of necessity lead him to the feudal past, but it prevented him from following the most radical contemporary leadership, that of the socialist Robert Owen. Southey could not help believing that the earth was not the permanent home of man, that in the nature of things evil would always exist, that men could only hope to improve conditions somewhat and never to change them utterly, and that the best to be expected was an amount of good greater than the unavoidable evil.

Owen's infidelity made Southey's participation in the radical movement of his time impossible, as it had done for Coleridge. In this dependence on religious faith Coleridge and Southey showed the way to their followers, who were unable to face a complete break with the social order, for all of their objections to it, until in the scheme of William Morris religion was left out of the requirements for an ideal society. As for Southey, he could admire Owen's practical benevolence, his charity and enthusiasm; he could agree with Owen's opinion as to what was wrong in England; he could praise the reformer's plan for employing the poor in agriculture and his coöperative associations, if kept within proper limits. But Owen was "building upon sand." Southey felt that Owen could have rallied support if he had connected his scheme with any religious belief, even a preposterous, outlandish one—anything would suffice to attract men as long as it was not exclusively material.

One further element in the conservatism of Southey seems to offer a contradiction to his humanitarian belief in the dignity and power of man. Southey had at times an almost pathological fear of revolution by the lower classes, which led him to say things which sound like bitter fascism to the modern ear. He insisted on the rights of property and was for suppressing by force any infringement upon these rights. In 1812, when it seemed that demagogues might rouse the people dangerously, Southey wanted to recall liberty of debate and of the press and to suspend habeas corpus. He distrusted democratic reform of Parliament and could not believe that the voice of the people had anything to do with the voice of God. He was even capable of saying, about the time of the reform crisis in 1831, that "we shall get through our difficulties, and the better if there be a war to help us." His view of man, essentially so humane and charitable, was therefore subject to a timid conservatism. He wanted the world changed in many ways, most of them favorable to the peace and happiness of man. Yet he could not give up the support of religion and property and therefore could not greatly disturb the society in which he found so much that was hostile to the quality of human life.

Southey expected that his ideally benevolent authority would do much to improve the life of the common man. He desired, too, the help of "well disposed and active individuals," who would accomplish what could not be done by legislative interference. He believed that a gradual reform could be effected in addition to governmental activity, by the sincere effort of the minister and the magistrate, of parents, masters, benevolent societies, and religious persons of the respectable classes, each doing all possible good in the sphere of his own influence. Much could be done for the relief of suffering humanity by such exercise of the duty which all individual men ought to feel toward God and their neighbor.

It was upon this foundation of unselfish benevolence that Southey rested his hope of human improvement. Like the other literary figures who shared his inspiration, he desired to add the moral, human note to the theory of economics. He was certain that no economist had as yet seen the proper relationship among men which would insure justice for all. No ponderous economic treatise had taught that the state of nature was not a state of hostility and war and that the interest of man was best secured through unity with his fellows. The object of a good and wise man was simply "to promote the welfare and happiness of those who are in any degree dependent upon him, or whom he has the means of assisting, and never wantonly to injure the meanest thing that lives; to encourage . . . whatever is useful and ornamental in society, whatever tends to refine and elevate humanity."

V. Carlyle

> We have faith in the imperishable dignity
> of man; in the high vocation to which,
> throughout this his earthly history, he
> has been appointed.—Carlyle, *Signs of the
> Times.*

IN READING CARLYLE we are reminded again of Thomas Mann's statement concerning the contradiction in humane optimism. Carlyle shows insight into the grossness and evil of individual men alongside the firmest belief in man's capacity for doing and knowing. The one underlies Carlyle's criticism of his own period; the other inspires his hope for the future.

Carlyle's eloquence and passion give a picture of the "condition of England" far more alarming than that offered by the Lake Poets. He speaks of a "chronic gangrene" from which there is no escape for the toiling millions. There had come upon England "days of endless calamity, disruption, dislocation, confusion worse confounded." The physical condition of millions who worked with their hands had fallen to a sub-human level. Indeed, the term "masses" applied to these people seemed to suggest, not persons at all, but an indefinite species who were used and then left to die "like neglected, foundered Drought-Cattle, of Hunger and Overwork." Carlyle wonders whether this is really the earth where so many human beings must work as hard as they can under wretched conditions for the merest existence, where the children, so lamented by Coleridge, shorten their lives in factories, where the effort to produce cheap and nasty but saleable things is carried on without thought of the people who make them, where the half-starved, brutalized conditions of the Irish laborers, a third of whom can hardly get enough potatoes to live on, is gradually reducing the lower mass of English workers, through competition, to the same level and where a new man born into the world seems to be a misfortune. The world, in short, for most of its less fortunate, laboring inhabitants, is a scene of physical destitution and want, a place which looks "black and vile," for all its great wealth, and "in the nostril smells badly."

Nonetheless, Carlyle feels that the poor have worse miseries to endure than poverty and want. They suffer from "the unendurable conviction that they are unfairly dealt with, that their lot in this world is not founded on right, not even on necessity and might, and is neither what it should be, nor what it shall be." They are isolated and left solitary by men who should look after them; they have lost all feeling of unity with the rest of mankind; they are inarticulate and incapable of speaking for themselves. Again, like Coleridge, Carlyle emphasized the need for hope in the spirit of man. It is "the last, first . . . the sole blessedness of man," without which he degenerates throughout his entire nature and abandons himself to the passing moment, no longer struggling for that elevation of himself wherein his true destiny lies. Without hope he loses "wholesome composure, frugality, prosperity" and falls into "acrid unrest, recklessness, gin-drinking, and gradual ruin."

It is here that one is struck by Carlyle's belief in human greatness. His outcry against the condition of the people—magnificent lament that it is—was no more informative than any commissioner's report. Carlyle's special contribution comes from his sense of the tragedy of waste in the lives of men. Like Matthew Arnold, he reported that his age excelled in mechanical arrangements, "while in whatever respects the pure moral nature, in true dignity of soul and character, we are perhaps inferior to most civilized ages." Carlyle shares the wonder of Coleridge over the possible good that England's great increase in wealth has done to the people. Is there any increase of blessedness in the hearts of men? Are they nearer the developmnt of their highest powers, the fulfillment of what makes them men, or has the struggle merely to live dragged them down? Carlyle mourns "that a white European man must pray wistfully for what the horse he drives is sure of,—that the strain of his whole faculties may not fail to earn him food and lodging."

Carlyle sees further waste in such a spectacle as the Peterloo massacre. The physical casualties are at least countable, but there went out of the spirit of man, which was intended for charity and understanding of others, feelings of rage and smouldering resentment. It was another perversion of man's proper end, mutual abhorrence wasting away man's capacity for mutual love. But of all the waste in human life which Carlyle felt to be the curse of his age, the loss of good through unemployment seemed most tragic. Carlyle has given us a superb statement of why the mere fact of man's having no work to do is so painful a tragedy. Unemployment is of all possible affronts to the dignity of man the most ruinous and wasteful. Carlyle saw the familiar sight of unskilled workers as the victims of technological unemployment. The workhouse awaits them as they find themselves unneeded by the world. It is the saddest picture to be seen in the world. "Idleness? The awakened soul of man, all but the asphyxied soul of man, turns from it as from worse than death." The poor laborer starved to death is not so sad as

a man willing to work; and unable to find work . . . seeking leave to toil that he might be fed and sheltered! That he might be put on a level with the four-footed workers of the Planet which is his! There is not a horse willing to work but can get food and shelter in requital; a thing this two-footed worker has to seek for, to solicit occasionally in vain. He is nobody's two-footed worker; he is not even anybody's slave. And yet . . . it is currently reported there is an immortal soul in him, sent down out of Heaven into the Earth, and one beholds him *seeking* for this!

Carlyle never tires of repeating that man, the apex of creation, capable of anything, should sit "enchanted" by the hundred thousand in workhouses, "pleasantly so named, because work cannot be done in them." The famous passage in *Past and Present* describing the faces of idle workhouse men, "their cunning right-hand lamed, lying idle in their sorrowful bosom," emphasizes the almost Shakespearian sense of the tragedy of waste which Carlyle feels. Unemployment is, then, the worst element in the "condition of England," because it prevents man from realizing himself as man, from giving force to the capacity that is in him. No one has seen or expressed more effectively the universal human need for self-realization than Carlyle. Everything that he deplored in his time was condemned against this as a background. His gloom only intensified with time, and he became sure that "the huge abominable Boil will *burst*, and the British Empire fall into convulsions, perhaps into horrors and confusions which nobody is yet counting on."

"How come these things? Wherefore are they, wherefore should they be?" Something must be wrong with "the inner man of the world." England's physical evil must be caused by some spiritual defect. Man has forgotten the thing which makes him man. "There is no religion; there is no God; man has lost his soul, and vainly seeks antiseptic salt." The spirit of mechanism is stupefying the highest powers of man. He is told that life consists in love of pleasure, in selfish pursuit of the material goods of Mammon. In believing this, man becomes the victim of "the most lamentable of Delusions. . . . Whatsoever is noble, divine, inspired, drops thereby out of life. There remains everywhere . . . the mechanical hull, all soul fled out of it." What is specifically human as distinguished from mere animal capacities is no longer dominant, and man forgets his destiny.

Now, in the management of practical affairs this triumph of mechanism shows itself in the adoption of certain principles. Carlyle's epithets are famous, more numerous, more pointed, and more indignant than the general phrases of Coleridge, who attacked the same thing. We read uncounted denunciations of the mammon gospel under the terms "laissez-faire," "leave it alone," "supply and demand," "cash payment the sole nexus," "time will mend it," "free competition," "devil take the hindmost," "Midas-eared mammonism," and the denial of all sisterhood and brotherhood as implied in the question of Cain, "Am I my brother's keeper?" All these terms referred to the ideas generally accepted in the conduct of business and employment of men in Carlyle's time. He found it especially odious that as a result of these principles men should isolate themselves from each other and have no specifically human relationship in return for labor.

Carlyle was peculiarly irritated by the notion that the payment of money to one man by another was the only transaction necessary when work was being paid for. He seems to have felt that there was some contaminating influence in money, as if the mere fact of exchanging money was injurious or at least irrelevant to the human qualities of those involved. The philosophy of Cain governs the millowner who says of his workers, "Did not I hire them fairly in the market: Did I not pay them to the last sixpence, the sum covenanted for? What have I to do with them more?" Cain had made in effect the same reply. " 'Am I my brother's keeper?' Did I not pay my brother *his* wages, the thing he had merited from me?" All this struck Carlyle as being unworthy of human beings. He tells his brother John of his disgust with London and its attitude toward human life: "a meaner, more utterly despicable view of man and his interest than stands pictured even in the better heads you could nowhere fall in with." Carlyle even wonders whether under the circumstances England can be called "society" at all. People seem bent on becoming free of one another instead of moving toward human oneness; one hears of "enfranchisement" and "emancipation," of the severing of human relations, of having "no business" except a cash-account business. "It is the silliest tale a distressed generation of men ever took to telling one another." It is absurd for the classes who should guide and govern to pretend that human affairs need no guidance from wisdom and forethought in place of folly and accident. "We are all bound together, for mutual good or else for mutual misery, as living nerves in the same body. No highest man can disunite himself from any lowest." Carlyle constantly warned England that unless its ideas were changed, it could not possibly expect anything better than the evils which disfigured its prosperity. Indeed, time would show that something far worse was in store.

Carlyle recognized the gloomy tone of his message, but defended himself by saying that "it is in general more profitable to reckon up our defects than to boast of our attainments." He was also very candid about admitting that his talent was better for denouncing what was wrong than for suggesting specific means of improvement. Nonetheless, he does offer some remedies, usually in very general terms; here again we encounter his estimate of man, which dictates the nature of what he has to recommend and what will remain valuable and inspiring to others long after his unfertile proposals for change are forgotten.

Although Carlyle hated the let-alone principle and its results, yet he had no respect for what was being done to make things better. We might have expected him to approve the immense amount of practical charity in his time, even if he had no faith in the extension of democracy, the new poor law, repeal of corn laws, or the five-point charter of the working class. We are told that

All so-called "reforms" hitherto are grounded either on openly-admitted egoism (cheap bread to the cotton-spinner, voting to those that have no vote, and the like) . . . or else upon this of remedying social injustices by indiscriminate contributions of philanthropy, a method surely more unpromising. Such contributions, being indiscriminate, are but a new injustice. . . . "Philanthropy, emancipation, and pity for human calamity is very beautiful; but the deep oblivion of the Law of Right and Wrong; this indiscriminate mashing-up of Right and Wrong into a patent treacle of the Philanthropic movement" . . . is altogether ugly and alarming.

Carlyle could not logically condemn all benevolence, given his own statements about the brotherhood of man. It was the notion that everyone should be given charity that he deplored; large-scale benevolence without careful distinction among its objects was one of his favorite victims. We encounter the usual array of compound epithets: such charity is a mere trade, "sugary disastrous jargon of philanthropy," "rosewater sentimentality," "universal syllabub of philanthropic twaddle," "specious fraternalism," "Exeter-Hall benevolence," "broad-brimmed Christian sentimentalism." Carlyle could not find any evidence in Christ himself, whom these universal philanthropists were professing to follow, of a "comprehensive universal soup-kitchen character." Indeed, if the Creator Himself is understood, He will be found stern and just, relentless toward the unworthy and by no means interested in universal charity balls. Let love and pity then be confined to the worthy; love alone will hardly do for the very flower of men, not to mention scoundrels and others past redemption. The correction of the evils of "let-alone" by such a version of benevolence was "contemptible as a drunkard's tears."

The formal effort of government to care for the suffering poor by the new poor law was also inadequate in Carlyle's opinion. The object of the new poor law was, apparently, to make relief so unpleasant that a man would apply for it only as an alternative to actual starvation. In this Carlyle saw further evidence of the bankruptcy, from the human point of view, of the prevailing economic theories, to which he gave his well-known title "The Dismal Science." His attitude toward economics is typically humanitarian. Since "the dismal science" lacked proper regard for humanity, it was irrelevant. Carlyle makes his imaginary prime minister in *Latter Day Pamphlets* say to "Respectable Professors of the Dismal Science" that he has read much, for his sins, in their inimitable volumes and is now familiar enough with

what of Divine Message you were sent with to me. Perhaps as small a message . . . as ever there was such a noise made about before. . . . Those Laws of the Shop-till are . . . useful in certain departments of the Universe, as the multiplication table itself . . . but . . . as the Supreme Rule of Statesmanship, or Government of Men—since this Universe is not wholly a Shop— No . . . here at last, in the Idle-Workhouse movement . . . I am fairly brought to a stand . . . beyond and above the shop-till . . . you shall as good as hold your peace.

The "dismal science" breaks down, because it lacks humane feeling; its prize exhibit, the new poor law, breaks down for the same reason. The workhouse is a failure, because it is simply beneath the dignity of man. Carlyle thinks that the old Spartan method of killing the superfluous population was better. "More humanity, I say, more of *man*hood, and of sense for what the dignity of man demands imperatively . . . this brutish Workhouse scheme . . . is but sluggish heartlessness, and insincerity, and cowardly lowness of soul."

Yet Carlyle saw a little virtue in the poor law, which at least recognized that no one should be allowed to remain idle, and it was "the probable preliminary of *some* general charge to be taken of the lowest classes by the higher." It represented the principle of supervision by a central authority over the multitude, who were obviously in need of being told what to do. Carlyle thought that the extension of democracy was the very opposite of what should be done, since it increased the wrong kind of freedom and was only more of the same, or worse than, the system of "let alone."

After all, what is it that the poor laborer really wants? "It is for 'justice' that he struggles." He wants and should receive, as the essential ingredient of justice, a "fair days-wages for fair days-work." Every man should be rewarded accurately according to his worth, according to "what he has earned and done and deserved." Carlyle cries out "Justice, Justice, in the name of Heaven; give us Justice, and we live; give us only counterfeits of it . . . and we die" But this means more than the payment of proper wages. The ever-toiling man desires, too, a superior "that should lovingly and wisely govern: is not that too the 'just wages' of his service done? It is for a manlike place and relation, in this world where he sees himself a man, that he struggles." Surely, of all the rights of man "this right of the ignorant man to be guided by the wiser . . . is the indisputablest. . . . It is a sacred right and duty, on both sides; and the Summary of all social duties whatsoever between the two." Wise command, wise obedience; a thorough understanding of the lower classes by the upper; the relation of the taught to their teacher, of the loyal subject to his guiding King, these are the vital elements of society. Let men discover the wisest and best among them and elevate them to leadership.

Carlyle thought that this leadership should ideally come from the English aristocracy. By their possession of land they made themselves subject to the law of their position. Each aristocrat should rule his own domain, should permit "nothing ugly or unjust or improper" to exist therein. Again, a return to something like feudalism is in order. The feudal baron knew that he could not bind men to himself as mere temporary mercenaries at so much a day; he had to have the love of his men in return for watching over their welfare. "It was beautiful; it was human!" Love, the impulse toward oneness with others, is one of the signs of man; separation, indifference, or hostility are beneath the level at which man as such must live in order to fulfill his destiny.

Carlyle admitted a certain degree of harshness and severity in the lot of feudal subjects like Gurth, whose condition had at least two special virtues: it offered a secure connection between him and other human beings in place of the so-called "free" separation of the modern worker, and better still, it offered permanence, the precious thing even in slavery itself. In any case, Carlyle would not mind the aspect of severity; in order to overcome the confusion of his time he was ready to accept coercion and regimentation. All workers could be organized into the "industrial regiments" of the new era, in which they would give "noble loyalty in return for noble guidance" by their "Industrial Colonels, Workmasters, taskmasters, Life-commanders, equitable as Rhadamanthus and inflexible as he." Every man would be forced to work, if need be on pain of death, so that there should be no idleness, no waste of precious human faculty.

While there is coercion, however, there must fundamentally be love as in feudal times; the captains of industry must bind their men "in veritable brotherhood, son-hood, by quite other and deeper ties than those of temporary day's wages!" Again, there must be permanence, for "Blessed is he that continueth where he is." Indeed, the time may come when the master-worker will find it needful "to grant his men a permanent interest in their enterprise, so that everyone from top to bottom will be "economically as well as loyally concerned for it." Carlyle even goes beyond the necessity for organizing labor to suggest a universal drill or discipline of all the people, leading in the end to military drill if need be, so that all men should learn commanding and obeying, "the basis of all human culture." He would begin with children and would strive for that feeling of "rhythmic human companionship" which comes to men who are being disciplined together in simultaneous movement and action. He would thus develop man's "heaven-born Docility or power of being educated . . . perhaps the deepest and richest element" in human nature; there would also grow up the spirit of association, the feeling of oneness with other men in place of modern hostility and isolation. As a result of the new spirit, the making of money would cease to be the English ideal. To be a noble master or a noble worker would then be the goal. The country's inventive genius would not compete so much for increased cheapness of goods as for a better distribution of those already cheap. Carlyle anticipates Ruskin and Morris in hoping for honesty and genuineness of goods in place of the increasingly poor quality produced for the sake of profit.

Regimentation and drill would be possible because of man's fundamental need for education and the ease with which his nature accepts it. This brings us to the common denominator of literary humanitarianism. Carlyle believed that, like unemployment, the lack of education was a tragic waste. "That there should one man die ignorant who had capacity for knowledge, this I call a tragedy . . . the miserable fraction of Science which our united Mankind, in a wide Universe of nescience, has acquired, why is not this, with all diligence, imparted to all?" Again, the mere fact of humanity gives a man the right to share in what his brother man has done and learned. Carlyle is amazed that this whole subject calls for any discussion whatever, "as if it stood not on the basis of everlasting duty, as a prime necessity of man." The desire to know is so completely normal that its frustration is a direct affront to humanity. But instead of having a chance to develop their normal human powers, "men, made in the image of God, continue as two-legged beasts of labour."

Carlyle felt so strongly on this subject that in 1835 he even considered trying for a job himself in the new scheme of national education. His recommendations for public action were not extreme. He felt that everyone in England should learn the alphabet and be taught to read; teachers ought to be sent everywhere, so that in ten years "an Englishman who could not read might be acknowledged as the monster which he really is!" Penalties might even be imposed by law on negligent parents and on every person unable to read. Schools should also teach proper behavior to the young scholar, "how he is to work, to behave and do" so as to develop "the talent of right conduct, of wise and useful behaviour." Carlyle insisted on religious training as well. The grand result of these educational hopes would be to awaken the "twenty-four million ordinary intellects" of the people so that they themselves could help to bring light and order into the chaos of their affairs.

Carlyle joined his predecessors in recommending emigration. While the demand for education grew more insistent in the work of Carlyle's followers, emigration became less important until William Morris offered an entirely new scheme for society, which would make it unnecessary for a man to depart, leaving evil behind him. Carlyle saw "the overcrowded little western nook of Europe" as a congested house; "our little Isle is grown too narrow for us," with millions cooped up in a kind of black hole of Calcutta, choking one another. It has come to this, that Malthus, talking about excessive increase of man as a danger to the human race, has made the birth of a new man seem an evil. Thus, the "condition of England" results partly from human wealth, from "increase of Men; of human Force . . . the most precious of all increases." Meanwhile, nine-tenths of the world was still vacant, or nearly so, mutely begging the superfluous masses of Europe for cultivation of its riches.

Carlyle repeatedly advocates emigration to America, and at one time he thought of going there himself with his entire family. In his earlier years he was unfavorably disposed to the American adventure, but in his maturity he became convinced that America offered justice, a fair return for honest labor. Carlyle thinks of a general system of emigration which would provide "a free bridge for emigrants." Every worker who could not be used in England should be helped to go elsewhere; in all quarters of the globe new colonies of Englishmen should be established. They would tend naturally to trade with the home country and would provide reliable markets for English goods, as well as relieve a desperate social pressure.

To these suggestions for organization of labor, leadership by those destined to lead, popular education, and emigration, Carlyle adds little in the way of practical measures. He shared to some degree Kingsley's fear for national health and suggested that sanitary regulations be adopted. He was angered by the pollution of England's rivers and contamination of the air by industrial waste. He hoped for a cleaning up of the manufacturing towns. He called for laws establishing "baths, free air, a wholesome temperature, ceilings twenty feet high . . . in all establishments licensed as mills." He anticipated Ruskin and Morris in urging parks and green fields for each manufacturing town, "a hundred acres or so of free greenfield, with trees on it . . . for its little children to disport in; for its all-conquering workers to take a breath of twilight air in."

When we add together Carlyle's specific measures, the total is unimpressive. He did not pretend, and rightly so, that he was ingenious as a planner. He thought of himself as commissioned to tell people that their way of life was wrong for certain reasons and that they had better mend it or suffer the consequences. How this change was to be brought about was another consideration, outside his special province. Carlyle's most valuable contribution lay in the ideas which were the basis for everything he had to say about life in his own time: his belief in the dignity of man and his constant assertion of man's greatness and potential destiny. This belief in man suggests why Carlyle, and Arnold after him, had so few practical measures to offer. Logically he must think that such specific measures are mere details and by no means the important thing. Man himself is the key to everything; if man will improve his own inner quality and will cultivate the elements and powers of his humanity as such, the world need not concern itself as to immediate measures.

Carlyle's grand project is therefore an improvement in the "soul" of man. Interference by the state itself has largely the same aim. It is a means to the end of elevating the quality of human life. If men complain of legislative interference on the score of loss of profits, the legislature should reply, " 'Yes, but my sons and daughters will gain health, and life, and a soul.' " So Carlyle speaks to his age only "with the hope of awakening here and there a British man to know himself for a man and divine soul." Let the English realize that "the crop of spiritual talent that is born to you, of human nobleness and intellect and heroic faculty . . . is infinitely more important than your crops of cotton or corn, or wine or herrings or whale-oil." This should demonstrate, too, that it is impossible to interpret man in material, mechanical terms. Carlyle's figure is like Newman's famous passage on the granite rock quarried with razors: "When we can drain the Ocean into mill-ponds, and bottle up the Force of Gravity, to be sold by retail, in gas jars; then may we hope to comprehend the infinitudes of man's soul under formulas of Profit and Loss." Anticipating Arnold, Carlyle points out that the dignity of man depends upon what lies within him; the elements which exalt man's life do not depend on institutions or mechanisms of any kind. Therefore, when man has ceased to think that material goods are all important—when mammonism has grown human again—when "bipeds-of-prey become men"— all reforms are possible. The right qualities of man's spirit being once more expanded, there will be no need for self-conscious benevolence and organized brotherly love. These virtues will proceed as they should, from the nature of things.

Carlyle repeats these admonitions endlessly. What does he mean by this recovery of "soul"? What must man know and believe concerning himself and his destiny before what is highest and noblest in him will manifest itself?

Man first of all must properly evaluate himself. The presence of an ideal, a spiritual force within him is what makes him man and it is this also which constitutes his kinship with God. Carlyle thought and wrote about this to the end of his life. In his eightieth year he could still write to his brother John, "daily I am taught again the unfathomable mystery of what we call a *soul* radiant with heaven." Man himself is in effect a symbol of God, and every man is "the visible manifestation and impersonation of the Divinity." Carlyle was fond of a remark by "the devout Novalis," which he repeats in *Sartor, Heroes,* and *Past and Present:*

"There is but one Temple in the Universe . . . and that is the Body of Man. . . . We touch Heaven when we lay our hand on a human body!" This sounds much like a flourish of rhetoric; but it is not so. If well meditated it will turn out to be a scientific fact. . . . *We* are the miracle of miracles,—the great inscrutable mystery of God.

Carlyle extends this high concept to the very "meanest tinker that sees with eyes." In a human face, even the most common of all, "there lies more than Raphael will take away with him."

We see here why Carlyle, like Coleridge, objected to lumping most of mankind together under the term "masses," as if each man

in himself were not an individual with a life of his own and as much
a manifestation of God as any other man.

Masses indeed: and yet, singular to say, if . . . thou follow them . . .
into their clay hovels, into their garrets and hutches, the masses consist
all of units. Every unit of whom has his own heart and sorrows . . .
every unit of these masses is a miraculous Man . . . struggling, with
vision or with blindness, for his infinite Kingdom . . . with a spark of
the Divinity, what thou callest an immortal soul, in him!

Man has therefore certain virtues and abilities which no other
creature possesses; the evil in life is due always to man's failure to
be true to or to develop these specifically human qualities. When
he renews these virtues, becomes faithful to them once more and
forgets the opposite tendencies which are beneath the dignity of
man and surrender to which has caused the "condition of England,"
then life will ascend to its proper level and man will have recovered
his soul. This principle is violated when people think that their
main object in life should be to prosper in a material way and so to
achieve personal happiness. Related to this tendency is the evil one
of human beings observing the law of animal struggle only, divorc-
ing themselves from other men and sharing no love or reverence
for them. Against these tendencies Carlyle would have men develop
those other qualities which are peculiar to man and which constitute his true greatness.

We may note in passing several things which Carlyle mentions,
but which are not as important as his more characteristic ideas. He
refers often to the desire for permanence as one of the signs of man.
The ape or the savage likes to be free to roam about, but the higher
the form of civilized man, the greater is his dislike of fluctuation and
his desire to maintain all relationships in his life for as long a period
as possible. Carlyle thought that even the Carolina negro slave was
better off, therefore, from a human point of view than the English
worker, who was unhappy in his "nomadic servitude, proceeding
by month's warning, and free supply-and-demand." Carlyle pointed
out, nonetheless, that one of the deepest needs of human nature is
the need for freedom, for release from all oppression by other men.
Yet man was held to aim at a higher freedom than political liberty.

The human need for orderly arrangement was suggested by Carlyle in his recommendation of discipline, because all men demand it. Carlyle was aware also of what Matthew Arnold later named the instinct for expansion. He discerned an "irrepressible tendency in every man to develop himself according to the magnitude which Nature has made him of: to speak-out, to act-out, what Nature has laid in him." This observation was partly responsible for Carlyle's doctrine of work. His plea for justice in life recalls his belief that hatred of injustice is also a sign of man's humanity. Injustice is intolerable to the spiritual principle in man, and rebellion against it is universally respected: "it is the common stamp of manhood vindicating itself in all of us," and the higher the quality of our humanity, the keener is our sense of injustice.

These qualities are all characteristic and entirely worthy of human nature at its best, but more important than these are the things which must be emphasized in and for man to combat his selfish isolation from other men and his desire for happiness through material means. Man should accept, whether he likes it or not, the fact of his kinship with all other men and his obligation to love and revere them. He must also surrender the notion that he is supposed to be happy in the usual sense of that term, and he must accept his destiny as one of serious labor imposed on him by the presence in his nature of the highest powers given to any creature under the sun.

Carlyle insists again that the spiritual element in man is the thing which unites him with every other man. All men were made by God, and all possess immortal souls. They have in common, therefore, the thing which makes them men. Like Ruskin, Carlyle never ceased to believe in the interdependence of all things in the universe, especially in the connection between men. There was not a thought or action of man "but has sprung withal out of all men, and works sooner or later . . . on all men! It is all a tree; circulation of sap and influences, mutual communication of every minutest leaf with the lowest talon of a root, with every other greatest and minutest portion of the whole." It is futile for men to deny that they are brothers. Even their very hatred and envy of each other show their common relationship, and their most insignificant actions are capable of affecting other lives.

Carlyle admits that every man must look at the world from a position which is in some ways peculiar to himself. Nonetheless, if
every man looks at life "faithfully," his view "will not contradict
his as faithful brother's view, but in the end complete it and har-
monize it," for " 'each man is the supplement of all other men.' "
In spite of his self-sufficiency, "man is infinitely precious to man";
there is no limit to his power of accomplishment if he will join with
others, for ten men united in love are "capable of being and doing
what ten thousand singly would fail in." It is pointless for men to
deny these things. The mere fact of their humanity imposes obligations upon them, so that "a good man by the very look of him, by
his very presence with us as a fellow wayfarer in this Life-pilgrim-
age, *promises* so much." We hear from Teufelsdroeck, in the tender
passage following upon his acceptance of the everlasting yea, how
the common destiny of man has inspired love and pity within him.
It is the same tenderness which Carlyle feels in his frequent urging
to "Pity thy brother, O son of Adam!" Teufelsdroeck sees that all
men must inherit sorrow and death; therefore they have earned the
love of their fellows.

Poor, wandering, wayward man! Art thou not tired, and beaten with
stripes, even as I am? Ever, whether thou bear the royal mantle or the
beggar's gabardine, art thou not so weary, so heavy-laden; and thy
Bed of Rest is but a Grave. O my Brother, my Brother, why cannot I
shelter thee in my bosom, and wipe away all tears from thy eyes!

If man will deny such human feeling, life will see to it that the
consequences are stern indeed. Carlyle's favorite example in proof
of this was the Irish widow who died of typhus and whose illness
infected seventeen other persons, who also died. In effect the widow
was asking for help because she was related to all mankind. But her
neighbors refused help, denying that she was a sister of theirs,
whereupon her kinship was proved by the death of those who
should have aided her. Only to another human being could she give
her disease; when she did so, these others paid with their lives to
show that humanity itself is relationship enough.

There is yet another tendency in man, allied to this feeling of
brotherhood. It, too, must be expressed if man is to develop all of
his highest powers and so recover his "Soul." This is man's admira-

tion of those whom he considers higher than himself. Carlyle never tires of repeating this, perhaps his most characteristic idea, which is implied in his constant demand for proper hero worship. It is the most important manifestation of man's boundless need and capacity for love. He feels safe only in companionship with his fellows, and "only in reverently bowing down before the Higher does he feel himself exalted." It is natural for men "to honour and love their Best," to seek out the intellect, the human worth among them, and to make this an "object of reverence . . . of devout prayer, and zealous wish and pursuit." The degree to which a nation of people tends to venerate human worth is the exact measure of its own human value. There is no violation of humanity more costly than failure to exercise the proper hero worship and to know accurately what is excellent and what is unworthy. Carlyle warned England constantly that it must perform its hero worship more adequately, for to do it better "means the awakening of the nation's soul from its asphyxia, and the return of blessed life to us." Nothing shows more clearly than this constantly repeated idea the estimate which Carlyle places on the presence in men, especially in those who are to lead others, of those qualities which are specifically human in the highest sense. Human life is so dignified, so precious—human worth so completely the only thing that matters—that nature and God have made recognition of greatness in man the test of whether a nation of men shall go down or shall live.

Having accepted his true relationship to his brothers, man must finally renounce his desire for material happiness and accept his solemn destiny of labor. Carlyle can only ask, what ever gave man the notion that he was supposed to be happy? There is in man a higher principle than love of happiness in the sense of having the "good things" of life, of enjoying pomp and ease, seeking pleasure and recompense, "sugar-plums of any kind." It is a calumny upon man to say that he is to be seduced only by ease. "Difficulty, abnegation, martyrdom, death are the *allurements* that act on the heart of man"; his life is not to be sold for any special wages of good things, but it must be given freely knowing that only a crown of thorns will be given in return.

How futile it is to imagine that slavery can be abolished by legislative action, when the very nature of things has imposed something like servitude on the whole of mankind. "We have simply to carry the whole world and its business upon our backs, we poor united Human Species; to carry it, and shove it forward, from day to day, somehow or other, among us, or else be ground to powder under it, one and all."

As long as man exists there will be what is called "evil" for him to conquer; it is precisely this evil, demanding the labor of man for its conquest, which gives man his opportunity. It is "the dark, disordered material out of which man's Free-will has to create an edifice of order and Good." It enables man to show his true greatness, which is in itself inseparable from his unhappiness. In speaking of Cromwell, Carlyle repeats Teufelsdroeck's remark: "the man's misery, as man's misery almost always does, came of his greatness." The essential tragedy of human life is a result of man's dignity and high place in the scheme of things. His misery is the price he pays for possession of the things which make him a man. If he wishes merely to be happy in a material way, he must then regret the fact that he is a man, not an animal. Carlyle used to say that the finer the human quality and spiritual worth of individuals, the greater their uneasiness and sorrow. For the race of men as a whole this is also true; since it is the highest form of life, it is most prone to misery.

Man, therefore, does not realize himself in a life of ease, but in working to the limit of his capacities as man. His only unhappiness, in the higher sense, is "that he cannot work; that he cannot get his destiny as a man fulfilled." Each human being is sent into the world to labour honestly according to the ability bestowed upon him, and "woe is to every man who . . . is prevented from fulfilling this the end of his being." He becomes a complete human being only when he has felt the "blessed glow of labour in him" and has plunged into the task before him. "Were he never so benighted, forgetful of his high calling, there is always hope in a man that actually and earnestly works." A man's work is all there is to show that he is really a man.

What a monstrosity, therefore, an idle man becomes. He is a contradiction in terms. Whether it is because he cannot find work or because he chooses to be idle and to permit others to work in his place, the inactive man violates human dignity. His human faculties "lie poisoning the thoroughfares. . . . For idleness does, in all cases, inevitably *rot* and become putrescent;—and I say deliberately, the very Devil is in *it*." Carlyle's insistence on having men coerced and drilled into work is due as much to admiration of human capacities as to contempt for the inability of most men to guide their own lives. Carlyle is willing to have compulsion and regimentation of the individual, if as a result each man's capacity shall be brought to fruition; almost anything is preferable to waste of human power.

Work is, therefore, an end in itself, because man is an end in himself. Work must be done, because man will not develop his highest powers in any other way; it must be done for its own sake, otherwise it is irrelevant. Only bad work and bad men will result if inspired by a materialistic aim. "No man has worked, or can work, except religiously," and herein lies his only happiness. What man really wants "is always that the Highest in his nature be *set* at the top, and actively reign there." The happiness of life will come, then, not from "the quantity of Pleasure we have had, but the quantity of Victory we have gained, of Labour we have overcome. . . . Let us on, then, in God's name!"

Carlyle's perpetual repetition of these ideas brings into relief the seeming contradiction in his estimate of individual men. He sees clearly how sordid and contemptible human beings can be in spite of the great dignity of the human race as a whole. If Carlyle seems to contradict himself, so does man, who is at times capable of being as base as he is great. "Are not both Heaven and Hell made out of him, made by him, everlasting Miracle and Mystery as he is?"

Carlyle has reserved some of his choicest epithets for those among mankind who represent the depths rather than the heights of human nature. "My indigent, incompetent friends. . . . Vagrant Lockalls, foolish most of you, criminals many of you, miserable all": so speaks the imaginary Prime Minister who is to bring order to future England. Carlyle tells his friend Sterling that man is a very strange fellow, indeed, "partaking much of the nature of the Ass." In reality only God is great, "and man is little and mean and a fool." There is folly in his heart, intolerance and pride and anger; Teufelsdroeck, who has considered it well, finds that man is "a blockhead and dullard; much readier to feel and digest, than to think and consider."

So Carlyle was violent against Democracy. "There are fools, cowards, knaves, and gluttonous traitors true only to their own appetite, in immense majority, in every rank of life; and there is nothing frightfuler than to see these voting and deciding." The whole process of consulting the mass of men at election time "is as ugly an exhibition of human stupidity as this world sees." Carlyle believed in human brotherhood, but he would not allow the "base and foolish" in his fraternity until they had returned to the right level of virtue. Profound as his belief in man's high calling was, yet he made distinctions. Leadership must come from the chosen few who will maintain the nobility of life "in spite of all the tremendous majority of blockheads and slothful belly-worshippers, and noisy ugly persons."

Nonetheless, if most individuals are foolish and contemptible, the powers of humanity itself are the most precious of all earthly things. "We will put up with many sad details, if the soul of it were true," and certainly human nature in its details offered Carlyle much to put up with. We are confronted everywhere in Carlyle by a strange mingling of pessimism and hope. Humanitarians are necessarily optimistic, yet Carlyle could write to his brother John, "My own thoughts grow graver every year I live." He was gloomy about the future and the possibility of improving the "condition of England." Aside from the fact that the English were intensely conservative and opposed to change—a trait which Carlyle approved of—it was clear to him that generations would have to pass before the problems originating in his time could be solved. He confessed sadly that his own remedies could only be striven for, at best, but never achieved. Probably not more than one in a thousand would heed his message, because it was necessarily an unpleasant one. He felt "how visionary these things look; and how aerial, high and spiritual they *are:* little capable of seriously tempting . . . any but the highest kinds of men." In a moment of despair he is found writing to Mill: "God be merciful to me! I surely ought to be in some other Planet than this."

And yet Carlyle could not entirely escape the hopeful implications of his ideas. In another letter to Mill he speaks with his usual emphasis about the seriousness of life, pointing out that "there is nothing for you but to fight,—or sit there and be butchered by Destiny. 'Nevertheless,' as our Scotch Preachers say, 'I hope better things, tho' I thus speak.'" There is something to be thankful for in the toil and anguish of life, and the wise man will see 'that in this very bitterness there is a medicine for his Soul." Man has no idea of his power of endurance, of the fund of life there is within him which enables him to survive pain and be stronger than ever once it is gone. Let him realize "what long corrosions one can stand, and not be worn *thro'* with them; may *be* worn purer and cleaner by them, and see them one day as indispensable blessings!" Meanwhile "the materials of human virtue are everywhere abundant as the light of the sun," even though they lie undeveloped.

Since it is true, however, that man still has every faculty of soul and body that he has ever possessed, he may once again "be all that he has been, and more." He may move forward to "higher and nobler developments of whatever is highest and noblest in him." In *Signs of the Times*, one of his first efforts to deal with the problems of his age, Carlyle said in so many words what we may accept as his final conviction: "We have a faith in the imperishable dignity of man; in the high vocation to which, throughout this his earthly history, he has been appointed." Through all the gloom of his mature years there was still hope in Carlyle's heart that even he could help to make some addition to the wisdom, justice, love, and manful effort of the world. When he became forty-nine years old, Carlyle wrote to his mother, a beautiful and moving letter in which he reviews the troublesome years and decides finally that life is something to be thankful for. It is the language of sadness, of the most complete realization of all the bitterness that life can offer, yet it is not the language of despair. Carlyle ends the letter in these words: "My ever-loved Mother, I salute you with my affection once more, and thank you for bringing me into this world, and for all your un-wearied care of me there. May God reward you for it,—as assuredly He will and does; I never can reward you!"

It is fashionable nowadays, when speaking of Carlyle, to point out that his literary style is a much greater achievement than the ideas which it was trying to express. This is true, yet the style derived much of its character from the nature of Carlyle's ideas. Carlyle himself remarked that one's style, like one's own skin, is inseparable from what it contains. In his own work the Biblical tone of solemnity was perfectly suited to the prophetic, admonitory things which he had to say. Furthermore, his style took on a special quality because of what he believed concerning the seriousness of life and the relentless compulsion on man to fulfill his destiny. Carlyle's style became what it was, then, because he thought of man, of human life, in a certain way. Its dark, restless energy, multiplication of epithets, its constant fervor and intensity, are most conspicuous when Carlyle is expressing his deep convictions about man and what is expected of him as such. And it is precisely in these convictions that Carlyle's contribution lies. They made his style what it was, and in this one particular the thing said was equal to the manner of saying it. When Carlyle had spoken out for our common humanity, for the value of man, and had expressed his belief in a great human destiny, he had said whatever useful thing he had to say. It was useful to his own time, and it will be useful to any other age, such as our own, which needs to be reminded of it.

VI. Kingsley

> O, my friends, think of this. Think of what
> you say when you say, "I am a man." Re-
> member that you are claiming for your-
> selves the very highest honour—an honour
> too great to make you proud; an honour so
> great that, if you understand it rightly, it
> must fill you with awe, and trembling and
> the spirit of Godly fear.—Kingsley, "Hu-
> man Nature," in *The Good News of God.*

IT HAS BEEN OBSERVED that the great doers of practical good on this
earth are not recruited from the ranks of clergymen as often as they
should be. The effort to improve conditions of life for all mankind
is frequently conducted by men who have nothing to do with organized religion. This is so true that one almost assumes a connection between radical social reform and irreligion, a connection
which, unfortunately for social progress, was established in England by Robert Owen and tended to neutralize his humane efforts.

If this is the rule, it is tested by the exception of Charles Kingsley.
If he strove for Heaven, as befitted his calling, he could still be
devoted to improving the life of man on earth. Kingsley achieved
a working synthesis between his religion and his radicalism; he
made it seem as if he had to be a humanitarian reformer because of
the implications which he saw in religion, not in spite of them. His
belief that cleanliness was akin to holiness seems at times just short
of that pathological obsession of Swift in his later years. It is one
of Kingsley's many distinctions that he could be urging men's
thoughts constantly toward the highest exaltation of the spirit and
at the same time could attack the filth and squalor of England's
slums, reminding men that this was the sordid result of forgetting
their humanity. Kingsley himself saw no contradiction in his dual
interest. A man has no "real love for the good and the beautiful,
except he attacks the evil and the disgusting the moment he sees it."

And so Kingsley fought all his life to elevate the physical condition of the people. Even though the hardened arteries of toryism somewhat chastened his final period, his inspired letter to Thomas Cooper in 1848 offers a fair summary of the attitude of his life: "I would shed the last drop of my life blood for the social and political emancipation of the people of England, as God is my witness."

Kingsley's vocation was an asset to him, both in high-minded planning for the improvement of mankind and in fierce denunciation of evil. With evangelical violence he exposed the "condition of England," and he repeated year after year his accusations against the selfish materialism of his age. He could say truly of himself that "no man has felt more deeply, or spoken more openly on the faults of England, on the cruelty and the oppression, the carelessness and laziness, which there is, alas! even here." He interested himself in the plight of men who worked with their hands for a living, including agricultural workers and all the rest of the miserable lives of what he feared were "one half of English souls this day." Kingsley's indignation was certainly comprehensive, but it was especially directed against two areas. He emphasized more than any of his predecessors the filth and squalor of lower-class life, and he helped to expose the terrible conditions of the sweated tailoring trade. Underlying these efforts was Kingsley's painful sense of waste in England, particularly waste of precious human life.

The villain that Kingsley never allows us to forget is dirt:

> The habitual ingrained personal dirt . . . the dirt which extends itself from the body to the clothes, the house, the language, the thoughts; the dirt of thousands and ten thousands in our great cities, who literally never dream of washing, simply because it has been to them from childhood a luxury. . . . Are these creatures, at once, animals, savages, and children, to be left for pure water to the laws of market demand?

Kingsley asserted in 1850 that there was hardly a district of the poorer classes in London in which the supply of water was not deficient in quantity and quality and supplied in such a way as to defile and waste as much of it as possible. The companies supplying water had finally achieved a monopoly and now felt justified in giving as little as possible in return for the highest price. Water being hard to obtain, the poor did without it and let the resulting filth accumulate.

Furthermore, the people were ill-informed and could not judge for themselves what good water was. Germs were not visible, so the diseases which people contracted were not usually suspected of having any connection with drinking water. Kingsley also quoted the famous remark of Chadwick as to the number of Englishmen who die annually from unnecessary and preventible diseases; his own version is that "bad water and want of water together" kill and wound more persons every year in Great Britain than were lost in any battle of recent history. The most deadly visitation in Kingsley's time was cholera, upon which the crusader preached four different sermons.

If the water supply was inadequate for drinking and washing, it is clear that little provision would be made for disposing of sewage. The human suffering caused by the inevitable open sewer calls forth some of Kingsley's bitterest language. Adding emotion and art to a blue-book report, he devotes an episode in his novel *Alton Locke* to representing an open ditch into which poor Jemmy Downes had just thrown himself. A policeman's lantern glares

Along the double row of miserable house-backs, which lined the sides of the open tidal ditch—over strange rambling jetties, and balconies, and sleeping sheds, which hung on rotting piles over the black waters, with phosphorescent scraps of rotten fish gleaming and twinkling out of the dark hollows, like devilish gravelights—over bubbles of poisonous gas, and bloated carcasses of dogs, and lumps of offal, floating on the stagnant olive-green hell-broth—over the slow sullen rows of oily ripple which were dying away into the darkness far beyond, sending up, as they stirred, hot breaths of miasma. . .

Life for Jemmy Downes and his family had become impossible in these surroundings. He had been unable to earn a decent living and had tried to escape misery by drinking away what little he had. His family were obliged to live as best they could in the appalling conditions which had finally contaminated and killed them. Kingsley does not allow us to overlook a single pitiable detail. With hair-raising vividness, almost absurdly melodramatic, he describes the death of Jemmy's wife and children. As they lie dead, their humanity and its inevitable desire for love and protection is symbolized in their attitudes, which Jemmy has arranged before his own suicide.

There was his little Irish wife:—dead—and naked; the wasted white limbs gleamed in the lurid light; the unclosed eyes stared, as if reproachfully, at the husband whose drunkenness had brought her there to kill her with the pestilence; and on each side of her a little, shrivelled, impish, child-corpse,—the wretched man had laid their arms round the dead mother's neck—and there they slept, their hungering and wailing over at last forever; the rats had been busy already with them—but what matter to them now?

Such were the poor's surroundings and the worst physical consequences thereof. People lived scarcely above the level of animals and died because they were, nevertheless, human beings, incapable of enduring their degradation. Emerging from their stinking courts and alleys, they would come into the main streets of their districts, "those narrow, brawling torrents of filth, and poverty and sin. . . . A ghastly, deafening, sickening sight it was" for Kingsley, who never forgot it and never ceased to cry out against it.

The conditions of work were even worse than the home environment, as Kingsley painted them. He could not understand public apathy before the spectacle of these impoverished victims of "luxury and neglect." With elaborate sarcasm, Kingsley acknowledged that the public was sorry for the thousands ruined by hard labor; sorry for the Sheffield grinders, who know that they will die young and lead a merry life while it lasts; sorry because of the diseases and miseries suffered by workers in various trades; sorry for the children who work long hours and grow up to be something hardly recognizable as human.

We are sorry for them all, as the giant is for the worm on which he treads. Alas! poor worm! But the giant must walk on. He is necessary to the universe, and the worm is not. So we are sorry for half-an-hour; and glad . . . to hear that charitable people or the government are going to do something to alleviate these miseries.

For one group of working people Kingsley made a particular plea. Armed with appalling documentation, he exposed the sub-human conditions of labor endured in the sweated tailoring trade. Work was frequently let out to contractors, middle-men, or "sweaters," as their victims called them, whose object was to make a large profit while paying the smallest possible wage. Often they made no effort to provide decent conditions of work; men were crowded into stifling garrets or small rooms with no proper ventilation and forced to work up to sixteen or eighteen hours a day. This might also include Sunday, to which the men had to agree, lest they should lose their jobs. "Why not?" asks Kingsley. "Is there anything about one idle day in seven to be found among the traditions of Mammon?"

It happened on occasion that there was not enough work to go around among a given set of tailors, since it was an advantage to have more than enough men on hand; yet the sweater might still refuse to let a man leave his confinement. He had to remain, on the chance that some new work might come in. We are told in *Alton Locke* of

half a dozen men imprisoned in that way, in a little dungeon of a garret, where they had hardly room to stand upright, and only just space to sit and work between their beds, without breathing the fresh air, or seeing God's sun, for months together, with no victuals but a few slices of bread-and-butter, and a little slop of tea, twice a day, till they were starved to the very bone.

The wages offered for this martyrdom were beaten down to a level which, even if it had been paid in full, would have provided only the barest livelihood. In a good week a man might earn from 9 to 12s., but he would be forced to live in the same room used for work. This would mean that the sweater had to deduct 6 or 7s. a week for board and lodging.

In addition fines of all sorts were imposed, deductions were levied on various pretexts, so that a tailor was lucky to end the week with a shilling or two for himself. If he were irregularly employed, he could not hope for more than a shilling or so a day and would end the week owing money to his employer. It was possible for a man,

therefore, to make a coat and receive nothing for his work. Some
of the men would pawn their own clothes to obtain a little money,
or if they were in debt to the sweater, their clothes might be held
as security so as to make them actual prisoners for months. Kingsley
pointed out wrathfully that the government itself was partly responsible for these evils. It would let out contracts for uniforms
without inquiring into conditions, but demanding the cheapest
price. As a result, tailors working on army, police, or post office
clothing could not expect more than 1s. 6d. for a fourteen-hour day.
A protest against this was officially answered by an M.P. with the
remark that it was not the business of government or of anyone else
to interfere with the laws of political economy, which held that
wages were governed by competition only.

The result of such a dreary and impoverished life was loss of
vitality, which made the tailor an easy prey to disease. Rheumatism,
typhus, dysentery, and very commonly consumption shortened his
life; he never had any real chance to expand his humanity or, indeed, to know what it really meant to live like a human being.

After presenting this dismal picture, Kingsley might have thought
that his point was made. But there was still the moral result to be
considered. A kind of recklessness developed among these vic-
timized people. Kingsley could hardly blame them for their search
after forgetfulness. This took the form of drinking—usually gin,
which the sweated tailors consumed in enormous quantities. But
drunkenness was also common among other members of the laboring poor, a habit which Kingsley deplored, but could not condemn
considering its background. Kingsley saw this drinking as a symp-
tom of disease in a barbaric civilization, "a far deeper disease than
any which drunkenness can produce; namely, of the growing de-
generacy of a population striving in vain by stimulants . . . to fight
against those slow poisons with which our greedy barbarism, mis-
called civilization, has surrounded them from the cradle to the
grave." People drank alcohol partly because they could not get
decent water; because the air, both at home and at work, was unfit
to breathe and had a deadening effect which alcohol removed; because they could not get themselves or their homes clean and wanted

to forget their self-disgust; because they were overworked and tried
to gain artificial strength in order to carry on.

Kingsley would repeat these things, continuing to ask the public
what they could expect. The circumstances of life made for a steady
dehumanization of these people; their machine-like labor made
thought and feeling unnecessary—their unclean homes after a day
of exhausting labor gave them no repose, destroyed their self-
respect, and dragged them to a level "with the sights, sounds, aye,
the very smells, which surround them." The despairing monotony
of their lives, with no hope or chance of anything better, produced
a kind of brooding wretchedness most pitiable to behold. Alton
Locke comes upon a crowd of some thousand common laborers; he
is struck "with the wan, haggard look of all faces; their lacklustre
eyes and drooping lips, stooping shoulders, heavy, dragging steps,
gave them a crushed, dogged air, which was infinitely painful, and
bespoke a grade of misery . . . habitual and degrading." Kingsley
was convinced that the English race in all classes had noticeably deteriorated since the beginning of the century and that the poorer
population was in danger of permanent degradation. With appalling
carelessness, society "wastes her most precious wealth, the manhood
of her masses!" The manufacturing process gives the key to the
social system; it is sometimes more profitable to allow a certain
amount of waste than to conserve everything. It pays better.

Capital is accumulated more rapidly by wasting a certain amount of
human life, human health, human intellect, human morals, by producing and throwing away a regular percentage of human soot—of
that thinking and acting dirt which lies about, and . . . breeds and
perpetuates itself in . . . the dark places of the Earth.

Such were the evils which Kingsley exposed with inspired energy; yet an even more powerful attack was made on their underlying cause. There was scarcely an ailment of mankind or the world
which was not in the end related to the "very ogre that is eating
us all up," the eleventh commandment to "buy cheap and sell dear,"
an open warfare of every man against his brother. Kingsley was
willing to admit that laissez-faire, in its extreme meaning, might be
suitable for men who were already ideally developed as human be-

ings. In proportion as their humanity was perfected on all points, so might they "be safely left to the suggestions of their own hearts and reason." But, alas! men have not been true to their higher selves; they have fallen into slavery to their passions and lusts, have become selfish and lawless. Laissez-faire was directly responsible for the water problem in London, since it had resulted in a monopoly completely indifferent to service or to justice. Kingsley shakes his head over poor John Bull, who could not see what unrestrained competition might do to the supply of water.

In your selfish, short-sighted cunning, you thought you would get your water a little cheaper by trusting it to the self-interest of a few . . . and letting them beat each other down . . . behold, you are literally filled with the fruit of your own devices, with rats and mice and small deer, paramecia, and entomostraceae, and kicking things with horrid names. . . . Oh John! John! The love of money is the root of all evil!

The English are beset by "isolating, individualizing selfishness," as well as a stubborn slowness to change anything, right or wrong. The government itself is poorly organized, and in many parishes is in the hands of the very people whose interest it is not to invoke sanitary reform. The operation of laissez-faire in the market place was also to blame for the waste of human life through hard conditions of labor. "England has been sacrificing her sons and her daughters to the devil of covetousness of late years, just as much as our forefathers offered theirs to the devil of selfish and cowardly superstition." The preachers of modern political economy took no account of the value of human life and, indeed, were actually afraid, with Malthus, that there were too many people in the world anyway. They could hardly be concerned to save the lives of children who were dying prematurely in the cities, and by so doing overcrowd England still farther "with those helpless and expensive sources of national poverty—rational human beings." Kingsley confessed himself "a stranger and a pilgrim in a world of laissez-faire. . . . I shall resist it, as I do any other snare of the devil . . . because I look forward to a nobler state of humanity." Kingsley shared Carlyle's prophecy of some dreadful upheaval or retribution against

England and feared the ruin of society through "the indignation and fury of its victims."

Long after the demands of Kingsley's clerical life had taken him out of the immediate social arena, his polemic against selfishness went on. Over against this narrow law of man's being, he set its opposite, the denial of self. Indeed, "God will only reform society on the condition of our reforming every man his own self." It is here especially that Kingsley shows his noble perception of human dignity, of the price man must pay for having been called to so great a destiny. He, too, fought laissez-faire, the "science de la misère," because he believed that it took no account of what it means to be a man and was therefore contrary to the nature of things.

To be a man is to stand at the apex of creation. Kingsley never tired of repeating this, and in one form or another it occurs in every volume of his important work. It seemed to him "that the most precious thing in the world is a human being; that the lowest, and poorest, and the most degraded of human beings is better than all the dumb animals in the world; that there is an infinite, priceless capability in that creature, fallen as it may be." It is true that man is an animal, but "an animal with an immortal spirit in it," which is capable of more than pleasure and pain, mere carnal things; "it can feel trust, and hope, and peace, and love, and purity, and nobleness, and independence, and, above all, it can feel right and wrong." Man has "the most beautiful, noble, and perfect nature in the world," because in some mysterious way, alone among created things, man was made after the likeness of God. Herein is his glory, and herein lies his penalty. There is a voice in the human heart which speaks of this resemblance to God and which tells man that from this kinship with his maker arises his supremacy among living things. Kingsley, like Carlyle, shares the reverence of Novalis: "Every man should be honoured as God's image . . . we touch Heaven when we lay our hand on a human body."

To be a man, however, is also to be tormented by a clash between two tendencies of one's own being. Man finds himself— again he is unique in this—puzzled by his own nature, which seems divided into mutually destructive impulses. Kingsley states this dilemma in religious terms:

How is it that while I am like the animals in some things, and yet feel as if I ought to be, and can be, like God in other things? How is it that I feel two powers in me; one dragging me downward to make me lower than the beasts, the other lifting me upward. . . . It seems . . . my body, my bodily appetites and tempers which drag me down. Is my body me, part of me, or a thing I should be ashamed of and long to be rid of? I fancy that I can be like God. But can my body be like God? Must I not crush it, neglect it . . . before I can follow the good instinct which draws me upward?

The answer is that God sent Christ into the world to take on man's nature, "without changing, or lowering, or defiling Himself"; this proves that man must originally have been created in God's likeness.

But in the course of time man fell and took up, instead, the likeness of brutes; the fault was not in his body, but in his spirit, which yielded to the flesh and became its slave instead of its master. So Christ came and lived as a man to show what a man really could be, that the animal can be conquered, that all men can rise into a resemblance to Christ himself. Hence the perpetual conflict in man, which is the more intense as manhood is nobler and healthier; a voice assures him that he is destined to be better than he is; he is discontented and longs after some good and noble state which he must attain for his happiness. And how is this to be attained? Kingsley tells us that man comes to the fruition of his humanity and fulfills the law of his being when he realizes in himself the sublime paradox: he must lose his life in order to save it, he must deny his desire in order to fulfill it.

Now this denial of self is the supreme contribution of Christ, which he displayed as the one perfection of humanity; the presence in man of self-forgetfulness shows the degree of his kinship with Christ and God the Father, shows in short, the degree to which he has become a man. Everything that is "truly manful, and worthy of a man, is like Jesus Christ," and he who would be a man must strive to be like Christ "in everything he says and does." So will he conquer his likeness to the brutes that perish and attain to self-sacrifice "as the highest duty and the highest joy of him who claims a kindred with the gods." For it is the special mark of the brute and of the flesh in man "that it does what it likes. It is . . . self-indulgent, cares for nothing but itself and what it can get for itself."

But man is destined to do more than what he likes, namely, what he ought. Here Kingsley repeats Carlyle's warning that men are not here to be happy as they conceive of happiness in the narrow, personal sense. They were not put into this world to get pleasant things, but to do God's will; not to claim their so-called "rights," but to perform their duties toward others, imposed "by the mere fact of your being men and women living in contact with each other." They will recognize goodness, not happiness, as the end of their being, yet in the surrender of their self-pleasing happiness they will achieve the only joy worthy of man. Kingsley here does not entirely avoid the gloomy contradiction of Carlyle as pointed out by Matthew Arnold. He sees at least dimly that men must be promised happiness, although they continually strive for it in the wrong way; they should realize that they really were born for happiness, but that it will come to them only if they "discipline self till she lays down, and ceases clamouring for a vote in the parliament of men."

As we should expect of a clergyman, Kingsley does not believe that this exaltation of man above himself can be achieved without divine assistance. For him "the true dignity of man lies in true faith in God." Man alone is too weak and ignorant for conquest of himself; he must therefore ask for guidance from the spirit of God. Kingsley gives us again the inevitable comparison to the life of animals. He urges that an animal can live and die all by itself, "selfish and alone," for God has provided an animal with all that it needs for its own continuance in nature. But it is just because man is nobler and has a being "intended for all sorts of wonderful purposes" that he needs the help of others. He cannot exist a day without his fellow men. He needs others to do what he cannot do for himself. "In proportion as he is alone and friendless, he is pitiable and miserable."

If this is true at the physical, personal level, it is even more true of man's spiritual life, which needs the help of God through religion to sustain and fulfill itself. We are presented again with the great paradox: as nothing is so harmful to one's own interest as a constant concern for one's self, so man achieves his highest dignity when he humbly confesses his own shame. He is noblest when

awakened to the mystery of his own actual weakness, his possible strength; his own actual ignorance, his possible wisdom; his own actual sinfulness, his possible holiness; and then, by a humility which is the highest daring, by a self-distrust which is the truest self-assertion, vindicating the divine element within, by taking personal and voluntary service under no less a personage than Him who made him; and crying directly to the Creator . . . I am thine.

Such is the principle of self-sacrifice which Kingsley would oppose to self-interest and laissez-faire. The struggle must be fought out by every man within himself, each in his own way. No one could surpass Kingsley's reverence for man and his belief in a great human destiny. Yet he was greatly influenced by orthodox religious belief. He could not allow man the inherent strength to fight upward toward the triumph of his higher self. Man could do nothing without the active spiritual assistance of God. The creator had not, therefore, actually made the spiritual element in man the stronger in itself. It would be stronger only if it asked for special divine aid.

This denial that man has the strength within himself to fashion a better world finally prevented Kingsley from becoming more radical in his demands for social reform. Man could go only so far by himself, constantly hampered by his brutish nature, over which he alone could not prevail. This is quite another thing from saying that man has two tendencies in his own nature and that he is free to choose the higher of these, which is in itself strong enough to overcome the lower, and that man alone is the master of his fate, capable of achieving his high destiny. This view can come into humanitarian literature only when orthodox religion is no longer a controlling factor in a writer's thinking. We must wait for William Morris to express such a view of man uncolored by organized Christianity.

We may now inquire into the kind of world Kingsley would expect from the operation of self-sacrifice. He constantly referred to the triumph of the Kingdom of God in this world when the "diabolic tyranny of Mammon" shall have fallen and the money-changers and devourers of human beings "are crying to the rocks to hide them." This concept is based on the oneness of mankind, but again it has a religious background. Just as "all the misery and the burdens of this time, spring from . . . selfishness," so will they all disappear when selfishness gives way before the spirit of brotherhood and love. This spirit again is inseparable from the fact of man's humanity. The higher the form of humanity, the greater the feeling of oneness with all other men. The reason for this unity is that all men acknowledge the common fatherhood of God. All men are members of the same human and divine family; every man must love and care for his neighbor, who, being also a child of God, is his brother. When this spirit of love and justice takes hold of mankind, then the kingdom of God will have come to the earth and there will be no end "to the wealth, the comfort, the happiness of the children of men."

Kingsley, in so many words, denies the workability of socialism, since it makes no appeal to this religious sense of unity. A common object of gain is not as strong as a common object of admiration and the feeling that all are descended from a common father. Kingsley not only urges men to accept this brotherhood one with another; he warns them that it is bound to assert itself, whether they like it or not. God has simply bound the human race together for good or for evil. Kingsley can do no better than to illustrate his point by Carlyle's famous story of the Irish widow who died of typhus because of her fellow-men's neglect, whereupon she took seventeen others to the grave with her. In some obscure way likewise, Kingsley seems to feel that the needless disease and suffering of men are paradoxically a sign of human dignity. They prove that man is punished for giving way to animal selfishness and neglect of others and so emphasize the true law of his being. Things which result from a violation of human dignity are also a proof of it; they show that man has a high calling by showing what happens when he pretends that he does not, since they show the consequences of refusing to accept his human obligations.

We might expect that Kingsley would demand a great deal of material charity from one person to another as a sign of the new brotherly spirit. Yet like Carlyle he could be impatient of charity, especially when it was indiscriminate. He saw no real service beyond the moment in pulling out one's purse to alleviate individual hunger or illness. This would not solve the poor man's basic problem and might do actual harm in encouraging deceit and beggary. Aside from such institutions as hospitals, many charitable efforts seemed to Kingsley "only means for keeping the poor in their degradation by making it just not intolerable to them." Later he modifies this view somewhat and praises the good done by benevolent gentlemen and ladies to combat the miseries of the underprivileged. He actively solicits the help of the upper classes and asks that they help their brothers "by restoring to them a portion of that wealth which, without their labour, you would never have possessed." His final view of personal charity seems to have something in common with his opinion of poor rates. This charity of the state simply shows that the poor are members of the same body as others and that men are in the end forced to help them, if they won't do what is right of their own free will. Besides being bad in that they discourage caution and independent effort, the poor rates simply prove that an injustice has been done. They are an admission "on the part of society that the labourer was not fully remunerated." Therefore, charity is a confession of neglect, a late and partial compensation for suffering which should have been prevented. Its very necessity is a humiliating sign of the diseased state of the nation.

Men must show their sense of brotherhood and love in a more practical form. For one thing, and supremely important it is, they must not permit the poor to live and work in unwholesome surroundings. Again we have the inevitable comparison between man and the animal: "You may breed a pig in a sty . . . and make a learned pig of him after all; but you cannot breed a man in a sty, and make a learned man of him; or indeed, in the true sense of that great word, a man at all." Kingsley modified his views on many points as time went on, but his belief that sanitary reform was a sacred duty never changed. The social and moral state of a city depend directly on its physical state—that is, on the land, water, air, and lodging provided for its inhabitants. Clean surroundings mean greater self-respect, greater physical and moral decency. They also mean the end of drunkenness on a large scale, because "*ceteris paribus*, a man's sobriety is in direct proportion to his cleanliness." Given a healthful and refreshing atmosphere in which to live and renew his strength, the worker will not be driven to the tavern for comfort and forgetfulness.

This reform of sanitation was for Kingsley one of the surest results of the Kingdom of God on earth. Once more we encounter the religious basis for Kingsley's practical effort. For him it was the will of God that all human beings should be clean in body as well as in spirit. He believed this partly because of his reverence for man's body as a divine temple and his belief that we shall have bodies in our state of perfection after death. Therefore it seemed "impious" to him that personal health and beauty should be neglected. The example of Christ himself on earth was called to support Kingsley; he went about, when a man, conquering physical misery and showing that God loved life and health, not disease and death. Baptism itself was a symbol of God's desire for the pure washing without and within of His entire human family so that His Kingdom on earth should be one of well-being for all.

There would be something almost comic in the humorless intensity with which Kingsley repeated his message, if his own unselfish devotion to duty and the obvious practical usefulness of his crusade did not redeem it. He could write to his publisher in 1857 that he would no more turn away from his work in sanitary reform "than from knocking down a murderer whom I saw killing a woman." Dirt and filth were in reality murderers and criminals,

C

The victims had no change against them when neglected; the poor had no choice but to sink into a degradation in keeping with their surroundings. One is reminded here of the observations of Pico della Mirandola *Concerning the Dignity of Man*. Pico says that the most wonderful thing about man is that he is free to choose the direction in which he will go; he is free to decide which part of his nature will control his life, whether he will, indeed, be like the angels or will succumb to his lower self.

Kingsley would say that this merely reinforced his point. The wretched circumstances of the poor deprive them of this very choice upon which the dignity of man rests. Given their squalor and filth, they cannot help falling down to its level of brutishness; they have no chance to decide whether they will follow the high human road upward or the animal road downward. Indeed, they are hardly aware that such a choice should be open to them as men, that there is anything in their nature which desires a higher expression than their squalid conditions of life will permit. Therefore they must be helped into a better physical world. Kingsley preached, wrote, and lectured on this theme to the end of his life, encouraging the formation of societies to promote sanitation and advocating for the masses pure air and sunlight, pure food and water, clean dwellings, public baths, and drinking fountains. Without these as a beginning, nothing could be done toward the practical realization of the Kingdom of God.

Not having Arnold's consistency, Kingsley was willing to offer a variety of schemes to implement his general principles. He thought that sanitary reform would be greatly aided by popular medical instruction; every large town should open a school of public health. Lectures at low fees should be offered dealing with physiology, the functions of the body, the causes of diseases common in cities, the value of pure air and water and wholesome surroundings. This project of public instruction was so dear to Kingsley that a year before his death he suggested professors of the laws of health for Oxford and Cambridge, their lectures to be compulsory for young landowners and future clergymen.

More specific attacks on urban filth would follow public education. Sewage disposal should be overhauled, and the substances causing so much suffering when left in towns should be used as fertilizer for the surrounding country. More important was the need for an abundant supply of water. In great detail Kingsley instructs London in the proper use of springs near the city, from which an enormous volume of pure water could be taken. His hope is that eventually all towns will give to the very poorest houses a constant supply of pure water so that everyone may use as much as he likes. In addition, public baths and lavatories will enable the poor to keep themselves and their belongings clean. The same opportunity should be given for pure air, ideally on the ground of duty and humanity, but certainly by force of law, so that ventilation is obligatory for every room in which people work and for every new house, whenever built.

At one time Kingsley had hoped that some philanthropist would undertake sanitary reform as a capital investment. He is finally convinced that only the government can accomplish these changes. Government should paternally aid and support the people until the feeling of responsibility and brotherhood is strong enough to make government unnecessary. Indeed, the English government had best see to its duty if it wishes to survive and not be overthrown in favor of a despotic regime which will at least be an active one. Kingsley feels that democratic pressure might well be applied to force the desired reforms if need be. The laborer with a vote should unite with the educated classes, the clergy, the press, and scientific men to defeat any candidate for Commons who was unfavorable to sanitary reform. Thus, the lowest class, which suffers most from unwholesome surroundings, and the educated class, which is best able to form intelligent judgments, would be more strongly represented and governmental action would follow.

With a clean and wholesome world to live in, much of the poor man's struggle to elevate his life would be won. Kingsley believed that the superior worker should fight along with his class to elevate all men who labor. He should stay among them to regenerate and defend them, not try to "get on" by himself. Once the poorer class has achieved dignity and wholesomeness of life, they will be happy in their work and will not struggle to desert their class. They will accept their work as a duty to which they are called by God, as a sign of their participation in the human scheme of things, an indication of their acceptance of one of the chief obligations of human dignity. But in their pitiable state under the law of selfish competition, they could not see in their work anything but a means of further degradation. In order to lift themselves upward and improve their conditions of work they should form associations.

Kingsley here simply applies his doctrine of the oneness of mankind. The coöperative principle recognizes that mankind is united whether it wishes to be or not and that men should make practical use of that unity by working together and helping each other instead of defying their natural oneness by competition. Kingsley believed that this would succeed in all phases of labor from agriculture on the coöperative principle—in which associate laborers would form large farming units, dividing profits and living together in model houses with common kitchens, schools, and churches—to making and selling clothes in groups. The workers should organize among themselves for buying and selling the necessaries of life, but especially the tailors should pool their work for their own profit. They could eliminate the sweater and sell their products more cheaply; by sharing and coöperating they could put an end to exploitation.

Kingsley believed so strongly in coöperation, that he could recommend small associate home breweries, where the laborer might get his beer cheaply and also avoid public houses. As for the model workshops, Kingsley again urged that philanthropists of means might invest in them at the outset. Such an investment would return a profit, especially if the hitherto indifferent public would resolve to deal only with associated workmen and they with each other. Unfortunately the early efforts at association were not successful. A dozen attempts were made, but in a few years all had collapsed. Workers failed to coöperate with each other; incompetence and dishonesty contributed to other causes which put a temporary end to the associative principle. Yet Kingsley's effect was more permanent than he knew in planting the moral seed of coöperation. Matthew Arnold might have told Kingsley that it was not his business to do anything more "practical" than this.

Kingsley, however, was abundantly fertile in other proposals to improve the state of the "laboring poor." He at one time advocated the charter and its democratic principles. He sympathized deeply with the people whom he saw at Chartist meetings: "the oppressed, the starved, the untaught, the despairing, the insane; 'the dangerous classes,' which society creates, and then shrinks in horror, like Frankenstein, from the monster her own clumsy ambition has created." He sympathized, too, with their hopeless struggle for decency, and for a time he believed that the charter was the answer to the poor man's problems. But the charter turned out to be mere "machinery" and did not penetrate to the real problem of elevating men's hearts. The charter too was selfish in its way, demanding its will, and defiling itself by its roughness and self-assertion. It could not set up real democracy until it had assembled men trained in self-control, obedience to law, and public spirit—in short, men able to live in a corporate body.

Emigration was another favorite project with Kingsley. He believed that the trade unions, for example, might finance the annual departure of certain members. It was imperative that the pressure of numbers be relieved at home and that sickly millworkers should be given a chance for a vigorous life. As late as 1868 Kingsley regrets that the unions did not organize emigration.

More dear to Kingsley's heart, however, were various schemes for making art, amusement, country life, and education available to the people. Anticipating Ruskin and Morris, he hoped that the laboring classes would some day live outside the city in model lodging houses not far from their work. He dreamed of great blocks of buildings, with common eating houses, baths, reading rooms, amusements, and conveniences of all sorts, where the worker might live at low cost and be conveyed to and from work by railroad branch lines. The city would then be only a workshop, and men would spend their leisure in the pure country air amid natural beauty and peace. Chemical science would prevent vitiation of the atmosphere by foul vapors; green vegetation would be safe, the now polluted streams would again run clear, and "the desert which man has created in his haste and greed" would once more "blossom as the rose."

Inevitably Kingsley also had a plan for popular education. He could put "no limit to the possibility of man's becoming heroic . . . no limit to the capacities of any human being to form . . . a high and pure ideal of human character; and . . . to carry out that ideal in every-day life . . . to live worthy of—as I conceive— our heavenly birthright." We observe that Kingsley says "any human being"; this means that the same education should be available to all. The state has an absolute obligation to provide this training, so that every man may bring to the highest development all his human faculties. Kingsley reminds us "that men are not mere animals and things, but persons; that they have a Ruler over them, even God, who desires to educate them, to sanctify them, to develop their every faculty, that they may be his children, and not merely our tools; and do God's work in the world, and not merely their employer's work."

Education responds to an absolute need in human nature which suffers a painful dislocation when its need for light is denied. Kingsley shows this powerfully in the novel *Alton Locke*, whose hero struggles alone to satisfy the demand of his being. *Alton Locke* is for the most part a dreary performance, a document with a "purpose" whose artistic means to the end creak mechanically and whose melodramatic situations leave the modern reader unmoved. Yet it is redeemed by occasional touches of our common humanity. Such truth is achieved in Alton's longing for knowledge; he tries to escape the mechanical drudgery of his labor through dreaming and makes pathetic sacrifices for the sake of learning. "My soul escaped on every side from my civilized dungeon of brick and mortar, into the great free world from which my body was debarred." Kingsley suggests with telling effect that Alton's dreams are a manifestation of his human dignity. The desire to forget the machine-like dullness of his work. the desire to know. to be a man and not a mechanism—no amount of exploitation or denial of opportunity will overcome this: Alton will at least dream to escape being a machine. If he cannot have a man's life actually, he can at any rate imagine that he has it, so necessary is it that his being finds some human fulfillment.

In his hours away from work he struggles with pathetic and yet magnificent heroism to read, to learn all that circumstances will permit. He hungers after light, simply because he is a man and because it is light. ". . . might not those days of mine then have counted as months? . . . before starting forth to walk two miles to the shop at six o'clock in the morning, I sat some three or four hours shivering on my bed . . . my eyes aching over the page, my feet wrapped up in the bedclothes, to keep them from the miserable pain of the cold; longing, watching, dawn after dawn, for the kind summer mornings when I should need no candlelight." No bodily weariness could deter a man thus laboring toward the ends of his being. He read during every spare moment, "while walking to and fro from my work, while sitting up, often from midnight till dawn, stitching away to pay for the tallow-candle which I burnt, till I had to resort to . . . contrivances for keeping myself awake." To make such sacrifice unnecessary, Kingsley demanded that its meaning be accepted as true for all men. Let it be established that every child born into England "be developed to the highest pitch to which we can develop him in physical strength and in beauty, as well as in intellect and virtue." When there is universal education, there can be universal democracy, but not before. These opportunities should extend through the universities as well, where sons of workers should be allowed to enter by scholarships established for the able. Kingsley's personal contribution to education of the poor came in helping Frederick D. Maurice to found the Working Men's College, designed to give a liberal, not a vocational, training to men "conscious of unsatisfied and unemployed intellect." Based on close fellowship between teachers and students, the college is still active today.

Such are the changes which Kingsley demanded for the life of England, all resulting from fellowship in the kingdom of God on earth. His hope for things to come was largely shared by others, who formed with him the movement called Christian Socialism. Kingsley was the most eloquent popular champion of this movement, even though he was in no sense its original founder. The epithet "Christian" implies that Kingsley would interpret his special branch of "socialism" as connected "with a live and practical church." He conceived of the individual parish church as a "centre of civilization, mercy, comfort for weary hearts, relief from frost and hunger; a fresh centre of instruction, humanising, disciplining." The old cathedrals had performed a humane function in their time, standing as "the only democratic institution in the world; and the only socialist one too," for a poor man's only chance of rising on his merits was by coming to a monastery. This function of help to the poor Kingsley believed essential to the Protestant churches of his time, for "the very essential idea of Protestantism is the dignity and divinity of man as God made him!"

Kingsley continually urged the clergy to make good the promises of the Bible to the people, for the Bible shows that the cause of the poor is the cause of God. It promises "justice from God to those whom men oppress, glory from God to those whom men despise . . . the Bible . . . is the poor man's comfort and the rich man's warning." The clergy should therefore be priests of a universal church, ministering to the masses, "after the likeness of Him who died on the cross." Such a vigorous prosecution of their calling would bring the church into active life once more and make it and membership in it the hope of the new coöperative society. Its condition in Kingsley's early maturity was described by the famous sentence in *Yeast;* Kingsley has Barnakill and Lancelot Smith enter St. Paul's Cathedral: "the place breathed imbecility and unreality, and sleepy life-in-death, while the whole nineteenth century went roaring on its way outside." The church should stand for the common worship of God and symbolizes therefore the unity and common end of its members. The parochial tie recognizes fellow worshipers as associates and members of the human and divine family. It enjoins and makes concrete the duties of one member to another; it points the way to helping the man who lives next door or on the next street, because he is a fellow member of the parish. Thus the parochial system fixes the notion of duty in the small, personal relationships of daily life—the duty that lies nearest at hand. From this will come the larger sense of duty to country and so on to all mankind. The "Christian" element in Christian socialism is according to this view the element from which the socialism or common benefit derives.

In time the movement as such ceased altogether, and Kingsley seems to have modified his early enthusiasm and to have come around to a kind of Tory conservatism. His friend Dean Howson said of him that Kingsley was a "mixture of the radical and the tory," the latter aspect being "quite as conspicuous" as the former. He was a radical fighter against free competition until it began to appear from liberal legislation that working people might be able to work out their own economic salvation. By 1855, five years after the white heat of *Cheap Clothes and Nasty,* Kingsley confesses to having held back from the social movement, feeling that working men are not as yet fit for association and that much in the older order has to be destroyed before the new era can begin. He believes that association for distribution is workable, but co-operative production will require two generations of training before workmen are capable of it. Evidence of greater conservatism increases with time. Kingsley begins to feel that the laws of social economy and trade, "just as much as the laws of nature, are divine facts, and only by obeying them can we thrive." In 1856 he writes to a correspondent that he can "see little before the English workman but to abide as he is and endure," advising strongly against strikes and suggesting only emigration.

His warm admiration for the upper classes also grows more pronounced. His friend Thomas Hughes said that Kingsley was by nature and education an aristocrat. He believed that a landed gentry was essential to the country, even to true liberty and democracy. Kingsley liked the habits and ways of the landed aristocracy and "keenly enjoyed their company." As early as 1852 he had seen England's salvation in a union of the church, the gentlemen, and the workers against the competitive industrial system. In 1861 he pled for the House of Lords, whose safety was assured if the aristocracy would make themselves necessary to the people in a social sense; they should "study the duties of rank and property, as of a profession to which they are called by God," and become the most virtuous and liberal and trustworthy class in England. Kingsley keeps urging women of position to engage in social work, pointing out the amount of good which can be done through mercy and sisterly understanding of the poor woman's problems.

By 1866 Kingsley is able to commend the House of Lords as an admirable body, representing what is permanent and solid in the realm; it must be preserved lest the rights of property be injured, the rich be taxed for the benefit of the poor, and art and civilization be impaired. Kingsley confesses in so many words that "the harsh school of facts" has cured him of belief in universal suffrage based on essential equality among men. Society must first be sure that those to whom she gives the suffrage are neither knaves nor fools. By 1871 Kingsley is indifferent, feeling that the ballot bill may very well pass, since it is not likely to do either harm or good.

Kingsley, too, eventually drew near to feudalism. He rejoiced to hear of any relic of the old patriarchal bond, the permanent relationship between master and man. He regretted that the French Revolution had changed the "cordial and wholesome" relations between gentry and laborers which had come down from the Middle Ages. People who have property and station and education, however, should renew the old sense of responsibility and consider all human beings under their influence as weaker brethren who are to be taught and guided and helped on their way to manful freedom in their own right. An ideal master is presented in the person of Lord Ellerton in *Alton Locke*, who conducts his estate unselfishly. He has lowered rents, set up churches and schools, improved cottages, lent his books to all of his people who wanted to read, opened his art gallery, and in general transformed his estate into a vast associate farm with communal living arrangements and a system of divided profits which gives every worker an interest in the farm. By 1871 Kingsley declares openly for a general return to the old medieval system and advocates binding the tenant to the landlord and making every man responsible to a superior who should represent him to the crown. He confesses that this is now an impossible ideal, but one which might in time realize itself in a more civilized country.

It would be unfair simply to follow Kingsley through the sadly familiar pattern which is the way of the world with men: a fiery and idealistic youth, passionate for reform and human betterment; a calmer middle age, subdued by the demands of career and the opportunities of the fruitful years; a disillusioned, or at least mellow, old age, when obstacles to change seem insuperable, when things as they are seem as good as weariness can hope for, when life nearing its end seeks its lowest common denominator and is willing to settle for what is anciently established and safe. If Kingsley would modify his means to the end, he never ceased to hope for the regeneration of the mass of English labor. Even though he was a clergyman, he did not despise life in the world; he anticipated another life after death, yet he saw a clear connection between the quality of life in both worlds.

I have no heart to talk to you about the next life [he tells his people] unless I can give you some comfort, some reason for trusting in God in this life. I never saw much good come of it. I never found it do my soul any good—to be told, "*this* life and *this* world . . . are given up irremediably to misrule and deceit, poverty and pestilence, death and the devil. You cannot expect to set this world right—you must look to the next world."

So he did what lay in his power to improve the somber days of those who labored. In the national area he never abandoned the fight for sanitary reform. He wanted only to help "save the lives of a few thousand working people and their children," in return hoping only for the blessing of God. In his personal life Kingsley followed his advice to others, "to do the duty which lies nearest us" and to perform cheerfully "those simple everyday relations and duties of life, which are most divine, because they are most human." He was painfully struck by the monotonous, cheerless lives of English working people; to bring some color and pleasure to those near him, Kingsley conducted a series of readings and entertainments in the evening: music, poetry, stories, lectures on health, accounts of travel, village concerts, and the like were offered as frequently as his exhausting clerical life would permit. His unselfish labor for others, his almost saintly tenderness, his generosity and consideration for those about him show that he had fulfilled in his own person the reform which was to be the source of future good for all men. That the happiness of mankind lay in seeking this inner goodness and in nothing outside the human spirit remained the core of his teaching to the end. He admitted the usefulness of money as a means, but the constant struggle to get it seemed like the snarling and fighting of dogs over a bone. Every man should take it as the guiding principle of his life, that "the sure riches, either for a man or for a nation, are not money, but righteousness, love, justice, wisdom."

In the end, for all of Kingsley's outcry against evil, which his contemporaries had to hear whether they would or not, for all his multifarious schemes of practical operation and improvement, this simple doctrine remained his chief contribution. Here he was in touch with the unchanging truth, continuing the tradition of great spiritual leadership. But not only did Kingsley point the way to that inward perfection which was to save the world, he held out the hope to mankind that it would succeed in this self-resurrection. Again, he is like every great humanitarian; with fierceness and gloom he will cry out against the world, he will point to the certain doom which awaits mankind unless it reforms itself by the most stupendously difficult of all changes—yet he will in the end tell the world that he is hopeful of its success, that it can achieve for itself the very perfection which he has represented as so essential, but so distant. He is simply convinced that the world "can be better, happier, wiser, fairer in all things than it is now." Even from the very fact of the world's adversity, Kingsley's religion enables him to draw a ray of hope. He seems to feel that adversity is good in that it gives man a chance to show his humanity in its higher manifestations. It is a sign of divine favor that man is abused and afflicted, since in the endurance and conquest of affliction he shows the extent of his highest powers. Adversity is meant therefore "to make you wiser, hardier, more sure of God's love; more ready to do God's work whithersoever it may lead you."

Kingsley's optimism grew in the face of the strongest possible belief that the world was evil. He thought the world to be worse "than anyone else thinks it;" he was more "unhappy than anyone else about all the injustice and misery . . . in it"; yet he was perfectly certain, "as sure as if we saw it coming to pass here before us, that the world will come right at last." In spite of all the waste, destruction, and folly of mankind, "God is stronger than the Devil, life stronger than death, wisdom stronger than folly, order stronger than disorder, fruitfulness stronger than destruction." It is possible for all men to become as excellent as any one man has ever been, if they will revere and strive for perfection when it shows itself among them. Man's character is eventually raised to the level of that to which he looks with reverence; "what man has done, man may do" with the help of God and his own humble desire.

When Kingsley was only twenty-three he was buoyant, cheerful, determined. He expressed then a hope which the remainder of his life merely confirmed: "the realm of the possible was given to man to hope, and not to fear in." The feudalism of his old age does not detract from this sign that Kingsley bore the mark of all great humanitarians—the union of compassion, humaneness, and optimism.

VII. Arnold

> . . . the whole body of society should come
> to live with a life worthy to be called *hu-
> man,* and corresponding to man's true
> aspirations and powers. This, the humanisa-
> tion of man in society, is civilisation.—
> Arnold, *The Future of Liberalism.*

So FAR the defense of human dignity has fallen conveniently under three headings: exposition of evil, denunciation of the doctrine
of every man for himself as the cause, and recalling to mankind its
high destiny, with specific recommendations for the conduct of
life in a better society of the future. Matthew Arnold's work is
at once simpler and more complicated than this. He devotes little
time to exposing the evil and dwells incessantly on the cause, if,
indeed, one should not say that the cause is for Arnold the main
evil of his time. Arnold speaks generally of the misery of the people, how

> The complaining millions of men
> Darken in labour and pain—

Like Carlyle he sees that "poverty and suffering are the condition
of the people, the multitude, the immense majority of mankind."
He is struck by the false picture of England's "unrivalled happiness," which for him is contaminated by the "external hideousness
of London," the element of grimness, the dismal workhouse, the
gloom and barbarity of lower-class life. He points to the "vast,
miserable, unmanageable masses of sunken people,—one pauper
at the present moment, for every nineteen of us," who have been
called into being by the system of free trade, untaxed bread, and
expanding manufactures. This system has merely created an immense number of new poor people by offering work in periods
of short-sighted, temporary expansion, only to leave them to the
mercies of an uncertain future in times of depression—more poor

people, in short, to eat what bread there is, instead of more and cheaper bread for those already alive.

Arnold speaks also with compassion of the injustice done to Ireland, of the suffering of the Irish masses from time immemorial. But he rarely does more than to say that there is physical misery among the poor; that a man is poor and socially unequal to other classes is enough for Arnold to know. He does not agree that this national disgrace can be removed by charity, by sincere "Hebraism," or by the so-called "economic laws" as given out by the *Times*, Herbert Spencer, and Company. What is needed to solve the problem of large numbers of miserable poor people is knowledge how to prevent their accumulation in the first place. And this knowledge Arnold sets himself to obtain. If there is evil in English society, what are the causes of it? What deficiencies in mind and character, what imperfect beliefs or attitudes of mind are prevalent in England? These imperfections within men are the cause of any evil in their outward social arrangements. It was to the exposing of these inward deficiencies and their cure rather than to the details of human suffering that Arnold devoted most of his mature energy.

Furthermore, Arnold scarcely ever mentions "the dignity of man" in so many words, yet more than anyone under consideration here he is concerned with what this phrase means and with urging that man become what he should be because of what he can be. With wonderful patience and clarity he ground away at his task. He wanted above all things to be useful and so he wished to make himself understood. "One gains nothing on the darkness," he wrote, "by being, like Shelley, as incoherent as the darkness itself." With great good humor he turned aside a compliment to his clearness of diction: "it is the very simplicity of our understanding that incapacitates us for the difficult style of the philosophers, and drives us to the use of the most ordinary phraseology." But Arnold's simplicity hides a most impressive achievement. In turning his attention almost completely inward upon the defects of men in his time, he discovered wherein the true dignity of man consisted, what forces militated against it, and what reform was

needed in order to place mankind once and for all upon the road
to its high destiny. He saw clearly the needs of the world, and
had a sense of what was permanently practical in the affairs of
mankind. The finest literary critic in the English language, he
emerges likewise as a great reformer.

The deficiencies in English life and character, as Arnold sees
them, are set against the deal of human life, which is to seek perfection, to obtain the "culture" which was the core of Arnold's
message. Culture and the imperfections in English life are mutually
opposed in certain ways. Here is one of many statements of this
conflict:

... nearly all the characters of perfection, as culture teaches us to fix
them, meet in this country with some powerful tendency which
thwarts them and sets them at defiance. The idea of perfection as an
inward condition of the mind and spirit is at variance with the mechanical and material civilization. . . . The idea of perfection as a *general*
expansion of the human family is at variance with our strong individualism, our hatred of all limits to the unrestrained swing of the individual's personality, our maxim of "every man for himself." Above all
the idea of perfection as a *harmonious* expansion of human nature is
at variance with our want of flexibility, with our inaptitude for seeing
more than one side of a thing, with our energetic absorption in the
particular pursuit we happen to be following.

The first of the three main English weaknesses is, then, the
so-called "faith in machinery." By machinery Arnold wishes to
describe things which are only means to an end, not ends in themselves. The English are accustomed to think of machinery "as if it
had a value in and for itself" or served some special end in itself,
not realizing that "only our perfected humanity is an end in itself." Arnold lists under this heading such things as freedom, population, coal, railroads, wealth, and religious organizations, all existing outside of man himself. Men have always been likely "to regard
wealth as a precious end in itself," but never more so than in
Arnold's England. They are enthusiastic about the expansion of
industry and think that success in business will create a fine civilization. They believe also that a tremendous, swarming population, regardless of whether it can be decently supported in the

world, is a fine thing, because it flows from "divine and beautiful laws," which are inevitable and "not to be quarreled with." Along with this, they desire freedom from outside interference so that they can all become as prosperous as competition will allow. If it is a good thing to be rich, then people should be left alone to become richer.

The second of England's weaknesses is the desire of people to do as they please, to assert their ordinary selves and their personal liberty. "Men, all over the country, are beginning to assert and put in practise an Englishman's right to do what he likes; his right to march where he likes, meet where he likes, enter where he likes, hoot as he likes, threaten as he likes, smash as he likes. All this . . . tends to anarchy." This freedom would be very well if most people had already achieved a high degree of elevation within themselves; but they have not, since they have used their freedom to express their "ordinary," not their "higher," selves. Arnold, too, was never prone to flatter mankind, regardless of his belief in human possibilities. Man is a "poor inattentive and immoral creature," mostly unsound, his aims and doings more often than not very faulty. For such a creature to be self-satisfied retards and vulgarizes him; hence the critic should fight against this self-satisfaction by holding up a remote ideal of perfection to be pursued. Otherwise, roughness and crudity gain control and bring on social disintegration. Unfortunately for any hope of improvement, conditions are such as to increase self-assertion rather than to curb it. Arnold sees the dilemma faced by anyone who says that in order to change the world men have to change themselves: prevailing conditions are the very things which make it hard for men to change themselves. So the pursuit of individual self-will is ruining English society, which in turn encourages and perpetuates the very thing that endangers it.

The third of England's tendencies away from perfecton is her failure to strive for harmonious development of all sides of human nature and to be narrowly absorbed in a part of man's duty as if it were the whole. For the sake of convenience and of simple clearness in his argument Arnold repeatedly divided our humanity into certain instincts, or "senses," which taken all together made up our total human nature. These were the "senses" for conduct, for expansion, for beauty, for intellect and knowledge, for social life and manners. Englishmen generally had ignored nearly all these instincts in favor of one—that for conduct and action, the moral side. This is one reason why they believed so firmly in their own independent way of doing things. The English have a great contempt for dreamers and failures and think that energetic action will make up for imperfect knowledge. They set up some kind of rule or end as desirable and then go after it with great energy, with assurance and self-satisfaction, not considering whether the end is a right or a rational one or whether it calls forth the best self of man instead of his ordinary self.

Arnold is fond of saying that the English prefer doing to thinking, that they have energy and honesty rather than quickness of intelligence. The English have become inaccessible to and impatient of ideas, because they have succeeded so well, as they think, and for so long without them. Arnold flatly says of England that "perhaps in no country in the world is so much nonsense so firmly believed."

He never liked Carlyle, because the latter preached earnestness of action "to a nation which had plenty of it by nature, but was less abundantly supplied with several other useful things." Thus, the English had no adequate ideals to respond to the rest of man's specifically human instincts. Only the sense for expansion in man was at least one-half developed, in addition to conduct. Expansion simply means the effort of man to develop himself with the utmost fullness and freedom, to become in life all that he is capable of becoming. Two things are necessary for satisfaction of this instinct: freedom and equality. The English had achieved freedom with a vengeance, so that one-half the instinct for expansion was fully satisfied; but inequality still obtained and made a perfect civilization impossible, especially for the inferior masses, who were depressed and degraded. Such were the consequences of England's over-concentration on a part, rather than the whole, of man's humanity.

Arnold found that in the end "all questions raise the question of religion." In speaking of religion, he meant Christianity, based upon the Bible. His estimate of the value of Christianity and its Book can hardly be exaggerated. Christianity was simply indispensable for modern civilization. The Bible itself had endured because men could not get along without its directions for achieving the true aim of life. In short, Christianity was "the greatest and happiest stroke ever yet made for human perfection." Yet, once more the English had failed to understand true religion and how it should be practiced so as to respond to man's need for the fullest development of his highest powers. People wanted to be religious, but had a false notion of what religion really was. They had a true sense for conduct, but did not see wherein right conduct consists. They missed the true meaning of Christianity but were sure that they understood it perfectly. In what did the misunderstanding consist?

Christianity has been perverted by theologians and preachers, who have relied upon miracles, myths, and superstitions. They have tried to show that God is a person who thinks and loves, but is so immensely improved and bettered that He is man no longer. Then they have tried to show the existence of angels, a set of creatures betwen God and man. There is also the whole body of miracles, which the preachers of theology have tried to foist upon the people. Arnold reviews many of the stock arguments to show that miracles are pure illusions, rumors, and fairy tales and that their presence in religion has become offensive to men of common sense, who think that religion must be unsound and contemptible if it is based on such absurdities.

The essence of Christianity has also been falsified and misunderstood. The Bible has been misread into a complete misconception of what Christ and the Apostles were driving at. As a result, the popular religions value what is the mere machinery of religion, the outward forms and organizations, the doctors, the priests, and the churches, which in themselves have no importance. What is actually believed in as Christianity is not Christianity at all. Some believe that God is a terrible power, Whose wrath will one day come and Who has to be bought off by giving Him certain services in return for not sending men to hell.

Religion becomes, then, a kind of legal transaction. Its believers think that by "death and resurrection" St. Paul meant only the death of the body and its revival again in the future life. But "resurrection" really means a spiritual rebirth: one should die to all moral faults and be born again to moral perfection. So in St. Paul's sense resurrection takes place on earth when man becomes dead to his lower impulses and lives only for his higher self. Finally, these people who misread the Bible also think that they have found the final truth which the Bible teaches, that there is a definite church order outlined in the Bible which insists on a fixed scheme of doctrines and beliefs which people have to follow in order to be saved; this definite scheme, they think, is in their hands only and anyone who believes anything else is wrong.

These objections to the England of Arnold's time—faith in machinery, assertion of self, concentration on too narrow a portion of our humanity, and a grotesque misconception of the Christian religion—somehow meet and are concentrated in the English middle class, the so-called Philistines. It is true that all three classes shared in the weaknesses of England, but the middle class was most guilty. Arnold decided on the name "Philistines" because it suggested "something particularly stiff-necked and perverse in the resistance to light and its children." The Philistines are pleased with themselves and support each other with applause, disliking outside criticism, preferring plenty of bustle and action instead of self-examination or thought, clinging to narrow prejudices, violently opposing what will disturb them in their vulgarity. Their ambition is to be as rich as possible, so that they will become as splendid and as important as the upper classes. Their religion is prosecuted with energy. Arnold was fond of saying that at the outset of the seventeenth century the middle class had "entered the prison of Puritanism, and had the key turned upon its spirit there for two hundred years." Its members developed a form of religion which became the lowest form of intellectual life "which one can imagine as saving." They ignored generally the other instincts of man which compose his total humanity. They arrived at a life, in short, of which Arnold asks: "Can any life be imagined more hideous, more dismal, more unenviable?"

Because of the nature of this middle class, Arnold took a seemingly pessimistic view of England's future. If England is to remain unchanged, "it will be beaten by America on its own line, and by the Continental nations on the European line. I see this as plain as I see the paper before me." Arnold makes Arminius also warn the English of coming decline. "You are losing the instinct which tells people how the world is going; you are beginning to make mistakes; you are falling out of the front rank. . . . Unless you change, unless your middle class grows more intelligent, you will tell upon the world less and less, and end by being a second Holland." England must therefore transform itself or face disaster. But if Arnold saw England's weaknesses, he also believed that it would find the power to conquer them and so rise to great spiritual leadership in the world. What must England do in order to achieve a perfect, in place of a very faulty civilization?

At this point a question arises of great importance in any view of the humanitarian man of letters and his proper function. Arnold says that "criticism must maintain its independence of the practical spirit and its aims." He believes that Carlyle and Ruskin have lost the right to be dispassionately critical of theory, now that they have descended into the so-called "practical" realm. After he denounces the English constitution for being a "colossal machine for the manufacture of Philistines," Arnold asks how Carlyle is to say a thing like this "and not be misunderstood, after his furious raid into this field with his *Latter-day Pamphlets?* how is Mr. Ruskin, after his pugnacious political economy?" Actually, if the critical man of letters wants really to be useful, he should avoid offering detailed reforms; let men once get the right ideas firm and clear, "the mechanical details for their execution will come a great deal more simply and easily than we now suppose." Yet Arnold could not be entirely indifferent to the way practical politics were going. He considered that everyone in England had to be a politician to some degree, "and I too cannot help being a politician." Yet he was a politician of a liberal sort not to be found elsewhere in his world, a liberal interested in improving the quality of human life, of civilization. If the development of our humanity is the chief problem, then Arnold was the most practical of all writers, as in fact he considered himself to be. For he analyzed his society in the first place because he saw in it a threat to man's total humanity. He ventured into the practical realm only as far as this threat to humanity demanded. Defective practical affairs were important because they manifested certain deficiencies in human beings; it was these human deficiencies that Arnold was after, not their results in external details. Only the greatest of English critics could say, "I wish to decide nothing as of my own authority; the great art of criticism is to get oneself out of the way and to let humanity decide."

This ability to ignore the personal feeling of the moment, to take a long view toward what is best in the end governs Arnold's opinion even of that least offensive of practical operations, private charity. Here we might expect more indulgence from a man who in his own personal life was the soul of generosity, kindliness, and warmth of heart. He admits to his sister that there is probably no safer employment, or one productive of more happiness, than beneficence.

But do not you feel sometimes anxious to attack the condition of things which seems to bring about the evils on which your beneficence has to be exercised? When once you have got it into your head that this condition *does* in great measure bring the evils about, and that it is in great measure remediable, I think one can hardly rest satisfied with merely alleviating the evils that arise under it.

Arnold saw that his method was slow, but he believed that it conformed to nature which would have all profound changes come about gradually; in all that he wrote he aimed at this gradual effect. "Our ideas will, in the end, shape the world all the better for maturing a little."

The remedy for those human failings, from which all the evil in Arnold's time had come, is to seek the total perfection of man's human powers—in short, to develop culture. The striving toward culture is inevitable, its triumph absolutely essential for the realization by man of his destiny; for it responds to the instinct of self-preservation in humanity which desires the development of all its specifically human qualities. The human race finds its ideal in "making endless additions to itself, in the endless expansion of its powers, in endless growth in wisdom and beauty." It therefore must seek its fulfillment through culture, which places perfection "in the ever-increasing efficacy and in the general harmonious expansion of those gifts of thought and feeling, which make the peculiar dignity, wealth, and happiness of human nature." But the final mark of the inevitability of culture is that it demands universal perfection; it does not reserve itself for a few; it makes no distinction whatever among human beings, but demands for all the same human perfection. Arnold realized, perhaps more perfectly than any of his fellows, the basic propositions of our civilization: the value of the single individual and the oneness of mankind. The cultural ideal is not possible "while the individual remains isolated. The individual is required, under pain of being stunted and enfeebled in his own development if he disobeys, to carry others along with him in his march towards perfection." The sympathy which binds humanity together is so great that we are, indeed, as Christianity says, "members of one body, and if one member suffer, all the members suffer with it. Individual perfection is impossible so long as the rest of mankind are not perfected along with us." The poor creatures in the East of London must also be carried along in the march to perfection;

if we ourselves really, as we profess, want to be perfect . . . we must not let the worship of any fetish, any machinery, such as manufactories or population . . . create for us such a multitude of miserable, sunken, and ignorant human beings, that to carry them along with us is impossible, and perforce they must for the most part be left by us in their degradation and wretchedness.

In this respect culture becomes the most "practical" of social measures, since it opposes by its very nature the degradation of the masses.

Here follows the great explanation by Arnold of how culture

is to be achieved. If it is the great help for England out of her difficulties, at all costs it must be placed within the reach of everyone whose humanity is capable of responding to it. If men can be educated to it because it deals in matters which expand their humanity, then the education which produces it must be offered to all who need it, particularly the middle classes. It is to be achieved, says Arnold in his most famous passage, by "getting to know, on all the matters which most concern us, the best that has been said and thought in the world; and through this knowledge, turning a stream of fresh and free thought upon our stock notions and habits, which we now follow staunchly but mechanically." Men will therefore acquire culture if they think and observe and read with a purpose; they will discover wherein human perfection consists by consulting "*all* the voices of human experience which have been heard upon it, of art, science, poetry, philosophy, history, as well as of religion."

Arnold arrives, like the other humanitarians, at education as the way outward and upward for mankind. In general, he felt that three "practical" reforms were necessary for a new English civilization: the reduction of that great inequality of condition and property now based on the English land system; a genuine municipal system; and the reform of education, especially for the middle classes. Of these the most important was education, since if its improvement were happily accomplished, all other changes would come gradually and easily. Of the details and arrangements for regulating public education, Arnold characteristically said that it was not his business to discuss them. Yet he does allow himself, in reviewing education in France and Germany, to outline an elaborate scheme for the reconstruction of English education, especially above the popular level. It is Arnold's only extended departure from the position of the critical man of letters who avoids detailed reform while offering spiritual guidance to the rest of mankind.

Yet here Arnold is both a humane critic and for once a special practical expert who is called upon to deal with a problem; he got his living by the inspection of schools, so that he must be allowed to separate his functions without inconsistency here. He describes a complicated scheme of administration and government, beginning with a central minister of education and extending through a high council, through provincial school boards to the conduct of school affairs for the whole country. Yet he has more of value to offer when he speaks of the proper content of education, of the best that has been said and thought in the world. He concentrates largely upon publicly endowed middle-class education and what it should contain. He was convinced that nothing effective could be done to raise the lower class except through an improved middle class; in order to take power away from the aristocracy, which was doing nothing effective, the middle class would have to transform itself. Once elevated by culture, this class would then dominate society as a whole, ruling intelligently and humanely and lifting the suppressed orders to its level. Its secondary education, like the already accepted popular schooling, should be public and compulsory, with education put as a bar or condition between every man and what he aims at in life.

In what should this public, middle-class education consist? What is the best that has been said and thought in the world? It is here that Arnold distinguishes himself as the most powerful voice, with the possible exception of Newman, ever to speak for humane letters. He offers, in the first place, the invaluable principle of simplicity in education. There should be broad lines of study for almost universal use, and the student should learn whatever is set out for him on these lines. It should not be great in quantity, but, "if we can get it well chosen, the more uniformly it can be kept to, the better." Arnold's simplification is even greater than that proposed nowadays by President Hutchins and his collaborators at St. John's and Columbia. In one of his letters he says that twenty books would be enough "in the direct teaching of the young and to be learnt as textbooks. Young people may read for themselves, collaterally, as much as they like." Further, most of the few things chosen from the best, will be found in the body of humane letters. Once more Arnold invokes the instinct for self-preservation in humanity and asserts flatly that the nature of man demands more of the study of letters than science, for the majority of mankind.

Letters will "call out their being at more points, will make them live more." Their humanity will be developed in all of its instincts by letters.

The study of letters is the study of the operation of human force, of human freedom and activity; the study of nature is the study of the operation of non-human force, of human limitation and passivity. The contemplation of human force and activity tends naturally to heighten our own force and activity; the contemplation of human limits and passivity tends rather to check it.

That literature must be chosen, then, which best conveys to men the "capabilities and performances of the human spirit." This means poetry in general, but especially the literature of ancient Greece and Rome, and the Bible. Poetry stands for Arnold at the very top of man's effort to express the best that is in him; it is "the highest and most beautiful expression" of humanity, the speech in which man comes nearest to the truth. Here man offers his finest criticism and interpretation of life and here a weak, defective human race must come more and more for sustenance. In the course of time science will seem incomplete without poetry; ". . . most of what now passes with us for religion and philosophy will be replaced by poetry. . . ." And the instinct for self-preservation in humanity will probably demand that it should be largely Greek and Latin poetry. This is because of the power in man of his sense for beauty; it seemed to Arnold that Greek literature and art especially served this instinct for beauty. Consequently man's desire to preserve and develop himself in his total humanity would maintain Greek as part of his culture. Likewise the need of man to know himself and the world through education, would direct him to the ancient humanities. This recalls a spectacular contradiction in Arnold's essay on "The Modern Spirit in Literature," wherein he spends most of his time discussing Sophocles and other Greeks and Romans in order to show what the term "modern" implies. The discipline offered by the study of humane letters will, finally, enable men to understand the Bible properly and so transform their mechanical notions of religion. For the Bible, too, has to be read and interpreted as a piece of literature, whereas heretofore orthodox theology has applied abstruse reasoning and a scientific spirit to its reading. The religious language of man is really poetry, which theologians have mistaken for science. The Bible is written in the language of poetry and emotion. "Approximate language thrown out, as it were, at certain great objects which the human mind augurs and feels after." To understand it, men need to know the way in which other men have thought, something of the history of the human mind, the way men have of using words and what they mean by them. The study of letters will give this knowledge through its fruits "of flexibility, perceptiveness, and judgment."

Such is the meaning of culture in Arnold's terms; it proposes the harmonious development of all the human powers of every man in society, so that no obstacle shall lie in the path of every man's progress toward his full human dignity. It assumes that only a man, because he is human, can be considered an end in himself; it demands that the oneness of mankind as a whole should govern the struggle of every man for his own perfection. No plea for equality, for the elevation of degraded men to their proper level, can be more complete and final than this. From an acceptance of these principles every possible good in the "practical" realm would have to follow; Arnold's descent to the ultimate groundwork for all human progress is infinitely more far-reaching and "practical" than the most complicated reform of outward arrangements; his uncompromising demand for complete human development is far more ideal and optimistic than the most lyrical schemes of social betterment for the lower classes. But all this demands one more ideal change, or is perhaps necessary to the accomplishment of this change if not a result of it. Arnold, too, insists on the paradox offered for the guidance of the human race by its greatest spiritual leaders. "He that loveth his life shall lose it," he that forgets himself and counts the happiness of others as essential to his own will find the only real happiness there is for man.

Arnold points out repeatedly that "happiness is our being's end and aim." But the question is, in what does real happiness consist? The spiritual leader must show men that they look for happiness

where it will never really be found; he must not, like Carlyle, baffle
them entirely by preaching labor, righteousness, and veracity as
means to happiness and then say that men were not meant for happiness at all. He must set up an ideal for ordinary men to follow, an
ideal "higher than that of the ordinary man, taken by himself." If
ever there was a notion, says Arnold, "tempting to common human
nature, it was the notion that the rule of 'every man for himself' was
the rule of happiness." But it turns out that this is a false notion.

The "Divine Plato" is called upon to say "that we have within
us a many-headed beast and a man"; the ancient conflict between
the flesh and the spirit goes on constantly, and every man is aware
of it. He feels one force

a movement of first impulse and more involuntary, leading us to grat-
ify any inclination that may solicit us, and called generally . . . man's
ordinary or passing self, of sense, appetite, desire; the other, a movement of reflection and more voluntary, leading us to submit inclination
to some rule, and called . . . man's higher or enduring self, of reason,
spirit, will.

For a man to obey his higher self means "happiness and life for him;
to obey the lower is death and misery." And herein lies the unique
wonder of man that he is thus able to stand against himself and to
make a choice between the dignity and the meanness of his spirit.
Yet man is weak and needs the inspiration of a noble example to
help in the triumph over his lower self. This inspiration is offered
by Christ, who preached, and exemplified in his own practice, the
qualities by which man's ordinary self is most essentially counteracted. Most people are unable to follow abstract moral rules; knowing this, Christ lighted up and inspired morality with "a joyful and
bounding emotion," enabling weak humanity to do what it knows
to be its duty. This morality plus inspiration is well marked by the
term "righteousness," the elements of which are revealed in the
Bible. This revelation makes the Bible absolutely indispensable in
the struggle of mankind for perfection.

Now, this message of Christ cannot be drawn as a table of rigid
external commands. It is simply an idea meant to sink down into the
souls of men, to work quietly there. It is, of all the ways to right-

eousness men can think of, the one most certain to succeed. Arnold summarizes it in what he calls the method, the secret, and the sweet reasonableness of Christ. The "method" is "inwardness," the setting up of a new inward movement for obtaining the rule of life. Christ said not to attend so much to outward acts as to the state of one's heart and feelings. Conduct, the three-fourths of life, was keeping the thoughts in order; in all the concerns of conduct Christ admonishes man to watch what passes within him. His "secret," then, comes to insure man's true happiness. It simply asks self-renouncement. If offers the greatest of all spiritual truths for human guidance, that in self-renouncement there is joy and life. The conquest of our ordinary self involves such pain and gloom and fear that the secret of Christ was needed to lighten and inspire the process. He simply showed that ceasing our concern with our apparent self and leaving it to perish was not to thwart or frustrate the true law of our being; it was to recognize that renouncement led us to our proper destiny. The bliss of man was, therefore, to be found, not in some fantastic paradise of the future, but in the resurrection preached by St. Paul. This resurrection was to occur now, a resurrection to righteousness. It was a spiritual rising in our earthly lives, a dying first to our ordinary selfish impulses and the rising to a life of obedience to the eternal moral order.

Men should then cease to think constantly of their so-called rights; if they will face the truth, they must confess with Arnold that they have no rights at all, but only duties. Political science can set up rights for a man and maintain them, but not so the "method and secret" of Christ. "Man sincere, man before conscience . . . finds laid out for himself no rights; nothing but an infinite dying, and in that dying is life." Yet, even in this great truth Arnold characteristically finds danger if it is too mechanically followed. Christ's "sweet reasonableness" is needed if his "method and secret" are not to be ill employed. For "the human spirit is wider than the most priceless of the forces which bear it onward," and there is danger in setting up renouncement as a stock maxim without flexibility or common sense to mellow it. Let the extremists in religion, the Philistine dissenters, realize that freedom lies in service, "not in service to

any stock maxim, but an elevation of our best self, and a harmoniz-
ing in subordination to this, and to the idea of a perfected humanity, all the multitudinous, turbulent, and blind impulses of our
ordinary selves." Christ's "sweet reasonableness" recommends this
to us not in any stark, mechanical, Philistine way, but so as to make
it seem "the most simple, natural, winning, necessary thing in the
world." When this is widely understood and applied, it will transform the world.

So every man learns the way to happiness. It is the way demanded
by his humanity, which turns out to have within itself the principle
of its own perfection. The more nearly human a man is, the more
nearly perfect he is, and from this achievement of his full dignity
alone follows his happiness. And by this attainment of his individual perfection he fulfills his oneness with the rest of mankind, the
dependence of his own perfection upon that of other men. Mankind
as a whole must be raised into the true law of man's being; every
individual contributes to this when he follows the "method and the
secret." For Christ had an unfailing sense of what made the solidar-
ity of men, of the fact that "the law of the spirit makes men one; it
is only by the law in our members that we are many."

Thus, when he charged man to renounce himself, he also gave a
positive command to "love one another." This love for our neighbor is the completion of our happiness in self-renouncement, and is,
indeed, the logical, inevitable result of it. Man recognizes that "my
neighbor is merely an extension of myself"; therefore, any effort to
live isolated from one's neighbor is an offense against oneself and
thwarts one's own desire for happiness. Thus, the two ideals of
individual dignity and the oneness of mankind are mutually dependent, neither possible without the other. Arnold applies this
directly to the sharp divisions among the classes of society which he
deplored. These divisions are overcome for those people in each
class who are curious about their best selves and wish to follow reason and the moral order to perfection. This desire, says Arnold,
"always tend to take them out of their class, and to make their dis-
tinguishing characteristic not their Barbarianism or their Philistinism, but their *humanity*."

This attainment of full humanity is in keeping with the popular ideal of an immense transformation of things into a better and happier future society. The multitude everywhere has wanted to be happy on this earth; it has desired a social transformation away from the great inequalities of wealth and position which Arnold found such an obstacle to human perfection. He denounces any tendency on the part of the church to defer to the propertied and satisfied classes and to preach submission to the poor, who are to wait for change beyond the grave. This violates the message of Christ, which enjoined self-sacrifice on everyone and service to the common cause. Those who cling to riches and personal enjoyment, "who have not brought themselves to regard property and riches as foreign and indifferent to them, who have not annulled self and placed their happiness in the common good," these, as Christ said, will hardly enter the Kingdom of God. And what is the Kingdom of God? Simply "the ideal society of the future," in which all men will be unified because they have perfected themselves by forgetting themselves.

The human search for perfection through the elevation of the best in man, the striving for a perfect expansion of his humanity, brings us finally to Arnold's extraordinary concept of the state, "the nation in its collective and corporate character." The idea that the state should represent the highest development of the nation as a whole, should be the outward expression of man's nearest approach to right reason and the eternal moral order would seem spectacular enough at most periods of man's history. It should appear brilliant now, when under fascism "the State has maimed and crushed individual activity," has operated as an alien power "not originated by the community to serve the common weal, but entrenched among them as a conqueror with a weal of its own to serve." But when the true possibilities of the state are understood, it becomes clear that state-action may be favorable to the individual's perfection. Arnold uses ancient Greece again, to show a place where state action was omnipresent and the individual was at his highest point of free activity. In pleading for the state, however, Arnold sees that he must overcome the current English view of the state as an outside, intrusive power, frustrating individual action. People were afraid of state action, also, because they conceived of the state "as something equivalent to the class in occupation of the executive government," and naturally supposed that the ruling class would abuse power for its own purposes. They did not realize that with a new concept of the state they could once and for all break the power of any single class over the others.

This suggests why Arnold was opposed to feudalism in any form. Not only did the presence of an aristocratic class living in ease, comfort, and pleasure offer a false ideal to the middle classes and plunge the lower classes into despair of ever attaining it for themselves; not only were aristocracies unable, with their lack of flexibility and total want of ideas, to rule in an era of expansion; it was simply that no class could or should rule England alone. Arnold asked that men "rise above the idea of class to the idea of the whole community, the State, and . . . find our centre of light and authority there." The reason men find it hard to get above the idea of class is that they live in their ordinary selves, which do not carry them beyond the ideas and wishes of the class they happen to belong to. Now when the state power is wielded by a given class, it is precisely this ordinary, inferior self which gets control. Let the state then offer an ideal of reason and right feeling; let there be a public establishment of our best self, "commanding general respect, and forming a rallying point for the intelligence and for the worthiest instincts of the community, which will herein find a true bond of union." In the end the individual will have to act for himself and perfect himself, but for a long time the state must oppose the individual's ordinary self and so help him to stand alone in perfection. Thus, the individual faces an overpoweringly difficult task; he must somehow set up for himself a thing which will help him to perfection, and yet in order to establish this helpful agent he must already have achieved and recognized in himself the very perfection which this agent is meant to create after he has established it.

But if he succeeds, man will have a power capable of conferring enormous collective benefits upon him; especially the present middle and lower classes will develop a life incomparably better than they could, unaided, provide for themselves. The individual will become a member in a partnership, not a dependent receiving favors from a parental benefactor; it will be a partnership likewise, as Burke is invoked to say, " 'in all science, in all art, in every virtue, in all perfection.' " The state, representing the best self of its members, will stand against all lawlessness and excess of the ordinary self, bringing about that firm and settled public order which is requisite "if man is to bring to maturity anything precious and lasting now, or to found anything precious or lasting for the future." We must come back finally to culture as the means of achieving the state, as well as of developing our total humanity. For the state depending on the emergence of our best self, also depends on culture, for

this is the very self which culture . . . seeks to develop in us. So that our poor culture . . . flouted as so unpractical, leads us to the very ideas capable of meeting the great want of our present embarrassed times! We want an authority, and we find nothing but jealous classes, checks, and a deadlock; culture suggests the idea of *the State*. We find no basis for a firm State-power in our ordinary selves; culture suggests one to us in our *best self*.

No one shows better than Arnold that wonderful quality of all humanitarians; great optimism in the face of knowledge of human weakness. If belief in education is the essence of the humane ideal, it would be difficult to find a nobler plea for education, a firmer belief in its good result than Arnold's. His analysis of the corrupting materialism of his time certainly did not flatter mankind; yet he could honestly say that men would surely come to a higher life in the end. "Instinctively, however slowly, the human spirit struggles towards the light." The struggle is attended constantly by failure, yet it must go on. Providence itself "forbids the final supremacy of imperfect things. God keeps tossing back to the human race its failures, and commanding it to try again." Man goes on hoping and always will hope beyond what he knows and can verify, but this is essential to progress. And when he makes a little headway, behold he finds that more is expected of him and that he is as far away from the goal as ever. Arnold also sees our humanity as a glory and a penalty:

we are called to develop ourselves more in our totality, on our perceptive and intelligential side as well as on our moral side. If it is said that this is a very hard matter, and that man cannot well do more than one thing at a time, the answer is that here is the very sign and condition of each new stage of spiritual progress,—*increase of task*. The more we grow, the greater is the task which is given us. This is the law of man's nature and of his spirit's history. The powers we have developed at our old task enable us to attempt a new one; and this, again, brings with it a new increase of powers.

And so Arnold could realize clearly that the reforms he demanded had no chance of attainment in his own time, and still believe that everyone was better for having aimed high toward great designs. "The endeavour will very likely be in vain. . . . But failures do something, as well as successes, towards the final achievement." As long as man is man let him remember Dante's admonition: " 'Consider whereunto ye are born! Ye were not made to live like brutes, but to follow virtue and knowledge!' " The day will come when men have largely solved the problems of Arnold's age, yet there will be new troubles, as the sparks fly upward. Men will "be mounting some new steps in the arduous ladder whereby man climbs towards his perfection; towards that unattainable but irresistible lode-star, gazed after with earnest longing, and invoked with bitter tears; the longing of thousands of hearts, the tears of many generations."

It is good to find that Arnold himself never ceased to labor for the perfection in his own person which he held up as an ideal for others. The truth of his message would not be canceled by a weak inability on his own part to practice what he taught. Yet such is the need in men for both precept and example, that one is glad to see in Arnold a human being who came as near as weak humanity will permit to a complete adherence to his own doctrine. He cultivated his "best self" on every side and was never content with anything less than the perfection which he held up as the destiny of man. He was an exception to his own remark that most of us "are what we must be, not what we ought to be,—not even what we know we ought to be." He conceived gentleness to be his special task; he was without the fierceness and savagery of Carlyle and Kingsley, even though his convictions were fully as deep as theirs. He hoped that his influence would be "a healing and reconciling influence"; he believed in the need of persuasion and charm and that even in ridicule "one must preserve a sweetness and good-humour." His kindness and Christian charity were also in keeping with what he conceived to be inseparable from culture: the effort to help others, to remove error, and to diminish misery, "the noble aspiration to leave the world better and happier than we found it." Above all he carried out in his hard, exhausting daily labor his noble doctrine of self-renunciation and realized its paradox by finding such joy as was possible for him in a period which depressed him profoundly. He spent his life and his magnificent talents in the dreary task of school inspection, seldom complaining of the small reward for his services, maintaining a consummate self-discipline and control and living like a Christian, without bitterness or envy. Arnold said the last word on his own reconciliation between theory and practice, a union so desperately hard for lesser men. On being praised for his gentle and patient treatment of school children, he simply wrote: "The great thing is *humanity*, after all."

VIII. Ruskin

> I speak either about kings, or masses of men,
> with a fixed conviction that human nature
> is a noble and beautiful thing; not a foul nor
> a base thing. All the sin of men I esteem as
> their disease, not their nature; as folly
> which may be prevented, not a necessity
> which must be accepted. And my wonder,
> even when things are at their worst, is al-
> ways at the height which this human nature
> can attain. Thinking it high, I find it always
> a higher thing than I thought it; while those
> who think it low . . . will find it always
> lower than they thought it: the fact being,
> that it is infinite, and capable of infinite
> height and infinite fall; but the nature of it
> . . . is in the nobleness, not in the catas-
> trophe.—Ruskin, "War," in *The Crown of
> Wild Olive.*

RUSKIN OFTEN SAID that the work of his middle years, during which
he devoted himself to "the condition of England," was in the last
degree distasteful to him. Yet, "tormented by agony of indignation
and compassion," he had to speak out "to disburden my heart of the
witness I have to bear." There was no one to whom he could turn
for guidance except Carlyle; he became weary of pen-holding, his
heart sick of thinking and working alone. He hated what he was
doing, and above all what he conceived to be the necessity for doing
it. He was interested in art and the teaching of art, in gardens and
pictures and birds. "I dislike having either power or responsibility,"
he said. "I don't want to talk, nor to write, nor to advise or direct
anybody. . . . I would give anything to be quit of the whole business." Yet he had no choice, given the misery and ugliness of the
world about him. The things he wanted to do were impossible anyway; he could not paint or read or look at minerals, "and the very

light of the morning sky . . . has become hateful to me, because of
the misery that I know of, and see signs of . . . which no imagination can interpret too bitterly. . . . I will endure it no longer
quietly; but henceforward . . . do my poor best to abate this misery." His "poor best" became an enormously complicated system
of social ethics, based upon the same belief in human dignity and
oneness which Ruskin had absorbed from other great spiritual leaders. This construction was worked out at immense personal cost
to Ruskin; it is a monument to his forgetfulness of self, his wonderful compassion and moral conviction, which made him turn aside
from his own desire and work for the benefit of others. In his own
life Ruskin, too, shows the way to the virtues by which mankind
might move toward the fulfillment of its dream.

In taking up the odious burden of preaching to England, Ruskin
spent less time in mere vituperation than did Carlyle. He was fond
of reprinting notices from the press containing horrible instances
of human suffering and degradation and letting them speak for
themselves. But he was the first among these literary humanitarians
to dwell upon the ugliness of England as a crime almost equal to
the loss of human dignity. This by-product of the industrial revolution had been noticed before, especially by Kingsley, whose emphasis was rather upon dirt than upon ugliness. It was left for Ruskin
and, especially, his disciple William Morris to expose the harm done
to England's beauty and to emphasize the meaning of such a loss.

A glance at certain government reports and other sources will
show that Ruskin is not to be dismissed as an over-sensitive aesthete
when he complains that England had lost much of her natural and
urban beauty. Aside from the loss of charm suffered in changing
to an industrial civilization, there is first of all the smoke nuisance.
The smoke from factory chimneys, gas and chemical works, distill-
eries, breweries, and the like, not only excluded the sun's light but
also made it very hard to keep one's person and one's home properly
clean. London alone suffered annual damage amounting to several
million pounds. In 1864 over three million tons of coal were burned
for manufacturing and home use, filling the air with quantities of
harmful acid and soot. This nuisance caused great expense in addi-

tional cleaning and painting and in the permanent injury done to furniture, books, pictures, and decorations of all kinds. People grew cautious about collecting the best obtainable works of art and handicraft, lest they deteriorate in the smoky atmosphere of their homes. The air of other cities was similarly contaminated, as Disraeli suggests through Lady Marney's description of Mowbray in the novel *Sybil*. Mowbray is a grand place, she says, "but like all places in the manufacturing districts, very disagreeable. You never have a clear sky. Your toilette table is covered with black; the deer in the park seem as if they had bathed in a lake of India ink; and as for the sheep, you expect to see chimney-sweeps for the shepherds." Harm was also done to public and private buildings. All coal contains sulphur, which when burned is released into the air and exerts a most harmful effect upon calcareous building stones; also, deposits of soot disfigure buildings, injuring especially ornamental stonework. One limestone church, for example, was covered in some parts with a black crust up to one and one-half inches in thickness, composed of a substance which not only ruined the beauty of the church but actually changed the original composition of the stone.

Yet the stain upon the beauty of cities was no more conspicuous than the harm frequently done to country vegetation. The growth of Manchester and the transformation of other industrial townships defiled the atmosphere and destroyed vegetation for miles in every direction. The injury done to vegetation by smoke from copperworks was traced in one instance beyond a distance of four miles, and it was discovered that certain delicate plants would not thrive within ten miles of London. The most harmful vapors came apparently from brick and tile works and from manufactories of earthenware and stoneware, which used inferior coal, from copperworks, and, before the passage of the Alkali Act in 1863, from places producing sulphite soda. In addition, a variety of manufactories along the banks of the Tyne evolved from twenty of fifty tons of muriatic acid gas daily. These various agents often prevented the healthy growth of wheat, barley, grass, clover, and oats. Plants would turn from green to yellow to white, often as if frozen. Grass was at times so contaminated that it was harmful to cattle; trees,

especially fruit and ornamental trees, were readily injured by polluted air. When we recall that sulphurous acid gas, for example,
causes the leaves of plants to droop when it is present in the air in
the proportion of only one ten-thousandth part, its destructive
force is apparent. Farmers could therefore complain of whole
estates left with scarcely a healthy shrub, of trees whose foliage
had turned yellow, brown, and finally black before dying completely. When leaves were so destroyed for several years in suc-
cession, the trees would often die completely. One estate was
forced to cut down about three thousand trees, all hopelessly
ruined.

Thus the aspect of cities and of the land itself was often blighted;
so, also, the beauty of England's rivers. The Rivers Pollution Commission gives a report upon the streams of the West Riding in Yorkshire which describes the crystal purity of the water in the higher
country. But as the water passed a series of woolen mills, for example, it became fouler after leaving each successive mill until it
was almost impure enough to be treated as an open drain. The River
Medlock, in 1844, was the receptacle for the drainage of a population numbering in all about 100,000. But the filth from streets and
houses was only a small item. The river also received the refuse
from numerous dyeworks, printworks, and factories, the whole
forming a mixture of intolerable filth, which gave off a villainous
stench. Other rivers in Yorkshire and Lancashire received the rins-
ings from tanneries, breweries, paper-mills, collieries, soap factories, and various chemical establishments. After taking up various such substances, a river often became a compound of earth, fat,
soap, coal, wool, hairs, and assorted chemical ingredients, which
stained the water with all possible colors and produced a putrid,
slow-moving mass from whose bottom decomposition sent up quantities of gas, causing the stream to bubble violently as it moved
along. The result was a repulsive substance in place of the once
beautiful stream. Such pollution went on with almost no hindrance,
the laws against it being so defective and so easily evaded that out-
raged sufferers from the nuisance protested largely in vain.

Ruskin never tired of mourning this loss of England's beauty, which seemed to him a reflection of the moral gloom and spiritual decay of men themselves. He uses a religious metaphor at times to describe his feeling that man had dishonored the dwelling place which God had prepared for him, as if there were a kind of consecrated holiness in the beauty of the world whose pollution was offensive to God. There seems to be a general indifference among the English to all this, Ruskin complains; the entire aspect of a place like London is repulsive . . . "rattling, growling, smoking, stinking,—a ghastly heap of fermenting brickwork, pouring out poison at every pore." A kind of instinct for the horrible in the English allows the destruction of beautiful things, which has been going on since the sixteenth century; it has extended even to the person of man himself, who has become on the whole "an ugly animal, and is not ashamed of his ugliness." From England, from English dwellings, from man himself—grace and glory have departed.

Yet there is something worse than external ugliness, a parallel result from the same cause, that is, the loss of human wealth which England has suffered. Amid the squalor, filth, and ugliness human beings live in such degradation that "existence becomes mere transition." Ruskin omits none of the familiar catalogue of human misery in nineteenth-century England: the children in dirty rags, trying to play happily in their loathsome surroundings, the terrible overcrowding in rotten and neglected houses, the pollution of drinking water into "hell-broth" and the consequent fever, the subhuman life of the cellars and all that it implied. In *Fors Clavigera* Ruskin speaks of having kept an index or file under the heading "misery," from which he constantly quoted excerpts, sometimes reprinting them in blood-red ink for public edification—all illustrating the human price being paid by civilization. We hear of Annie Redfern, aged twenty-eight, who was found dead in a cellar rented at 1s. 9d. a week. She had died with her three-year-old son clasped in her arms, and her body was removed to preserve it from the rats. We are told of the hundreds of gallons of opium sold weekly for the purpose of drugging babies to sleep while mothers were away at work. This recalls our horrible acquaintance "Godfrey," a thing so often mentioned in nineteenth-century history as to take on immediate reality, like a person willing to help others in the process of self-destruction. Ruskin quotes also a newspaper account of a man found sitting on a junk-pile, dead. The rain had been beating down on the body all night after the man had died of cold and neglect. He had been a bone-picker, obviously in the most extreme poverty. In his pockets were found a single penny and some bones.

Ruskin was constantly tormented by the knowledge of such bitter want. While England was alive with spinning wheels, black with the digging of coal, while her harbors were a forest of merchant ships, the people died of cold, nakedness, and hunger. The poor outnumbered the more fortunate ones by a thousand to one and occupied the social position of helpless slaves—their physical condition was an index of their moral state as well. Ruskin sadly reflects on the stupidity of the working masses, their lack of foresight in marrying and reproducing themselves promiscuously, with no prospect of offering a decent life to their children, their incredible ignorance of the most elementary religious knowledge, and many times over their fantastic consumption of liquor, which further enriched the upper classes. Ruskin understands, nevertheless, why the laborer drank himself deeper into poverty. He points out the need of education to give a sense of values and discrimination, the need for some decent amusement for even the better paid workers, where they may spend some of their time instead of ladling port wine out of buckets in the tavern. Ruskin admits in so many words that "if I were in your place, I should drink myself to death in six months, because I had nothing to amuse me." The cheerlessness of life seemed to leave its mark upon the faces of most people; Ruskin speaks of seeing seven or eight hundred people in a day without noticing a single happy face. This unhappiness was true of the very lowest middle class as well as of the starved and impoverished laborer. Ruskin is so weighed down by his knowledge of the anxiety and pain in life, that he feels constantly like one living in a great churchyard, "with people all around me clinging feebly to the edges of the open graves, and calling for help, as they fall back into them, out of sight."

England would have enough to be ashamed of if her laboring

masses suffered only from hunger and physical neglect, for which there is no excuse. But there is a subtler means of human degradation, which would be an affront to human dignity even if the low man were abundantly paid and physically cared for. This is the waste of men under the tyranny of machines, whose effect is to produce a race of less than men, to degrade their human powers, and to make their rightful destiny impossible. This raises once again the question of human greatness and wherein it consists.

Every "companion" of St. George's Company, Ruskin's private organization of men of good will, had to write out in his own hand and sign an eight-point "creed." In the second article the "companion" asserted his trust "in the nobleness of human nature, in the majesty of its faculties, the fullness of its mercy, and the joy of its love." Ruskin's pages are alive with tributes to the unique importance of man and his life in the world; to the unlimited capacity of man for nobility of mind and person; to his wonderful sensitiveness and depth of feeling; to the beauty and the glory which are to be found in every human countenance, even in the commonest features met "in the highways and hedges." But Ruskin, too, thought well of man and his possibilities for good in spite of the bitterest admission of human weakness and folly. "I am surprised," he says, "at no depths to which, when once warped from its honor . . . humanity can be degraded." He was helped to such an admission after years of trying to drive his ideas "into the gnarled blockheadism of the British mob . . . the desperate leathern-skinned, death-helmeted skull of this wretched England." Ruskin's experience taught him "how much baser the human material I had to deal with, was, than I thought in the beginning." He was often depressed when observing the populace generally. In one day of travel he had seen only a single human creature "on whom sight could rest without pain. The rest of the crowd was a mere dismal fermentation of the Ignominious." Ruskin admits freely that most men are dull and suited only to simple work in the world; that some are like stones and crush others, some are like weeds and entangle others, some are like logs and obstruct the way, some are like thorns and choke the good seed; that men in general are incapable of sat-

isfaction even with the best of what the earth can give; that every
glory of the human soul no matter how beautiful is exposed to its
special form of corruption.

But when every unsavory detail had been admitted, Ruskin insists that man is "nobly animal, nobly spiritual" in his nature. He
believes this because he has to, given his hopeful view of man's future; he is forced to take a high view of human nature, because he
is sure that men will become what they think they are. Let them
believe the false prophets who say that men are half-beast, half-
devil, and they will sink to that level. Even in his art criticism Ruskin
disapproves of pictures showing the extreme passions of terror and
ferocity on men's faces. He considers ferocity the least human of
the passions and dislikes pictures which represent it; indeed, he is
opposed to showing any extremely violent passion, because it is "destructive of human dignity." It is simply inappropriate to represent
the human race as being so degraded; there is too much kinship with
the Divinity in man, ever to allow a picture which should present
general human truth, to give an unwholesome, animal-like impression. The good that is in man is of divine origin; man's pleasure in
divine attributes and his willingness to dedicate himself and his
powers to God show the reflection of God in the soul of man. The
strength of his spiritual life is what makes him human. Thus, in so
far as man is true to the highest powers of his humanity, he is divine. His heart and conscience are of God, and we know "that in
his perception of evil, in his recognition of good, he is himself a
God manifest in the flesh; that his joy in love, his agony in anger, his
indignation at injustice, his glory in self-sacrifice, are all . . . proofs
of his unity with a great Spiritual Head . . . in these . . . he is
king over the lower animate world." If men adopt the high view of
themselves, therefore, they will see that by nature they are kind
and generous and that they are capable, even the lowest and weakest
among them, of making a gift to the well-being of all mankind.
This capacity for helping others is one of the ultimate glories of
being a man. Individual differences of power and function among
men are adapted "to each other's assistance, admiration, or support."
They increase human love and allow every man to bestow as well
as to receive, binding himself to others by a thousand necessities and

gratitudes and realizing his human destiny by becoming the complement of other men. A man is so wonderfully designed, therefore, that it is part of his nature to seek fulfillment in union with others, to go outside of himself for the satisfaction of the things which really make him a man, the things which he has in common with God.

This high view of man leads Ruskin to his hatred of any force in life which tends to degrade the individual man or to make impossible the full development of his nature and capacity. Ruskin believed that in his own time the machine was such a force. There was no question in his mind as to a decline in human quality among his contemporaries. There is

evil diversity, and terrible stamp of various degradation; features seamed with sickness, dimmed by sensuality, convulsed by passion, pinched by poverty, shadowed by sorrow, branded with remorse; bodies consumed with sloth, broken down by labor, tortured by disease, dishonoured in foul uses; intellects without power, hearts without hope, minds earthly and devilish; our bones full of the sin of our youth . . . well for us only, if, after beholding this our natural face in a glass, we desire not straightway to forget what manner of men we be.

To this obvious decline of mankind the machine has made an immense contribution, for all mechanical operation is degrading. To begin with, machines cause idleness, and idle men represent a loss to the world of unfulfilled human possibility. Not even Carlyle has surpassed Ruskin's magnificent lament in the *Stones of Venice* over the quantity of waste in life.

I do not wonder at what men Suffer, but I wonder often at what they Lose. . . . The fruit struck to the earth before its ripeness; the glowing life and goodly purpose dissolved away in sudden death; the words, half spoken, choked upon the lips with clay for ever; or, stronger than all, the whole majesty of humanity raised to its fullness, and every gift and power necessary for a given purpose, at a given moment, centred in one man, and all this perfected blessing permitted to be . . . crushed, cast aside by those who need it most. . . . These are the heaviest mysteries of this strange world.

For such loss and waste the machine is responsible when it does the work appropriate to human hands.

Yet even when machines do not deprive men of the chance to

work, they degrade those who use them, partly by lowering the quality of the thing produced and, worse than this, by making the men themselves into machines through a starvation of the very faculties of mind and spirit which make them men. Ruskin believed that most of English labor was spent unproductively, either in making the equipment for war or in producing goods of cheap and inferior quality, made to sell. These goods are not worth the human labor spent on them; they are made by dull, mechanical processes instead of by the use of the workman's own skill. They are made in defiance of "the value of the human soul, and the shortness of mortal time." They betray an indifference to art and to the thrilling spectacle of a strong man's skill shown in his work. The so-called "division of labor" submerges the individual even more deeply than a complete operation, however dull. The man's whole mind is never brought into play; he is lost in and becomes a part of the machine. It is not so much the labor that is divided, it is the men who are broken into fragments and crumbs of life. Their intelligence is not allowed to make a whole pin or nail; it must be exhausted in making only the point of a pin, or the head of a nail. A great human price is paid for the making of many pins in one day, as even Adam Smith was willing to admit. The pins and other wares are made with wonderful perfection and mechanical thoroughness, yet by an immensely important contradiction it is this very perfection which costs the laborer his own humanity.

Ruskin's elaboration of this idea in *The Stones of Venice* is one of his most impressive achievements and is essential to his thought as a whole. He tells us that "men were not intended to work with the accuracy of tools, to be precise and perfect in all their actions. If you will have that precision out of them . . . you must unhumanize them." Ruskin traces the mania for finish and execution to the fifteenth century, when great artists achieved great perfection and polish. Having seen this perfection in art, the world began to demand it in everything: all work had to be done in a complete and accurate way at the expense of feeling and originality. Finally, with the coming of machines the workman attained method and finish but lost his soul in exchange for them. In every workman there is some unpolished power, some rude and imperfect imagination which is completely lost in a society which demands technical perfection and finish. If the human and imperfect part of the man is not to be lost, the world must be willing to accept the faults and errors which are inseparable from all human effort. If a man is to be other than a tool, let him begin to imagine, "to think, to try to do anything worth doing; and the engine-turned precision is lost at once. Out come all his roughness, all his dullness, all his incapability; shame upon shame, failure upon failure, pause after pause: but out comes the whole majesty of him also." He is then able to do human work; "that is to say, affectionate, honest, and earnest work." Ruskin's case against the machine is therefore based upon its human cost.

Such was Ruskin's view of the ugliness and misery of the world in which he lived. No wonder he could say in the year 1878, after his long and futile war with the iniquity of England: "Probably there is not another so much vexed person as I at present extant of his grave."

In analyzing the reason why life has suffered so great a degradation, Ruskin adds various emphases to the views of his master, Carlyle. He also denounces priesthoods that do not preach and aristocracies that do not govern. Because the clergy have failed to teach the right gospel to elevate morality and have dined with the well-to-do and preached to the poor, instead of preaching to the upper classes and dining with the poor, they have been answerable for much of the prevailing evil. The upper classes have enjoyed "one large Picnic Party" and have neglected their duty of protecting and guiding the less fortunate. The gentry seem more intent on shooting birds than on performance of their real duty, "their task of painful honorableness." Instead of behaving like real aristocracy, the English upper classes are concerned to make the people work for them, while they, the leaders, take most of the wages, regardless of the ensuing human misery. Ruskin denounces this as nothing better than robbery, stealing the produce of a man's work from him, keeping him poor and ignorant so that he won't realize what is being done to him, and then despising him for the very degradation and crudity which is the result of his inferior position. This is how the class of people who should protect and help others have managed to get wealth into their hands. Their love of luxury is simply indefensible alongside the painful want of the masses.

But the chief cause of England's troubles is the political economy which is generally adopted. Ruskin's attitude toward the social and economic philosophy which felt especially triumphant at the very moment when he chose to attack it, would have seemed one of the most sublime pieces of impudence in the nineteenth century if people had bothered to notice it. At the very peak of mid-Victorian prosperity Ruskin could write the famous opening passage of *Unto This Last:*

Among the delusions which at different periods have possessed themselves of the minds of large masses of the human race, perhaps the most curious—certainly the least creditable—is the modern *soi-disant* science of political economy, based on the idea that an advantageous code of social action may be determined irrespectively of the influence of social affection.

There is a fine, Carlylean accent in the vituperation which Ruskin heaps upon those who say that they believe in classical economics. We hear that "nothing in history had ever been so disgraceful to human intellect as the acceptance among us of the common doctrines of political economy as a science." The whole structure is a tissue of absurdities. To begin with, it systematically denies the doctrines of the English national religion, which is supposed to be based on Christian love. The laws of the devil are declared, with "entire naïveté and undisturbed imbecility," to be more practicable than the laws of God. Adam Smith has set up a new religion, which says, " 'thou shalt hate the Lord thy God, damn His laws, and covet thy neighbour's goods.' " In addition political economy teaches that the individual should be free to seek his own interest under the so-called principle of laissez-faire. Ruskin believes that "of all the curses that poor, vicious, idiotic man can suffer, liberty is perhaps the greatest." It is the most treacherous of all phantoms, for there is not, should not be, and cannot be such a thing as the liberty preached by the "let-alone" philosophy. Discipline and interference, help and restraint are the real roots of human progress and power. Among the results of the "let-alone" principle Ruskin finds the pernicious "laws" of supply and demand and free competition. He simply denies that such principles exist. The so-called "law" of supply and demand is "false always, and everywhere" simply because it is beneath human dignity. It is the privilege "of the fishes, as it is of rats and wolves, to live by the laws of demand and supply; but the distinction of humanity, to live by those of right."

As for the notion that wages are to be measured by competition, Ruskin says that he has "no terms of English, and can find none in Greek nor Latin, nor in any other strong language known to me, contemptuous enough to attack the bestial idiotism" of such a theory. Finally, Ruskin denies the validity of classical economics, because it takes a low view of man, directly opposed to his own naïve and optimistic faith in human dignity. It makes the stupendous blunder of leaving out the soul of man from its calculations and assuming that the nature of man is like that of a predatory animal. The whole science of political economy is founded on the assumption that man's constant instinct is to defraud his neighbor. Thus, it is openly confessed that men are not to be considered as men, but as beasts of prey. Ruskin finds a sentence in a paper read before a social science meeting in Glasgow, 1860, which asserts that since the predatory and carnivorous spirit is a condition of human nature, the arrangements of civilized society should be based upon it. He considers this "the most vile sentence . . . in the literature of any country or time." It should "in the monumental vileness of it . . . be blazoned, in letters of stinking gas-fire, over the condemned cells of every felon's prison in Europe." Such a view of man declares that faith, honesty, largeness of heart, and self-sacrifice are the mere phrases of poetry. Ruskin may as well admit in that case, that he lives among thieves and murderers and that everyone around him is trying to rob everybody else.

Like Arnold, Ruskin was afraid that England would decline and in another century would be "among the dead of nations." But he proposed numerous plans for rescuing England from disaster. His recommendations are based upon a high view of human nature and

its possibilities; he assumes that men are or can become good enough
to conduct their affairs according to certain "laws" which he would
set up in place of the misleading "laws" of political economy. He is
very quick to denounce the false appearance of the virtues which
he believes man to be capable of. Like Carlyle, he has no patience
with the mere show of Christianity or the specious exercise of the
Christian virtues. But he does believe in a "Human Economy."

Ruskin thinks constantly in human terms and relates everything
to man and to human life. This was true of his criticism of art at
the beginning of his career and was maintained as a first principle
to the end of his long and unselfish labor. He tells us in *Modern
Painters* that his essays on art bring "everything to a root in human
passion or human hope." He prefers one school of architecture over
another because it has a better influence on the life of the man who
works. For Ruskin every work of art has value, "exactly in the ratio
of the quantity of humanity which has been put into it, and legibly
expressed upon it for ever."

Further, the value of anything must be measured in terms of life
and of the human effort involved in its production. This is one of
Ruskin's answers to "supply and demand," for the value of a thing,
he says, has nothing to do with quantity. A thing either avails
toward life, or it does not. Its value lies in its life-giving power. Its
cost is the quantity of labor needed to produce it: its price will be
the quantity of labor which the owner will take in exchange for it.
These ideas are heard like a constant refrain in Ruskin's work and
are inseparable from his belief in human dignity. If all value depends on life, then a country's wealth is in its human beings, and the
more and better the human beings are, the greater is the nation's
wealth.

Whatever "laws" Ruskin will set up to guide men away from
"the condition of England" are therefore based upon his everlasting
concern for and belief in human life as the measure of everything.
His desire to construct a better world is the product of his deep
compassion for the suffering of poor men, a generous sympathy
which is one of the most appealing things in his life and work. It
escapes mere sentimental humanitarianism because it is allied with

strong indignation and an immense intellectual effort at the reconstruction of the world. As Ruskin himself often says, it follows the current of the unchanging spiritual leadership of mankind. This feeling of oneness with the wisdom and the spiritual tradition of man is so strong in Ruskin that he half-jokingly tells the readers of *Fors Clavigera* how he begins for the first time "to admit some notion into my head that I am a great man." Not only must he have the firmness to do his work in the face of contempt and opposition on all sides, but also he sees that he is at one in viewing nature and life with the greatest of classic authors. Ruskin never pretends to say anything new—why should he, when the truth of all that he writes has been for ages "known to the wisest, and proclaimed by the most eloquent of men?" His friends must have found the following passage in *Fors Clavigera* more than a little absurd in view of their belief that his ideas were outlandish:

I do not enter into any debates, nor advance any opinions. With what is debatable I am unconcerned; and when I only have opinions about things, I do not talk about them. I attack only what cannot on any possible ground be defended and state only what I know to be incontrovertibly true . . . I should be ashamed if there were anything in *Fors* which had not been said before,—and that a thousand times . . . common truths, as clear to honest mankind as their daily sunrise.

For the sake of clarity and order among the endless details and applications of his ideas which Ruskin expounded in volume after volume, it will be convenient to state under four general divisions or "laws," his directions for carrying out in practice these timeless rules. Assuming that men behave as their spiritual tradition requires, they will be governed by the law of help, based on charity and unselfishness; the law of honesty; the law of reverence and loyalty in return for true government; and finally, embracing all of these and more, the law of justice.

The law of help follows from the very nature of man and the oneness of mankind, which is the first law of life. Ruskin sets this in opposition to the economic law of competition and holds that a being is able to achieve perfection only in union with others of its kind. To contend in isolation from other men for one's own selfish interest is therefore a law of death; competition and separation are principles of corruption, but the highest law tending to life is the law of help. It is, indeed, another name for "life" in Ruskin's view.

Once more we are led to the great paradox, endlessly repeated by Arnold. In all matters "whosoever will save his life shall lose it, whoso loses it shall find it." One of the worst betrayals "by the plausible impiety of the modern economist" was the persuasion that we do best for others when we do best for ourselves. Even at the level of material success, men are foolish enough not to see that they will prosper best if their neighbors also prosper. Nothing is so ruinous for men, even in commerce, as to concentrate upon themselves and their own interests. Yet they should not dwell upon the material profits of unselfishness; they ought to recognize that love of other men is the healthiest condition for their own minds. There is no true joy but in the love of mankind; the happiness which is the aim of life depends upon the fulfillment of that humanity whose precepts, like those of the skies, are simply these: " 'Execute true judgment, and show mercy and compassion, every man to his brother in your heart.' "

The affections, then, are the basis of political economy, not the instinct for competition and personal success. Ruskin is very specific as to how benevolence ought to show itself in practice. Those who are well-to-do should study how they can spend their money for the benefit of others, and by proper administration of what they have they should contribute most to the good of the community. Let them curb the desire for luxury and give to others what they do not need themselves. Men should be willing to die fairly poor, having done the greatest possible good with what they have beyond their own needs. They should give without thought of return or profit, as Ruskin did with admirable consistency. He gave more than half of what he had to the poor, and in the general conduct of his life he behaved with a generous concern for others and a disregard of worldly wisdom which, he observed with bitterness, earned him only the scorn of hack writers, who referred to "the effeminate sentimentality of Ruskin."

Nonetheless, he believed strongly in the right of property; he did not favor "the common socialist idea of division of property." A man who worked for a thing should be allowed to keep it and consume it in peace. Ruskin asks only that any riches not absolutely needed should be employed in the service of mankind. Such individual effort would do more for human happiness than the activities of government, important as these were in Ruskin's plans. Every Christian man who can do so should, in the literal Biblical sense, feed the hungry, clothe the naked, and give shelter to the homeless—all these in one's own house, if need be, and not in the poorhouse. Ruskin is less fanatical about indiscriminate charity than Carlyle; yet he, too, urges a wise beneficence, designed to do the greatest good now and in the future. Anticipating in part the third of Ruskin's "laws," charity should be more than alms; it should help people to find work in those services wherein they can be most useful and productive.

The law of help asks, then, that the poor be led in disciplined troops to fruitful labor so that they may earn and not beg their bread. Since there is no wealth but life, the law of help defines a new concept of riches; it reveals that he is richest who, "having perfected the functions of his own life to the utmost, has also the widest helpful influence, both personal, and by means of his possessions, over the lives of others."

Ruskin's law of honesty combats the principle, "so disgraceful to the human intellect," that one should always buy in the cheapest and sell in the dearest market without questioning any further the nature of a given transaction. Ruskin demands, rather, that a moral principle should govern the making of money; if honesty does not prevail, men cannot be happy; "food can only be got out of the ground, and happiness only out of honesty." In trade, therefore, the merchant should look to it, after the rule of Venice, that his "weights be true and his contracts guileless." There should be just laws of trade established, lest anyone sell dishonest or adulterated goods or give short measure. All transactions should be open and so designed as to give advantage to all parties concerned. Above all, there should be no labor wasted on "works of darkness," useless and poorly wrought things which pretend to be otherwise. For Ruskin

such a waste is the most criminal of all the offenses which the law
of honesty must overcome. To set a man upon the production of
"cheap and nasty" goods is to bind his thoughts, darken his eyes,
destroy his hopes, steal his rightful pleasure in work, and degrade
his humanity, which desires a proper outlet for its power. The man
himself must resolve that he will do only good work so long as his
right hand has motion; that he will refuse to be assigned to dishonest work, "whether the issue be that you die or live." Thus, any
given transaction for the merchant or the worker requires only the
single question: is it a just and faithful one? Once more Ruskin is
sure that to forget one's own interest is in reality to serve it, for if
two persons trade without cheating each other, they will make more
money than if they do cheat. But, again, this is not why a man
should be honest; it is simply beneath human dignity to be a fraud.
"If you ask why you are to be honest—you are, in the question
itself, dishonoured. 'Because you are a man,' is the only answer."

The influence of Carlyle is nowhere more conspicuous than in
Ruskin's third law: loyalty and reverence in return for proper guidance. The concept of liberty under laissez-faire is here denounced,
and the need of leadership for the inferior mass of mankind is constantly repeated. In spite of his belief in human possibility, Ruskin
accepted Aristotle's view of a large part of mankind as naturally
and eternally slavish. A man's quality is fixed for him at his birth;
much can be done by education and favorable circumstances, but a
great man cannot be made out of an essentially small one. Whether
men like it or not, the truth is that an everlasting difference is set
between one man's capacity and another's. Slavery is, then, not a
political institution *"but an inherent, natural, and eternal inheritance*
of a large portion of the human race—to whom, the more you give
of their own free will, the more slaves they will make themselves."
The plea for freedom and equality is inadmissible; freedom cannot
have any objective reality for mankind short of the freedom offered
by death itself. As for equality, Ruskin points out that if there is any
single notion insisted upon in his work more frequently than any
other, it is the impossibility of equality. He would rather see the
ancient Austrian tyranny restored to Europe than to risk the chance

of being dominated by the American trust in liberty and equality, "of which I detest the one, and deny the possibility of the other."

Since, therefore, the poor are to be always with us, and since the world is always to have numerous inferior, weak, and foolish persons, it is necessary that superior men should guide, "or on occasion even . . . compel and subdue, their inferiors according to their own better knowledge and wiser will."

Obviously Ruskin prefers the gentlest and the most humane relationship between master and man, in which genuine love for the one served is the chief motive. The upper classes ought so to guide and help those below them that the inferior ones may rise to the nearest level with themselves of which the lowly are capable. If this is done, there will be a natural return of love and reverence on the part of those who have received guidance and a corresponding advance in human quality. If one looks up to others, one is himself ennobled and therefore happy, because an essential need of human nature is satisfied. But most wonderful of all is the realization that true liberty for men resides in this very obedience. Far from slavery, the holding of ourselves at the disposal of another through admiration and respect is often the best kind of liberty, "the noblest state in which a man can live in this world." Once the duty of obedience is acknowledged by the masses, they will have a right to claim relief from their distresses, care for their weaknesses, and perpetual justice at the hands of those above them.

For it is the law of justice which contains the summary of all that need be done by men for one another. Ruskin wearily tells his readers that for years he has spent his life and strength in declaring "that all productive prosperity in this Christian nation depended on literal obedience to the command . . . 'Seek ye first the Kingdom of God and His Justice.' " The mere fact of the nation's great wealth does not in itself prove that its possession is a good thing; what matters is that justice should have been served in its acquisition. Expediency is therefore a false rule of conduct, since one cannot be sure what the result of a merely expedient action will be. Yet every man can know what is a just or unjust act; he can learn that justice will in the end be the most profitable of guides. Ruskin's idea of justice includes affection also, such affection as men owe to each other. This debt of affection is, however, not entirely paid by the charity demanded in the law of help. Ruskin goes so far as to say that charity itself must be preceded by justice, for "you cannot build upon charity. You must build upon justice, for this main reason, that you have not, at first, charity to build with. It is the last reward of good work. Do justice to your brother . . . and you will come to love him." The English Christians who go piously through the forms of Christianity without the substance, would do well to follow the poor Mahometan's maxim: " 'One hour in the execution of justice is worth seventy years of prayer.' "

We must now examine how Ruskin would have justice manifest itself. His complicated and various schemes are reducible to certain tendencies and aims, the most obvious of which concern the proper behavior of government toward its subjects. Ruskin was quick to admit that not every detail was likely to be perfect, but he believed that his reforms were right in principle. He was also careful to point out to the working classes that their own efforts for themselves would be more helpful than anything done by government. Nonetheless, all human government has an immense obligation to its subjects; it must be kind and just, liberal, merciful, and patient. It must in the highest sense of the term be paternal, which for Ruskin means " 'the executive fulfillment, by formal human methods, of the will of the Father of mankind respecting His children.' "

Now in actual operation, Ruskin hopes to see an observant authority, to look after and take care of men; a helpful one, to give aid where needed; a prudential one, to see that the proper sort of work is done where it is wanted and needed; a martial one, to punish rogues and force the idle to work; an instructive one, to teach people what they should know and to answer their questions; a deliberate and decisive one, to judge by law and to amend or make law; and finally an exemplary one, to show what is loveliest in the art of life.

The first concern of such a government must be the poor. Persons in authority should know the number and resources of the

poorest people and make sure that these at least are virtuous and
comfortable. Here Ruskin's principles seem better than their detailed operation. He would appoint for life an overseer or Bishop
to look after each group of about a hundred families and render an
annual account to the state of the life of every person under his
care. There would be no spying or coercion involved, but only
helpful supervision. Ruskin would hope in this way to make it impossible for any person, however obscure, to suffer unknown want
or to live in unrecognized crime. The benevolent pastors would
keep a kind of biographical record of each family so that the state
could know which persons to aid, reward, or punish as need be.
Over these pastors would be higher officers, commanding larger
districts; they would enforce or mitigate laws according to the pas-
tor's reports, basing decisions on the needs of each case and per-
forming the maximum of justice for every individual.

Perpetual assistance would in this way be available to the poor
throughout their lives, but the principal concerns of the paternal
government would be twofold. It must, to begin with, see that
people have food, clothing, fuel, and shelter. Ruskin points out
that the English government of his time habitually interferes in
matters military and divine. Why not look after bodily nourishment as well? The government, and indeed all Christians, should
make certain that no one lives in need of these four bodily requirements; so long as anyone is without food, especially, not a mouthful
should be sold across the border to a stranger.

The second duty of government is to provide education for the
people. Considering the movement of thought in which Ruskin is
participating, a strong claim for education on his part is inevitable.
He has a number of contributions of his own to make, which, as
always, he describes in great detail. He advocates a free and compulsory education, unrelated to the stupid passion "to get on in the
world" and founded on the assumption that each person is to remain in his own class. Ruskin is very hard on the comon desire to
"elevate" oneself in the world:

the idea of a general education which is to fit everybody to be Em-
peror of Russia, and provoke a boy, whatever he is, to want to be

something better, and wherever he was born to think it a disgrace to die, is the most entirely and directly diabolic of all the countless stupidities into which the British nation has been of late betrayed by its avarice and irreligion.

The fact remains that all people are not the same. Knowledge must be imparted according to the needs and the quality of each individual, and every person must be directed toward the occupation for which he is fitted—and in which he will be happy. This will avoid the plague of discontented and useless persons trying for a place beyond themselves. No amount of competition or teaching can add an ounce to the available brains that any man has; "the entire grace, happiness, and virtue of his life depend on his contentment in doing what he can, dutifully, and in staying where he is, peaceably."

Now the education that Ruskin has in mind would promote certain physical, moral-intellectual, and practical ends. He warns the English that it is going to cost them money. But men do not learn that they may live; they live that they may learn to become better men. First of all, the body should be made as beautiful and perfect in youth as possible. Students should learn the laws of health and right exercise—including riding, running, personal defense and offense, as well as music, which ought to be part of all popular instruction, presumably for movement and rhythm as well as for its own beauty. Ruskin would also include manual training so that everyone—"from the King's son downwards"—might become a good handicraftsman of some kind, thus learning to respect manual labor as decent and honorable, and to know many things besides, "which no lips of man could ever teach him."

Moral training is also required, for men must be taught to behave as they do not behave, to become better than they are. Since nobility, kindness, and truth are "the true power of our inherent humanity . . . the aim of education should be to develop this." Let the young be taught reverence, humility, compassion, obedience, truth, and accuracy of observation and thought. Let a child be ignorant of a thousand things rather than have "consecrated in its heart a single lie." Let the young be made capable of honesty and of delight, and above all, the summary once more of everything to be desired, let them get habits of gentleness and justice. Such moral training is to be given to all as befits our common humanity.

Although the purely intellectual discipline will vary with individual needs, yet knowledge is mental food for all; it is good that all men be able to consult with the wisest and greatest men. Every man should resemble the great genius in his childlike wonder at what is still to be known and his happy eagerness to extend his knowledge. He should be given every chance to satisfy this desire to know, through the establishment of national libraries, with a selection of the finest books accessible every day and evening. Furthermore, his intellectual education should strengthen the faculties of admiration, hope, and love by the study of nature, the sight and history of noble persons, and the setting forth of noble ends of action. No child should read what is not worth reading or see what is not worth seeing. Of specific subjects, Ruskin includes the natural and biological sciences, mathematics, history, and other subjects, such as drawing, for those especially gifted.

The actual schools might very well be of three kinds, with variation in subject matter. Schools for city children might specialize in mathematics and the arts; those for country children in natural history and agriculture; those for children who will be seamen, in physical geometry, astronomy, and the study of sea fish and sea birds. But wherever possible the intellectual discipline should include knowledge immediately bearing on practical life and the mastery of that calling in which one's living is to be earned. The young workman ought to be educated for his work before being allowed to undertake it; he should be practically serviceable on his entry into life. This should be accomplished by the government schools, which ought to maintain workshops and factories in connection with them, where necessary commodities of true and pure substance might be produced and sold and every useful art be exercised. For each youth, likewise, a place should be ready on leaving school. Every trade should have government establishments where the young could be received as apprentices and all unemployed could find work at any time. The commodities produced could be given to the poor when needed and their production so regulated that no one commodity would find its market glutted.

Finally, when people grow too old for work, they should also be honorably provided for. A laborer serves his country by toil and has the right to a pension just as do other persons for more spectacular services. Ruskin was concerned, also, to make a distinction between the relief given to distress caused by misfortune and that caused by idleness and fraud. The state must so act that it can give honorable relief to men in their old age; it can do this, if it has watched over their middle years and has recognized that those years were spent in the performance of duty which now merits a decent reward.

Yet Ruskin does not ask the government to solve every problem touching the life of its subjects. Important issues remain to be dealt with by what we now call "private enterprise," which Ruskin would not discourage by his governmental operations. He raises questions as to the proper relationship between employer and worker, involving adequate provision for the personal health and happiness of the worker; the proper payment to be made for all work; and finally the nature and quality of the work itself.

Ruskin's belief in paternalism leads him to demand that a master should make up for the loss of home influence upon the young person entering commerce. To do justice to those whom he employs, a master must deal with them as he would with his own sons. A father would sacrifice himself in time of need for his child; so must the employer in a crisis take more suffering on himself than he permits his men to feel. It is not enough simply to employ a man, therefore; he must be led to work at a task which will allow him the healthiest and happiest possible life. Like Carlyle, again, Ruskin believes that man's happiness depends on the release of his capacities in sincere work.

Yet Ruskin does not glorify hard human labor; he makes labor the basis of all price, because he sees in it a contest which spends human life. Labor is the quantity of defeat which has to be counted against every deed of man. It is " 'that quantity of our toil which we die in.' " A fine passage in *The Crown of Wild Olive* shows that

Ruskin was not blind to the human degradation involved in coarse labor. It is futile

to conceal the sorrowful fact by fine words, and to talk to the workman about the honourableness of manual labour and the dignity of humanity. . . . Rough work, honourable or not, takes the life out of us; and the man who has been heaving clay out of a ditch all day, or driving an express train against the wind all night . . . is not the same at the end of his day or night, as one who has been sitting in a quiet room . . . reading books . . . or painting pictures . . . of all hand work whatsoever, necessary for the maintenance of life, those old words "In the sweat of thy face thou shalt eat bread," indicate that the inherent nature of it is one of calamity; and that the ground, cursed for our sake, casts also some shadow of degradation into our contest with its thorn and its thistle.

Since labor of the common sort is inescapably degrading to some extent, every effort must be made to achieve pleasant conditions of work and to give the worker as much joy in his labor as possible. The pleasure he derives from his work is in reality part of his compensation for it, without which his labor is base and without human satisfaction. This point is also related to the nature of the thing made by work and anticipates the principal idea underlying the work of William Morris. One who employs other men must therefore see to it that they are as safe and comfortable as their employment permits. They are, in Ruskin's general scheme, supposed to remain in one position always; let them be made happier and wiser while staying where they are. Their work should be done in an orderly, human way under proper captains of labor, and it should be as carefully planned, disciplined, and rewarded as the military labor whose end is death itself. There should be regular periods for rest and play in true gardens; and workers and their children should have the same chances for happy recreation, for reading and fireside comfort as anyone else.

Justice demands even more sternly, however, that men who labor should be paid a life-giving wage based on a fixed, unvariable standard, which can be determined. One of Ruskin's favorite beliefs is that the best work is not done for pay and that love and trust will give more satisfaction than wages. He feels also that one of the fundamental distinctions between men is to be seen in this, that the best men consider their work first and the fee second. Indeed, it might even be said that "God means all thoroughly good work and talk to be done for nothing." It is a matter of statistics that "none of the best work in art, literature, or science is ever paid for," because as a rule people are inclined to pay only for being amused or cheated. But the man who works with his hands has a right to expect a just wage which can be arrived at scientifically. Let reputable physicians be asked to state the proper sustenance necessary for a laborer's healthy life in a given situation and the length of time he may work daily without shortening his life if so sustained. All masters should then allow a choice between an order for this quantity of sustenance or the wages being currently offered for that number of hours' work.

Ruskin further insists that since just payment has nothing to do with the number of laborers available, the law of supply and demand should not be recognized; wages should not vary with the demand for labor. Employers should use only good workmen at a fixed rate, so that inferior labor cannot successfully offer itself at low wages, thus forcing out able men or making them work for less because of competition. Ruskin would even have some regulation of the return given the employer for his efforts. He wonders why it is that the merchant has never been honored so freely by other men as, for example, the soldier, lawyer, doctor, or clergyman. Ruskin finds that these men are able to forget themselves in facing danger, doing justice, healing the sick, or serving God and are therefore recognized as superior beings. The merchant is held to be an "inferior grade of human personality" because he is "presumed to act always selfishly." He should rather think of himself as a public servant whose duty it is not only to get profit for himself but to offer society the finest product he is capable of obtaining. He should operate sanely for a smaller, more secure return instead of risking ruin to himself and his men through "impatient covetousness."

Finally Ruskin believes that what a man is required to make is more significant than what he is paid in wages. The whole question

of human dignity and the degradation of man below the level at
which he can fulfill his highest powers is once more involved in the
thing which man is forced to make. Ruskin says that the manufacturing cities make everything except men; they never think "to
brighten, to strengthen, to refine, or to form a single living spirit."
He demands a new understanding of the kinds of labor which are
good for man and a sacrifice of all convenience or cheapness which
is got by the degradation of the workman. Ruskin asks for healthy
and ennobling labor, expended upon the good and useful that makes
for life: food, clothing, fuel, shelter, which are then always ready
to sustain man, and not gunpowder or iron bars. The workman is
reminded of the law of honesty which demands that he do good
work whether he lives or dies. He should, indeed, prefer to die
rather than "*make any destroying mechanism or compound.*" In
particular, he should work by hand in preference to the use of
machinery, and he should be happy to cultivate the earth and to
grow the means of life. Not only is such work more healthful, more
human, and therefore more ennobling than mechanical labor; the
very nature of human life and its origin are symbols of the life-
giving power of the earth and the inevitability of man's dependence
upon it for existence and the fulfillment of his humanity through
labor. " 'Dust thou art, and unto dust shalt thou return,' is the first
truth we have to learn of ourselves; and to till the earth out of
which we were taken our first duty."

Ruskin admits that a large amount of "foul or mechanical work"
must be endured by any society; he recommends that such work
be done so far as possible by criminals and public enemies, especially work at mines and furnaces. Other inferior labor should be
reserved for those who, at least temporarily, are fit for nothing
better. Ruskin thus aims at an ideal of life wherein human employment shall be happy and noble. The upper classes especially should
lead the way back to the soil, forbid the use of steam machinery
over their land, and stimulate the use of human labor.

Ruskin is also concerned for beauty of the world outside of man,
lest there should be this one necessity of human nature for which
he has not dreamed the perfect satisfaction. He hopes for a future

England of great beauty, with cities limited in size, clean and
orderly in every corner, and surrounded by gardens, trees, and
streams. There would be an end of festering suburbs, of the enormous begrimed ugliness of urban England, of hideous and filthy
lodgings for the poor. Strong and beautiful dwellings would receive a healthy race, all of whom would be only a few minutes
distant from fresh air and green grass and a view of God's horizon.
Away from cities, the country would return to agriculture and
the land would be redeemed into ordered fruitfulness, its beauty
and peace restored by man's own labor.

Along with this change in the nation's aspect, Ruskin would
even enforce neatness and cleanliness of dress upon the people
themselves. He was at first inclined, in *Modern Painters*, to adopt
a national costume, influenced perhaps by More's *Utopia*. Later,
in *Sesame and Lilies*, he urges that people dress according to their
rank, and that changes of fashion should be limited by overcom-
ing man's frivolity and vain pretensions. Ruskin longs for a new
satisfaction of the sense of beauty and art in man, not only because
it is in itself wholly good, but because it fosters the very best impulses of human nature. People cannot have art and beauty amid
dirt and starvation. They must live in pure air, away from un-
sightly objects and mechanical occupations. If this freedom from
ugliness did no more than to restore English art, it would be so far
a priceless gain. But what is good for art is also good for the bodies
and souls of men. Ruskin wants a world which satisfies the human
instinct for beauty, because without that satisfaction human dignity is once more affronted. It is the "direct adversary of envy,
avarice, mean worldly care, and especially of cruelty . . . the
men in whom it has been most strong have always been compassion-
ate, and lovers of justice, and the earliest discerners and declarers
of things conducive to happiness of mankind." Ruskin even allows
himself to hope that despite the great differences among men, the
circumstances of life can be so changed as to develop gentleness
and refinement even among the worst-treated men and women
of the English race. Perhaps all men, if properly cared for, may
become beautiful and intelligent in the course of time, developing

the quality of "gentlemanliness . . . another word for an intense humanity."

Ruskin came to the end of his enormous labor on behalf of human dignity with a painful sense of failure and defeat. He could not accuse himself of a single deviation from his ideal; he did not turn away from his task, in spite of every discouragement offered by an indifferent world. In his whole life he had "never written a word either for money or for vanity, nor even in the careless incontinence of the instinct for self-expression, but resolutely spoken only to teach or to praise others." His devotion was repaid as he himself said the world would repay its best work; "some mocked at it, some pitied, some rebuked,—all stopped their ears at the cry." His leadership was not accepted, his work seemed to end in nothing. "Such as I am, to my own amazement, I stand . . . alone in conviction, in hope, and in resolution, in the wilderness of this modern world." Every project or aim of his life seemed perversely destined to result in failure. His battle for Turner in *Modern Painters*, his struggle for good architecture in his own time, his costly scheme of the St. Georges' Co. to buy English land and develop upon it the healthiest and most refined life for as many Englishmen as possible—these schemes came to less than Ruskin had hoped. "And still I could tell of failure, and failure repeated as years went on." Yet the result of this perpetual frustration was not a declaration that life itself is vanity. On the contrary, "the more that my life disappointed me, the more solemn and wonderful it became to me."

Ruskin was never blind to the evil of the world, never unaware of the fantastic odds against the realization of the smallest of his hopes for a better life. He could even rebuke his heroes, Carlyle and Emerson, for being too encouraging and comforting about the final victory of right and the fruition of the one good seed in a thousand. They should insist more on the power of evil and the weakness of good. "Medicine often fails of its effect—but poison never; and while . . . I have a thousand times seen patience disappointed of her hope, and wisdom of her aim, I have never yet seen folly fruitless of mischief, nor vice conclude but in calamity."

And yet, Ruskin's compassion, love, and sympathy were so great that for all of his perception of the evidence against him, he could make a contribution to the human dream based on the most optimistic assumptions of human greatness. He refused to believe that the ideal thing could never become the real thing, because "what is impossible in reality is ridiculous in fancy." Nothing could shake his "solemn faith in the advancing power of human nature," his belief that "there is no hour of human existence that does not draw on towards the perfect day." He saw that absolute justice was not attainable in any foreseeable future, yet "as much justice as we need for all practical use is attainable by all those who make it their aim."

Seldom has any man built a scheme of improvement for his fellows upon such a pyramid of optimistic assumptions. No one could set a higher goal than Ruskin or believe in it more sincerely. The lifelong question that dominated his existence was simply this: "What is indeed the noblest tone and reach of life for men; and how can the possibility of it be extended to the greatest numbers?" For the answer, Ruskin, like Arnold, looked not outside of man "but in the hearts of us," for it was written, " 'the Kingdom of God is within you.' " The mere law of averages in the long history of human folly would seem to demand that the world must soon discover this. It has made its experiments in every direction but the right one—by fighting, preaching, fasting, buying and selling, by pomp and parsimony, by pride and humiliation. It has tried "every possible manner of existence in which it could conjecture there was any happiness or dignity." But all the while it has forgotten that "to watch the corn grow, and the blossoms set; to draw hard breath over ploughshare or spade; to read, to think, to love, to hope, to pray,—these are the things that make men happy." Ruskin's humane optimism assures him that men will come finally to understand that only from such simple means will come the unity, peace, and dignity for which they struggle.

IX. William Morris

> It seems to me that the sense of beauty in
> the external world, of interest in the life of
> man as a drama, and the desire of communi-
> cating this sense of beauty and interest to
> our fellows is or ought to be an essential part
> of the humanity of man, and that any man
> or set of men lacking that sense are less than
> men, and lack a portion of their birthright
> just as if they were blind or deaf. This
> proposition . . . does certainly impose a
> duty upon us, the duty of guarding jeal-
> ously this birthright, this gift of humanity
> . . . no other pleasure is so sure and so last-
> ing as that which comes of our exercising
> this gift.—Morris, *At a Picture Show.*

Even had William Morris not come at the chronological end,
his work would offer the best climax in reading the literary humanitarians. At the mere economic and social level, Morris advocated a completely new society, and so pursued the common inspiration to a point where none of his predecessors would have followed him. There is something final and uncompromising about
Morris, as if he were determined to extend his principles to their
farthest limits. Then, too, Morris is clear and easy to understand.
He is at immense pains to make his ideas unmistakable. Nonetheless, he shows in the very extremity of his reforms that he was,
like his predecessors, not really a sociologist or an economist at
all. The more extreme his proposals became, the more poetic, un-
scientific, and emotional were his reasons for making them. "You
see," he tells us, "I am but a poet and artist, good for nothing but
sentiment." The wonderful paradox is that nothing in the life of
Morris showed him so completely to be a poet and artist as the
theory which he called his "Socialism." This is true of the other

men whose inspiration he shared; they wrote on social and economic subjects to defend the dignity of man, violations of which they could not endure, because they were poets and artists and as such represented in a high degree that human fulfillment which they could not help desiring for other men. Morris is the clearest and best example in nineteenth-century English literature of the poet and artist turned sociologist and economist, not because of a separate interest in an area of thought distinct from his poetry, but because he was a poet and artist and hence unable to escape the sense of oneness with all human experience.

Morris never ceases repeating his love of beauty and his corresponding hatred of ugliness. He was sensitive to the aspect of the late Victorian world, almost to the point of abnormality. All Ruskin's fierce outcries against the ruin of England's beauty are endlessly repeated by Morris. Not only is the external aspect of the world ugly, but the houses men live in, the things they choose to surround themselves with, the clothes they wear, the things they make by their labor, and worst of all men themselves have become ugly as well. A city like London is a "horrible muckheap"; the great towns of England are devoured by hideousness and squalor. "Civilization is passing like a blight, daily growing heavier and more poisonous, over the whole face of the country." Morris is unable to endure the "brutally vulgar and hideous" aspect of the houses, even those occupied by men of wealth and education. Architecture has simply been abandoned as an art expressive of genuine human power. Its most elaborate products betray only "hypocrisy, flunkeyism, and careless selfishness." Morris can find no language at all for the dwellings of the poor. They live in sweltering dog holes, "for whose wretchedness there is no name." Even the best of such places are unfit for human beings to live in. Morris admits that he knows of these things mostly from the reports of others, for he never dared to face them personally.

It was also depressing for him even to look at the aspect of a modern English crowd. He found the general color to be "a dirty sooty black-brown-drab with a few spots of discordant and ill chosen bright hues due always to the feminine part of it . . . the shape of our garments . . . is for the most part so hideous that it seems to be an indication of our degradation in the scale of life." As for the things produced by the daily labor of man, Morris continues Ruskin's denunciation. He considered it axiomatic that every new thing made to replace an old one in his day would be several degrees uglier. All production by machinery "necessarily results in utilitarian ugliness in everything which the labour of man deals with." The nineteenth century is able to make machines showing wonderful skill and invention, especially machines for commercial use and for destruction in war. Yet the work done by these machines is mostly dishonest work, resulting in "measureless quantities of worthless make-shifts." A great demand for cheap goods exists, so the manufacturers will do whatever is necessary in order to produce the desired cheapness. They will set men to making "cheap things and nasty" too, they will waste labor on "adulteration and puffery" of goods, on sham luxury and useless adornment, and on wares which are cheap enough to enable the poor to buy them. The poor have to live on poison and junk, since nothing else is within their means; so the labor of men is called upon to make such things for sale. Only mechanical drudgery is needed for such tasks; the workman hardly knows what the machine is making. His work is necessarily without beauty, because it is irksome to perform; it is inhuman work, burdensome and degrading. It can turn out, therefore, nothing but ugly things.

The ugliness of the world and of the things made by human labor leads to the degraded condition of the men who make them. These people live under conditions which it is "a shame even to think of." They are forced to compete against one another "for something less than a dog's lodging and a dog's food." They are crowded "like pilchards in a cask" into places where an existence worthy of human dignity is impossible. Their clothing has been known to grow so foul that the dirt becomes an integral part of its substance, providing an additional defense against the weather. Such conditions of life are real for the majority of men in civilized societies; they are "dirty, ignorant, brutal, or at best, anxious about their next week's subsistence." The artist cannot help thinking as he looks at these

"ungrateful and unbeautiful" human beings, that they belong to
the same species as the figures he has seen on the frieze of the
Parthenon and the ceiling of the Sistine chapel. They are related
as well to the magnificent heroes and heroines of romance; "nay,
when people had created in their minds a god of the universe,
creator of all that was, is, or shall be, they were driven to represent him as one of that same race . . . as though supreme intelligence and the greatest measure of gracefulness and beauty and
majesty were at their highest in the race of those ungainly animals."
Morris sees a group of field-laborers, burned and grimed until one
mistakes them for black slaves. The gracefulness and softness is
gone from the women; the men look heavy and depressed. Those
no longer young are "bent and beaten, and twisted and starved out
of shape." Their work has disfigured them and knocked them "out
of the shape of men fit to represent the Gods and Heroes."

This is the worst that Morris has to complain of. The laborer
is kept from fulfillment of the aim of human life and is prevented
from satisfying all of the instincts which make him a man. This
is true because he is poor, because the world around him is ugly,
and chiefly because his work is a degradation and not a pleasure
to him. The mere "struggle for anxious life" by any man is cor-
rosive of the best there is within him. Extreme thrift is in itself "a
degradation to man, in whose very nature it is to love mirth and
pleasure." Morris accused society of simply telling men that they
can be happy only if able to afford it; "unless you have a certain
amount of money you shall not be allowed the exercise of the social virtues: sentiment, affection, good manners, intelligence even,
to you shall be mere words; you shall be less than men, because
you are needed as machines."

Furthermore, an ugly world makes it impossible for its inhabitants to be complete men. Ugliness is a constant offense to the
instinct for beauty in man and results in slow degradation of his
manlike qualities. Without beauty, "what would be left to us indeed of all that makes life worth living?" But man fails even more
dismally to achieve the aim of life when his work is mechanical
drudgery which offers him no pleasure. There is a definition of the

aim of life which is either openly expressed or implied on every page of Morris's later work: "the pleasurable exercise of our energies is the end of life and the cause of happiness." This is true of all living things;

even beasts rejoice in being lithe and swift and strong. But a man at work, making something which he feels will exist because he is working at it and wills it, is exercising the energies of his mind and soul as well as of his body. Memory and imagination help him as he works. Not only his own thoughts, but the thoughts of the men of past ages guide his hands, and, as part of the human race, he creates. If we work thus we shall be men, and our days will be happy and eventful.

Morris does not believe for a moment in the "hypocritical praise of all labour" as good in itself. He accepts the law of nature that men must labor or perish, yet he believes that some compensation is offered for this compulsion to labor by the pleasure that men derive from doing their best. Morris wishes to remove from labor the curse or punishment described by Carlyle and Ruskin. He sees that man will be happy only if he can pleasurably use his energy; he will be miserable if he is unemployed, for then he has no outlet at all. He will be miserable, also, if his work is dull or painful, giving him no sense of joy or personal fulfillment. Work in the nineteenth century, Morris says, did not call for the exercise of the laborer's human powers at all; it was utterly unintelligent work, with "no sign of humanity on it; not even so much as to show weariness here and there, which would imply that one part of it was pleasanter to do than another." The inventiveness of the worker, his faculty of design and dexterity of craftsmanship handed down through generations of tradition—all this was left undeveloped. The result of such work was to make the laborer an unthinking mechanism, something less than a man. His life was cheered by no gleam of self-respect or hope except that of one day "shifting the burden of unhappiness on to some one else's shoulders." Morris is completely in sympathy with the means usually taken by the laborer to make his life endurable: "if I were to work ten hours a day at work I despised and hated, I should spend my leisure I hope in political agitation, but I fear—in drinking."

So far, Morris is developing ideas already present in Arnold and Ruskin. He begins to go beyond Ruskin in certain details when analyzing the reasons why the world has become so ugly and unhappy. The later work of Morris could not help reflecting the influence of the movement toward socialism which developed so powerfully in the late nineteenth century. Morris would probably have arrived at something very similar to this final position even if he had avoided any influence but that of his literary predecessors. Yet his analysis uses some of the terminology and attitudes of Marxian socialism, especially its historical materials. Why, then, is everything in the world so ugly, why are most men so wretchedly poor, and why must they do work which is a degradation to their humanity? Morris's general answer to these three inseparably related questions is the familiar one: the system of competitive commerce and the "innate moral baseness" which it breeds and in turn feeds upon. The aim of this competition is profit, and by its very nature it cannot be troubled by aesthetic considerations.

Is money to be gathered? Cut down the pleasant trees among the houses, pull down ancient and venerable buildings for the money that a few square yards of London dirt will fetch; blacken rivers, hide the sun and poison the air with smoke and worse, and it's nobody's business to see to it or mend it.

Modern commerce is not concerned beyond the rows of figures in the counting house. But having made profit at whatever expense to the world's beauty, the competing men of commerce add further to the sum of ugliness not only by making cheap and nasty goods for the poor but also by demanding that luxuries be produced for their own use. The money heaped up by greed "has raised up against the arts a barrier of the love of luxury and show, which is of all obvious hindrances the worst to overpass." Competition continues here among those who have made commercial profit, each trying to see which can live most luxuriously and ostentatiously instead of living simply, which alone makes for great art. In this ugliness and vulgarity Morris sees also a reflection of the sordid bareness of life endured by those who make the sham adornment. The pinched meanness of the laborer's life had worked itself

into the ugliness of those luxurious homes, and art had no chance
to live among men.

The death of beauty might have been tolerable if it had been
paid for by new life and happiness for the people. But poverty
and degradation in labor went on as before, "still facing . . . the
monster who destroyed all that beauty, and whose name is Commercial Profit." For it is essential to the competitive struggle for
profit that most men remain poor. A kind of warfare goes on constantly, and like all warfare it is wasteful and destructive; it assumes that one side is going to win at the expense of some other
man's loss. The winner grows wealthy and the loser poor. Morris
extends this concept of war to all units of the world:

the parts of the system dovetail into one another, so that no one can
escape from the conflict: nation competes against nation, class against
class, individual against individual; each of these wars sustains the
other and has its own peculiar waste; only as it is with other war so
it is with war commercial, that it is the common soldier that pays for
all, in the long run. In commercial war it is on the loss of the manual
workman that the whole system is built up; without him there would
be nothing to support the war.

The war in a given industrial society goes on, then, between two
classes and between individuals within these classes. The privileged
or upper class has an enormous advantage over its opponent, the
lower class. It possesses a monopoly of all the means of producing
wealth and is therefore able to force the lower class to work for its
own disadvantage: it takes everything possible from the lower
class, allowing its slaves barely enough to keep alive and to reproduce their own kind.

Morris estimates that in one way or another the monopolizing
class absorbs about two thirds of what the laborer earns. Since
the whole system rests on profit, the direct employer makes as
much as he can. In the end taxes are really paid by the laborer;
house rent is also required, as well as a commission for the middle-
men who distribute the goods made by the laborer. Finally, in order to protect himself against the insecurity of his employment,
an insecurity caused by the employer's gambling in the market,

the laborer has to pay dues to a benefit society or trade union. Thus, besides the profit to his immediate master, the laborer "has to give back a large part of his wages to the class of which his master is a part," a class which produces nothing and lives from the work of others by means of legalized thievery. Now the parasitical class cannot take all of the produce of the laborer; it must leave something, even though the laborer himself has no choice. Since he has only himself and his capacity for work to sell, the laborer has to work on the monopolist's terms or he will die. But it is not to the employer's advantage to let the man die; he wants to keep the man alive to work and to breed his own kind, just as any slave-owner or dealer in draught cattle does. Morris stigmatizes this principle as the essence of society in his time: to improve or to elevate the condition of the reserve army of labor would shake the foundations of society. When there is a demand for certain commodities, a given employer must have a large group of workers whom he can call on at will to supply the things for which there is a demand. If he could not get these laborers when he wanted them, his opportunity for profit would pass and other manufacturers, perhaps in other countries, would step in and take over the market. While the demand continues, there is work to do, but in time more goods have been produced than can be sold; then the market is said to be glutted, and the workers who are no longer needed are discharged until their services can once more be used. But even in years of so-called normal demand, there are more men available than there is work for them to do.

Labor-saving machines, which were invented out of the lust for profit from the surplus value of labor, are partly responsible for this. They get rid of many hands, they lower the quality of work required so that skilled labor is less in demand, and they force men to work harder and more productively while they are actually at work. To this must be added the employment of women and children to whom no one pretends to give a proper wage. The result is that men are forced to compete against one another for what work there is, and the cruelty of war forces its victims to make war in turn upon each other, already defeated in a war imposed on them from above. In order to get work, they undersell one another. The employer does not need to force them to work for the lowest possible wage; they will offer themselves in competition against each other for this wage, and so, driven by fear of starvation, they play the monopolist's game and help to concentrate into his hands the very power which grinds them down. Since they have only themselves to sell, they must take what price there is; if unwilling to do this, they must starve or go to the workhouse, where they will be treated like criminals under conditions purposely made intolerable so that no one will endure them before the time of his "industrial death."

Much the same is true of unhappy and degrading labor. Since the monopolist has no motive other than profit, he does not care whether the man who works enjoys what he is doing. His attitude is directly opposed to the artist's view, which holds that his work is everything. The artist wants to make the fullest use of all his human capacities and so produce the finest thing he is capable of. The commercial producer thinks that his wares are nothing; he is concerned only for their adventures in the market, and he conceives it to be his advantage to give as little as he can to the public. He therefore compels his men to do work which is unintelligent and unhuman, so that their lives are completely untouched by art or by any sense of pleasure or triumph in their daily work. And herein lies the worst insult to human dignity that Morris can expose in his own time. The "superstition of commerce being an end in itself, of man made for commerce, not commerce for man," constitutes the greatest possible denial of the dignity of man. Every man is an end in himself; he is being treated as less than a man if his happiness, his comfort, health, education, conditions of life and labor are sacrificed to an outside end. Because this was true in his own day, Morris could tell us that hatred of civilization was one of the ruling passions of his life. The profit motive was not something confined to a few who managed to deceive the better part of society and to carry on in the face of legal opposition. All government and law, the police, the army, the courts, and the full force of the executive branch was directed toward the end of maintaining this system. The true aim of human life was defeated by the very forces established for its benefit.

Such was the case of William Morris against late Victorian society: "I beg you to bring your commission of lunacy against civilization without more delay." The condition of the world being what it was, Morris could not be afraid of a further punishment for man in some other life. "Such a world," he tells us, "if it cannot be mended, needs no hell to supplement it."

Yet bad as it was, there was hope for its amendment. The earthly hell was made by men, but rather by their stupidity than their malice. It was now their task to destroy what they had done and to build a new world. As we come to our reading concerning the new society of Morris, we find exactly what his uncompromising honesty would lead us to expect. He proposes to establish a new world which is a complete negation of the old. He will not tolerate "mere palliation." He admits that the change will be gradual, since it depends greatly upon improvement in men's opinions, but it must be inexorably prosecuted. Under no circumstances must there be even partial tolerance of the profit system. There must be caution lest people be taken in by occasional concessions which are given by those in power only to quiet the demand for complete change.

Too great reliance must not be placed upon trade unions, for example, because they deal only with separate abuses and perhaps get a little money for the worker while accepting the system which keeps him in bondage. Emigration is also too limited to be useful, since it does not attack the basic evil which makes it necessary. Morris is even scornful of personal charity, considering the fact that most of the money given away in driblets to the poor was made by "dishonest and tyrannical means." It is an admission that wrong has been done, a kind of effort to make hell a little cooler without changing its real nature. Rossetti says that Morris never gave a penny to a beggar. He was bent on removing the conditions which caused beggary, by establishing an entirely new kind of society, which he described as "socialism." It is a peculiarly artistic and humane "socialism," most of which is not taken seriously by professional economists. It is the "socialism" which follows from the love of beauty and an optimistic, even poetic, belief in human dignity and oneness. It has more in common, with the literary predecessors of Morris than with the teaching of Karl Marx. It is a system directly opposed to ugliness, poverty, and degrading labor. It calls for a beautiful world in which a nonascetic simplicity of life is the ideal; it provides that there shall be no such thing as a poor man, and therefore no rich man either; it sets up an ideal of coöperation, of common ownership of wealth, of human association and helpfulness in place of the warlike struggle for commercial profit; it offers justice to all men, the opportunity to achieve the fullest development of their highest powers by education and the pleasurable use of their energies in happy labor.

The beauty of Morris's dream England extends from the outside world down to the smallest object made by man for his own use. It assumes, and cannot be separated from the restoration of art, the pleasure of man in his daily work. Since "those who are to make beautiful things must live in a beautiful place," Morris sets about to restore the natural beauty of England. In its own way, every square inch of the earth's inhabitable surface was beautiful, needing only the restraint of man to keep it from ugliness. In the utopian fantasy, *News from Nowhere*, Morris imagines that everyone has striven to make England an exquisite garden. The air is pure and clean, the river Thames beautifully clear and transparent; the grass is green, flowers bloom luxuriantly and send delicious waves of summer perfume through the air. The trees are thick and massive; the fields themselves are tilled as if they were gardens made for the pleasure as well as the livelihood of man. The cities, too, have been transformed beyond recognition, until the streets are as lovely as the natural forests. Morris had always insisted that buildings, especially men's houses, must be beautiful if art were to flourish. He therefore imagines all public buildings as representing the finest effort of the human mind and hand. All private homes are lovely in design, solidly built, and somehow reminiscent of the rural Middle Ages. In no private dwelling is there a sign "of waste, pomp, or insolence," and whenever possible there is a garden near the house. Morris imagines the city as a whole to be arranged in zones radiating from a center containing public buildings, theaters, and gardens. Everywhere there are parks and gardens for the enjoyment of all, extending to the outer zone, which is itself "a garden thickly besprinkled with houses and other buildings." The concept of architecture has been expanded to include not only large units for life and work but also every object or appliance needed to carry on a happy and dignified life. Necessary articles of daily use are works of art according to a principle which Morris italicizes and repeats, after his fashion: *"Have nothing in your houses that you do not know to be useful, or believe to be beautiful."* The beauty of everything used extends also to dress, which even for manual workers is beautifully decorated in bright colors. Morris imagines finally that the people themselves will be handsome, because they will be happier than human beings have ever been before.

This very human happiness is the goal. Men will be happier because they will receive what every man has a right to expect, since he is a human being and desires above all else the fullest development of his human powers. Every man may claim as his proper right a beautiful world to live in, a healthy body, an active, well-educated mind, and work which permits health and refinement, while allowing abundant leisure for rest and further development. Having made men themselves healthy and beautiful in a beautiful world, Morris plans elaborately for the human claim to education. He believes that the remedy for a corrupt civilization is simply a more complete civilization, to be achieved by "education on all sides." He predicts that as the nineteenth century might be called the century of commerce, so the twentieth may be called the century of education. He states the aim of this training to be the fullest development of individual talents. It is to be offered to all men, "not according to the money which they or their parents possess, but according to the capacity of their minds." Every man should be allowed his share of whatever knowledge there is, depending upon the bent of his mind. It should be determined what each person is fitted for, and he should then be encouraged and enabled to develop his inclination fully. Furthermore, every man ought to learn several handicrafts; he should also have some skill in the fine arts. He ought, in short, to be versatile and variously developed instead of the slave to a single routine task. The children in Nowhere, for example, can all swim, ride, and cook at an early age. As they grow older, the boys especially learn to mow, to thatch, to do odd jobs of carpentering; nearly everyone is able to carve. Most important of all is the life work for which education has prepared the individual. Morris admits a threefold human standard for this work: it must be worth doing; it must be of itself pleasant to do; it must be done in agreeable surroundings and under such conditions *"as would make it neither over-wearisome nor over-anxious."* No man should ever again speak of the curse of labor.

Now the first requirement that work be worth doing is allied with an ideal of nonascetic simplicity of life, by which men will lessen their material wants. If they can bring themselves to require only a few fundamental comforts and necessaries of life, there will never be any sham or pretension in work, any cheapness and nastiness called into being by public demand. This simplicity is the very foundation of refinement: when it becomes the ideal of life, the worker will not be called upon to make things which look as if they cost twice as much as they really did. The worker of the future will have a right to refuse to labor on poor or indifferent work; he may insist that he will do only good work, that every new thing he does shall be better than the last. He will, in a word, be an artist. "Nothing can be a work of art which is not useful . . . which does not minister to the body when well under command of the mind, or which does not amuse, soothe, or elevate the mind in a healthy state." This demand for utility is a strong insurance against producing inferior work. Morris would bring together the makers and the buyers of goods as closely as possible; he would avoid bargaining and the elaborate machinery of middlemen, so that a piece of goods would be directly obtained from the worker for a just price, he having made it because someone really wanted and needed it, not because he was taking a chance on someone's

buying it for as high a price as the traffic would bear. In Nowhere,
Morris even eliminated payment in money entirely. Since all the
citizens of Nowhere live simple lives and command the elementary
arts, there is no one who does not take pleasure in satisfying the
common needs of mankind. Men do not disdain to make things
for their own and for their neighbor's use; having discarded the
motive of profit in favor of service and usefulness, they have
ceased to be "hands" or "operatives" and have become men.

When a man's work is worth doing and results in a useful, excellent thing, he is certain to take pleasure in it. This joy in labor
is the summary of all that Morris has to teach mankind as it strives
for a life of dignity and happiness. When this is achieved, the reign
of art in human life will begin, for art means human happiness based
upon the expression by man of his pleasure in labor. Morris pleads
for the universality of art with all of his incredible energy, with all
the conviction of the most sincere and honest of men. Art is to be
like a universal language. It will destroy all degrading toil, all luxury, and all formality. It will be the enemy of ignorance, tyranny,
and dishonesty.

It will teach you to respect the highest intellect with a manly reverence, but not to despise any man who does not pretend to be what he
is not and that which will be the instrument that it shall work with and
the food that shall nourish it shall be man's pleasure in his daily labour,
the kindest and best gift that the world has ever had.

Morris has in mind what he conceives to have been the condition
of art and work in the Middle Ages.

During all this period the unit of labour was an intelligent man . . . a
man's work . . . used the whole of a man for the production of a piece
of goods, and not small portions of many men; it developed the workman's whole intelligence according to his capacity, instead of concen-
trating his energy on onesided dealing with a trifling piece of work;
in short, it did not submit the hand and soul of the workman to the . . .
competitive market, but allowed them freedom for due human development . . . this system . . . had not learned . . . that man was made
for commerce, but supposed . . . that commerce was made for man.

When work has once again become a pleasure, it will bear within
itself its own reward. Assuming that a man has a decent share in

the common life, he does not need, nor should he receive, anything more for his labor than the pleasure he derives from doing well the thing that he most enjoys. "You *can* give him nothing more worth his having: all other rewards are either illusory or harmful."

But if work is a pleasure only when it demands the use of all of a man's finest powers, what shall be said of the use of machines in the new world and of the performance of those odious tasks which are inseparable from all civilized life? Morris anticipates this objection; he admits that rough, crude work has to be done which will always be distasteful. He provides for this by saying that no one in his true society will ever be asked to do rough work for any great length of time; much of the burden of crude labor is due to its long continuance. Furthermore, no one will be asked to do such work exclusively, without pleasurable variety; it will be put, in so far as possible, on a volunteer basis in a society of free men who will do it because they are making a useful contribution to the community. Actually, the machine itself can be used for much unpleasant work whenever the nature of the task compels it or when "the machine does what mere human suffering would otherwise have to do." Morris follows Ruskin in asserting that machines should never be used for any work which it would be a pleasure to do by hand. Machines can do everything "except make works of art," and in a society capable of subordinating them properly, they might be used to lessen the amount of time spent in unattractive labor. If after all of these conditions, there remains work which is still a torment to the laborer, Morris believes that it should be left undone and society should do without the thing which such labor produces.

The last demand on behalf of man's labor is for agreeable conditions of work and abundant leisure for rest and expansion after it is done. Morris imagines the centers of labor to be pleasant buildings set among his beloved gardens. Science has seen to it that no smoke, litter, or filth is thrown off to poison the air and water. The factories are rather units of a rich intellectual and social life, with libraries, dining halls, and places for study and recreation. Here every person learns to develop his special gifts; varied social, musical, and dramatic entertainment is offered as well. These things are all possible, since in a society not competing for profit, men need work only about four hours a day at their regular tasks, thus having abundant leisure for rest and the cultivation of their sense of beauty and their desire to create beautiful things. Morris imagines that actually "a great deal of the best work would be done in the leisure time of men relieved from any anxiety as to their livelihood, and eager to exercise their special talent, as all men, nay, all animals are." The time may come when distaste for work will seem ridiculous and idleness will be looked upon as a disease. In Nowhere, at any rate, it is only in books of history dealing with an era of slavery that men discover that there was once unwillingness to work.

There remains the removal of poverty and competition among men before the ideal society can be achieved. As we review these various elements, we must not forget their complete interdependence; no one of them is conceivable without the realization of all. There could not be a beautiful, happy world if anyone in it were poor or if the commercial system of competition for profit were not replaced by association and common ownership. It is this principle of union and association which would strike at the very basis of the danger to human dignity in Morris's time. Every human being should struggle for the happiness of the human race as a whole and so come to the fulfillment of his own destiny. Here Morris completes his own kinship with the spiritual leaders of mankind. This last poet-humanitarian is unmistakably inspired by the same belief which has unified the work of the others: every man is an end in himself, but mankind taken together is one, and only in fulfillment of the highest destiny for the whole can the dignity of the single man be realized. The accumulated stock of human achievement is the birthright of every man, simply because he is a man inseparable from the human corporation. This sense of union will distinguish the society of the future, in which no one will be "ashamed of humanity or ask for anything better than its due development." The individual will feel himself a member of a unified whole and will shrink from any action against the common interest.

There will be no classes, no warlike struggle among the units of the human family; all will be friends working for the common good, and in their fellowship they will realize a good life for all and inescapably a good life for each. It is assumed that no masters will exist in the new world. Morris leaves Ruskin and Carlyle far behind in asserting that no man is good enough to be a master over others: "equality of fellowship is necessary for developing the innate good and restraining the innate evil which exists in everyone." The notion of poverty is also unacceptable: actually Morris believed that even in his own time there was plenty of wealth for universal comfort, if only it were fairly distributed. In Nowhere, of course, the term "poor" is not even understandable in terms of the reality of life. And if there are no poor, there can be no rich, not even one, as *The Dream of John Ball* reveals. There should be a general equality of condition in which all men work enough to satisfy their needs. The livelihood of every individual ought to be assured to him, following a clear principle: "to *everyone* according to his needs, *from* everyone according to his capacities." In order to be certain that work is not done for profit, there must be common ownership by all men who work—which will be all men—of the means of making labor fruitful. The national plant and stock, the land, machinery, factories, means of transit, and other facilities must be held in common and be regulated in the general interest. No man must ever need to fear that he will be out of work or that he will not be justly paid for what he does. Every man should be free to use his share of the common wealth as he pleases, so long as he does not turn it into an instrument of oppression over others. Finally, the principle of association as against competition is to include nations as well as individuals. Morris believes that the disappearance of the profit motive will see the end of nationalism and therefore "of perpetual war, sometimes of the money-bag, sometimes of the bullet." He imagines a system of free communities living in a federation, managing their own affairs by democratic consent, yet acknowledging some kind of center so as to simplify transactions and intercourse with one another. "What we now call a nation," he says, "is a body whose function it is to assert the special welfare of its incorporated members at the expense of all similar bodies; the death of competition will deprive it of this function; since there will be no attack there need be no defense." The nation will cease to exist as a political entity and a great decentralization of government will prepare the way for the "Federation of Independent Communities." Morris believes that the whole nature of government itself will be changed when the commercial system ends. He hopes for the rule of society by a kind of public conscience made up of the aspirations of our better selves. In *News from Nowhere* he throws off all realistic restraint and dreams that there will be no politics of any kind, no civil or criminal law, no machinery for law enforcement. This could be true, because government in the nineteenth-century sense of the term existed to defend the system of profit and private property. Since there will no longer be inequality or injustice, there will be no reason for crime, and consequently no reason for legal machinery. In matters which concern the whole community, the will of the majority is accepted by all and such regulation as is necessary becomes a matter of general assent.

Finally, Morris is careful to lay down certain principles for achieving the society of his dreams. He recognizes that the change must be gradual, but it will be hastened by adoption of this motto for himself and his fellows: "Educate, agitate, organize." To begin with, discontent with the present state of society must be spread among all the people: this will be followed by a longing for the new world and the end of resistance to its coming. The privileged of England themselves must be urged to renounce their class and cast their lot with the many when class-antagonism arises. The lower class in particular must no longer remain ignorant, but must become aware of their problems as a class. They must realize their real capacities as men and the power which will be theirs if they stand solidly for their class interests against those of their oppressors. Once they are so educated, they will go on in unity toward the new world.

As for agitation and the first steps toward social action, Morris finally admits that much can be done through parliamentary action. He was at first inclined to oppose this as a mere compromise, but in the end he grants that political action may be used as a means. Those sympathetic with him should form a political party in order to gain control of the government and so have power to reform society. This would be part of the third need, organization, especially of the working classes. Union and brotherhood alone will produce a power equal to the force which must be overcome. Accordingly Morris advocates a vast federation of all workers, an immense revolutionary body organized to present a united front against the commercial system. In a remarkable chapter in *News from Nowhere,* called "How the Change Came," Morris imagines the eventual operation of this body and the manner in which it might finally bring about the new society. Morris constructs the future revolutionary scene with extraordinary ingenuity. "The Combined Workers," as they are called, will force upon the masters certain ameliorations of their condition by the constant threat of a general strike and by supporting other strikes with their large fund of money for this purpose. At the proper time they will demand that all natural resources, raw materials, and instruments of labor be surrendered to them. This will be the signal for an outright civil war, in which the vested interests will make the first use of armed force by firing with mechanical guns on a meeting in Trafalgar Square. The leaders of the people will try to accomplish what they can through parliamentary action, but this will fail. The workers will then make use of their greatest weapon: they will call a general strike and all the usual operations of life will come to a standstill. The civil war, most destructive and vicious, will continue for about two years, with the victory inevitably going to the lower classes. Once the war is over the workers will reconstruct society, and the new era will be at hand. These events will probably take place about the year 1952.

It is easy to find in these elaborate plans for a future world and the preceding revolution some of the ideas which are associated with Marxian socialism. We must ask whether Morris arrived at

his convictions through the inspiration which he held in common
with his literary predecessors, or whether he owed his final view
to the powerful example of Marx. It seems clear that the men of
letters from Coleridge to Ruskin were largely uninfluenced by
professional economists; they knew very little about economics
themselves and did not reflect in their literature many of the influences tending toward a new social order. Robert Owen was
of interest to Coleridge and Southey and probably to Kingsley;
Carlyle seems to have known the work of St. Simon, and Ruskin
that of Fourier. Yet it cannot be maintained that the man of letters absorbed these contemporary influences with complete conviction into his work; his theme was from the beginning, and
remained to the end, the dignity of man and the oneness of mankind. No matter what the details of his recommendations for society were, before Morris he remained fundamentally conservative and desired reform from within the prevailing system.
Whether there had been parallel movements in thought in the
nineteenth century toward a new society or not, the man of letters would have gone on making his protest and asking that men
improve their own souls; his work was in reality only a continuation of the spiritual leadership which is as old as man and his un-
fortunate selfishness. Morris is the only one of the writers sharing
this inspiration who insisted on a complete break with the social
order of his time. Was this true because he was the only one who
wrote most of his work after the publication of *Capital* by Marx
and was in the center of a strong English movement toward socialism? Or did he come to his extreme position largely through
his own effort and through the inspiration of the movement of
which he was a part and which, in the work of Ruskin, had already
constructed an elaborate scheme of social ethics? It is hard to prove
that a thing which happened under one set of circumstances would
have happened just as certainly if these circumstances had not been
present at all. Yet it seems clear that Morris owed more to himself
and his literary predecessors than to Marx or the English movement of the 1880's. The evidence for this is at twofold: the testimony of the poet himself and that of other authors and the special

nature of that reconstruction of the world which Morris called his "socialism."

Morris himself is very explicit as to his indebtedness to other writers, but never says that he owed his ideas to Marx. He speaks with appreciation of More's *Utopia*, which R. W. Chambers says "did more to make William Morris a Socialist than ever Karl Marx did." [1] He mentions "the honoured name of Robert Owen," who symbolized the nobler hopes of his day and advocated coöperation and brotherhood, although he failed to see the meaning of the class struggle. He pays tribute to Owen and Fourier for their effort to restore man's pleasure in labor. He had read Mill's posthumous work "in which he attacks Socialism in its Fourierist guise. In those papers he puts the arguments . . . clearly and honestly, and the result . . . was to convince me that Socialism was a necessary change." George Wardle, a friend of Morris, says that the poet had not read "any destructively socialist book" before joining the English movement then led by Hyndman. He had read lives of Owen and Lassalle, the history of Chartism and the work of Cobbett.[2] Morris praises Carlyle as "the glory of England" who had warned men away from sham and pretense, and one of the few Victorians who had rebelled against the general complacency of his age. At Oxford, Morris was influenced by Kingsley as well, "and got into my head therefrom some socio-political ideas which would have developed probably but for the attractions of art and poetry." He speaks with appreciation of Matthew Arnold and confesses, "if I had not read his article on equality . . . I doubt if I should have had the courage to say a good deal of what I have already said."

But it is Ruskin of whom Morris repeatedly speaks as "my master towards the ideal." Ruskin it was from whom Morris learned to give form to his discontent. He was able to confess himself "so much taught by him that I cannot help feeling continually as I speak that I am echoing his words." He did not like to be praised at Ruskin's expense, "who you must remember is the first comer, the inventer." Ruskin's work showed that the inevitable change ex-

[1] *Thomas More*, New York, 1935, p. 125.
[2] May Morris, *Morris as a Socialist*, Oxford, 1936, pp. 603 ff.

pected by Morris was already under way long before there was
any hope of its realization: "the pessimistic revolt of the latter end
of this century led by John Ruskin against the philistinism of the
triumphant bourgeois, halting and stumbling as it necessarily was,
shows that the change in the life of civilization had begun, before
anyone seriously believed in the possibility of altering its machinery." Most important of all is the admission that Ruskin is the
source of the most essential idea in the later work of Morris. One
of the numberless repetitions of the creed that "art is man's expression of his joy in labour" is followed by this remark: "If these
are not Professor Ruskin's words they embody at least his teaching on this subject." Morris singles out the great essay in *Stones
of Venice* "On the Nature of Gothic" as "a marvellous inspiration of genius" in which Ruskin expresses the very essence of
Morris's own teaching on architecture and art. This essay "in future days will be considered as one of the very few and inevitable
utterances of the century"; it makes art the motive power for the
realization of pleasure in labor and shows that Ruskin has made a
solid contribution to the new worth of society. It is pleasant to
know, by the way, that this admiration was mutual. Ruskin is supposed to have remarked to a common friend, "Morris is beaten
gold."

There is no such literal statement of indebtedness to Marx. If
a great influence had existed, Morris would certainly have spoken
of it in the unmistakable terms which he applied to everything else.
If he really owed much of his "socialism" to Marx, he himself
seems not to have realized it. On at least one occasion he disclaimed
in so many words the influence of Marx and admitted his debt to
Ruskin: he was supposed to have confessed that he arrived at his
ideal society through reading Marx. On being questioned, he re-
plied characteristically:

You see, most people think I am a socialist because I am a crazy sort of
artist and poet chap, and I mentioned Marx because I wanted to be
upsides with them and make them believe that I am really a tremendous
Political Economist—which, thank God, I am not! I don't think I ever
read a book on Political Economy in my life—barring if you choose

to call it such, Ruskin's "Unto This Last"—and I'll take precious good care I never will! [3]

The study of economics of any kind was distasteful to Morris, and he was frank to admit that "I don't think I should ever make an economist even of the most elementary kind." He was led to his "socialism" by hopes and dreams for the future, which as the Arab king said of arithmetic, "would otherwise be too dull for the mind of man to think of." His dislike of economics in general extended to the work of Marx in particular; although "I thoroughly enjoyed the historical part of 'Capital,' I suffered agonies of confusion of the brain over reading the pure economics of that great work. Anyhow, I read what I could, and will hope that some information stuck to me from my reading." It seems clear that Morris enjoyed "the admirable account of the different epochs of production" in Marx and the whole account of the change from the eighteenth-century workshop to the modern manufacturing system. He pays various tributes to Marx as one who helped make modern socialism what it was, and he was among those who did honor to Marx in 1884, a year after his death. Morris describes the procession to Highgate cemetery "at the tail of various banners and a very bad band." This participation took place shortly after Morris had actually begun to read Marx; he had joined the Democratic Federation in the winter of 1883 and being now a member of a socialist body he "put some conscience into trying to learn the economical side of Socialism." His daughter says that Morris began to study Volume I of *Capital* in a French edition in 1883, since no English edition appeared until 1886 and English Socialists had only Hyndman's *England for All* available for the study of Marx's theories.[4] He seems to have learned more about Marx in talking with friends like Bax, Hyndman, and Scheu than from his own reading; he speaks also of attending propaganda meetings which instructed him. He collaborated with Bax in writing articles on Marx for *The Commonweal*, and after 1884 he was able to give

[3] Quoted by J. B. Glasier, *William Morris and the Early Days of the Socialist Movement*, London, 1921, p. 142.
[4] *Morris as a Socialist*, pp. 73–74.

some elementary exposition of Marx in his lectures. He was glad of these opportunities for "hammering some Marx into myself." The mere chronological evidence, therefore, shows that Morris was already fixed in his "socialism" before he had begun to think about Marx. We have finally his own unmistakable word for this. In 1894 he was reviewing his career in *How I Became a Socialist* and remarked that his present view of socialism was the same as he had entertained from the beginning. When he joined the Democratic Federation in 1883, he says, "I was blankly ignorant of economics; I had never so much as opened Adam Smith or heard of Ricardo, or of Karl Marx." By 1883 he had already been writing and lecturing on art and the need of recovering man's pleasure in labor for about five years; his most characteristic ideas were already fixed once and for all and had little to do with any formal or professional economic doctrine. He felt obliged to join and to understand as well as he could the radical movement of his time, which had small connection with the literary movement of which Morris was the climax. But before long the poet saw that he was out of place among the other English Socialists. As William Gaunt says in *The Pre-Raphaelite Tragedy*, "Nobody knew anything about art or thought that art had got anything to do with Socialism." [5] The creed of Morris was a separate creation of his own and finally made participation with other radicals impossible.

Whatever further testimony is needed can be found by recalling the kind of "socialism" that Morris believed in. He took much from Marx's analysis of social evil, its causes and history, although even here he says little which he could not have obtained from his literary masters. He has in common with Marx, at any rate, especially in his work after 1884, the notion of the class struggle, the inevitability of a Socialist revolution, the exploitation of the working masses by others who prey upon them while contributing nothing of value, common ownership of the means of production, the dilemma that the man who works has only his person to sell while the employer owns everything needed for production, and to some extent the idea of surplus value in labor which is taken as profit by

[5] Pages 200–201.

the employer. Nonetheless, these are only details which are added to Morris's own fundamentals and about which he did not care to argue with his fellows. He incorporated such materials into his work "because he did not feel disposed to bother about doctrines which, whether true or false, hardly interested him." [6] What mattered to the poet was the fact that most human beings were miserable because they were prevented by exploitation and poverty from developing their humanity to the fullest extent. Glasier [7] reports that once at a Glasgow meeting someone asked Morris whether he accepted Marx's theory of value. His reply was characteristic:

I do not know what Marx's theory of value is, and I'm damned if I want to know . . . I have tried to understand Marx's theory, but political economy is not in my line, and much of it appears to me dreary rubbish. But I am, I hope, a Socialist none the less. It is enough political economy for me to know that the idle class is rich and the working class is poor, and that the rich are rich because they rob the poor. . . . And it does not matter a rap . . . whether the robbery is accomplished by what is termed surplus value, or by means of serfage or open brigandage . . . we Socialists have got to . . . work together for . . . a system of coöperation wherein there shall be no masters or slaves, but where everyone will live and work jollily together as neighbours and comrades for the equal good of all.

It is the dream of human happiness and the beauty of life which inspires Morris; everything else is only a means to this end. He was at home in the simplicities of the small England of the Middle Ages and was uncomfortable before the intricacies of scientific economics. The story of Arthur as read in Malory and the communism of the round table, the stately hall in which workers might dine together seemed closer to the poet's dream of human brotherhood than the somber and forbidding dialectic of Marx. A socialism which had as its main thesis that every man should be an artist was more like pre-Raphaelitism than Marxism. Human dignity and the oneness of mankind, the joy of man in his labor, the restoration of handicraft, the human need for beauty in every aspect of life—these

[6] J. B. Glasier, *William Morris and the Early Days of the Socialist Movement,* p. 143.
[7] *Ibid.,* p. 32.

ideas are hardly traceable to the influence of a writer who makes "no recognition of art as a primary factor in human experience, or art as a mode of knowledge or as a means of apprehending the meaning or quality of life." [8] *News from Nowhere* is a poet's dream, not a work of scientific analysis. It is "as far removed from Marx's *Capital* as the Gospel of St. John from the Book of Judges." [9]

A world fashioned according to the dreams of a poet and aesthetic craftsman cannot therefore be the same as the construction of a scientific analyst, however impassioned. "I am an artist: art is that by which I live; it feeds me body and soul, and without it the world would be empty to me." Believing with all his soul that beauty and human happiness were inseparable, Morris labored with suicidal energy to give "some share in the happiness and dignity of life to *all* the people." Since mankind is one, the blessings of happiness bestowed by art must be shared not only by the few, but by all. If the life of a single human being is prevented from its fulfillment by ugliness and want, then no man shall say that he is complete and untroubled. The personal effort that Morris made to restore the pleasure of man's labor by making beautiful things resulted in an arts and crafts movement. But a cruel irony prevented it from spreading to the work of all men, and Morris was defeated in even that small segment by which he hoped to bring the human dream nearer to fulfillment in his own lifetime. Morris produced books and prints which were a joy to himself and others, yet they were bought only by rich men, as his interior decoration could be used only in rich men's houses:

as long as the craftsmen remained a member of a separate class—unfused with society as a whole—a rival organization side by side with the industrial system—so long was his work undone and even a failure inasmuch as he had simply helped to add another caste to the existing castes without merging all into one. The Arts and Crafts movement perpetuated some of the contradictions he had encountered himself. Its

[8] Herbert Read, *Poetry and Anarchism*, London, 1938, p. 25.
[9] Arthur Bryant, *Pageant of England*, New York, 1941, p. 200. For the opinion that Morris was in reality a Marxian Socialist see Granville Hicks, *Figures of Transition*, New York, 1939, pp. 86–93. However, Marx and Engels seem to repudiate men like Morris in so many words. *The Communist Manifesto* sneers at humanitarians.

products were expensive necessarily in relation to the machine economy. Therefore they were sold to the rich and thus became a novel luxury instead of the normal employment of the country in whose production and enjoyment all would share.[10]

And so once more the world, as it has a way of doing, saw to the defeat of one of its best men.

Morris is the only figure in this history who does not invoke religion in some form: Morris never mentions orthodox religious belief as an aid to, or a part of, the world to which he would lead mankind. His break with the accepted way of life in his own time included the Gods as well. Faced by the misery and ugliness of civilization, he took no comfort in the usual consolations of religion. He saw the "operative," as the man was called, working at a machine to produce an imposture, and "all the religion, morality, philanthropy, and freedom of the nineteenth century, will not help him escape that disgrace." The poet was about to despair before the monstrous evil of his age: "This was a bad look-out indeed . . . especially to a man of my disposition, careless of metaphysics and religion, as well as of scientific analysis, but with a deep love of the earth and the life on it, and a passion for the history of the past of mankind." The poet found wanting the religious and philosophical preaching which somehow never seemed to touch the reality. People have maintained and profited materially from the injustice of life, but have professed to believe in codes of ethics and religion which called for honor and justice among men. Morris proposed to make of his socialism the means by which religious theory should govern the actual conduct of human life. Some doctrines "have gone so far as to bid us to hear one another's burdens, and put before men the duty . . . of the strong working for the weak, the wise for the foolish, the helpful for the helpless; and yet these principles have been set aside in practise . . . and naturally so, since they attack the very basis of class society. I as a Socialist am bound to preach them to you once more." But these doctrines were not to be offered with any sanction other than that of human beings; Morris advocated no motive beyond "the responsibility of

[10] William Gaunt, *The Pre-Raphaelite Tragedy*, pp. 243–45.

man towards the life of man" in place of man's dependence on some abstract idea. He saw Christian ethics absorbed into an all-embracing system of morality, his "socialism"; once it was triumphant, no separate system of ethics would be necessary, and the pursuit of true human fulfillment as the aim of life would make obsolete the ancient systems of theological morality which had failed to perfect the earthly life of man.

Morris was used to hearing how outlandish his ideas were, how fantastic and unreal his hopes. He resented being written off as a dreamer, as if to dream were in itself to ignore or to defy reality.

It is a dream, you may say, of what has never been and never will be; true, it has never been, and therefore, since the world is alive and moving yet, my hope is the greater that it one day will be: true it is a dream; but dreams have before now come about of things so good and necessary to us, that we scarcely think of them more than of the daylight, though once people had to live without them, without even the hope of them.

But if the poet dreamed and fancied and hoped, it was not because he failed to see the obstacles in his path. May Morris builds up an impressive picture of her father's astonishing common sense—his endlessly patient analysis and criticism of the numberless schemes of all kinds that came to his notice. His feet were solidly on the ground in the day-to-day work of the Socialist movement. He made a considerable success in business and might have become rich in the approved, practical fashion had he attended solely to the affairs of Morris, Marshall, Faulkner and Co. He strove constantly to "brush away the cloud of sentiment from modern phraseology; always trying to realize for himself and point out to others the actual probable development of the movements of the time, their strength or weakness." [11] He was willing to admit that his hopes for the world might in some ways add to the troubles of life. He saw that the fact of human dignity is at once a glory and a penalty and that the nearer human life approaches to the fulfillment of its aim, the more difficult it becomes for man to maintain its quality. Morris does not give a dreamer's reply to this dilemma: "consider after all that the life

[11] *Morris as a Socialist*, p. 297.

of a man is more troublous than that of a swine, and the life of a freeman than the life of a slave; and take your choice accordingly." The poet's choice was toward ever more intense and difficult human life, and in his effort to achieve it he became one of the great servants of mankind. He could look upon a world in which it was impossible for him to spend a carefree day, yet he refused to "despise the present or despair of the future." There was change and stir in the world about him, and he believed that these were signs of life leading to the bettering of mankind. His years ended in exhaustion, after inconceivable labor in the service of the human dream, and he was determined to the last not "to let the earth be joyless in the days to come "

Conclusion

> I suppose that if some half-dozen men at any time earnestly set their hearts on something coming about which is not discordant with nature, it will come to pass one day or other; because it is not by accident that an idea comes into the heads of a few; rather they are pushed on, and forced to speak or act by something stirring in the heart of the world which would otherwise be left without expression.—Morris, *The Lesser Arts.*

IT IS A LONG ROAD from the mild proposals of the Lake Poets to the impassioned dreams of William Morris. Yet Coleridge and Southey had the same reason for being conservative feudalists that Morris had for being a "Socialist." From beginning to end the belief in human dignity and brotherhood is the reason why this work is done at all. Certainly these men did not stand to profit personally from denouncing the society in which they lived. On the contrary they were turning away from the main business of their lives and with great weariness and vexation of spirit were attempting to force men into conformity with truths that have remained their only salvation in all ages. In return they could expect only the usual repudiation and resentment which has always been the payment of those who stand against the general course of society. It is true that they were not offered the hemlock or the cross of Socrates and Christ, but only because they were not taken seriously enough by their contemporaries. If it had seemed to many other Victorians that these men had any real chance of success in their effort, mankind would once again, with its invariable suicidal perversity, have thrown off with angry discomfort the men who stood ready to teach the one thing needful; so jealously does man guard within himself what above all else he must surrender. The seed of his own destruction is his instinct to preserve himself the way he is; he will protect this instinct at any cost and will not be attentive to the Arnolds and the Morrises of the world. Yet these men worked on, from the strongest possible sense of duty and by their very effort they emphasized the truth of their own teaching. They showed that such pitiful and halting progress as would ever be made toward the fulfillment of the human dream must come from that forgetfulness of self which remains the greatest of all paradoxes: he who thinks not of himself is his own best servant, and he who is one with mankind realizes most fully his own separate destiny. In saying this again, the humanitarians became the great benefactors of their own age, just as the spiritual leadership of every new generation can do no better human service than to repeat the same message in whatever terms are comprehensible.

In looking back it will be simplest to judge this achievement at three levels: as practical reform, as poetry, and as theology. We have seen how uncomfortable Matthew Arnold was in any practical controversy; he saw the great risk which the poet, the artist, or philosopher undergoes when he leaves his special area of abstract principles to show the world in detail how it should get on with its practical affairs. The poet is uneasy when dealing with such matters and cannot feel that they are his proper business; like Ruskin he may even resent the fact that these things are so badly done by persons whose charge they are that he himself must intervene to show what ought to be done. Nonetheless, it is remarkable that the artists we have studied arrived through their own spiritual inspiration at the concept of a new society in which human dignity and oneness would have a better chance for realization. Such a new society was certainly not desired by the Lake Poets: if we omit their youthful enthusiasm for Pantisocracy, which went the way of many other visions of Coleridge, we see that their final position was on the whole very conservative. Their insistence on hereditary classes, defense of the existing poor law, opposition to democracy, and their belief in the practice of Christianity by all classes as the means of social progress, show how completely they were still attracted to the society in which they lived. One test of conservatism we may apply to the Lake Poets and their followers, that is, the plea for emigration, which is sounded perpetually until Arnold and Ruskin where it receives only minor mention; it is finally eliminated entirely by Morris. The belief in emigration shows that salvation is looked for within the framework of society as it is; instead of changing conditions at home, so that greater justice and equality will result, men are to be sent elsewhere to begin a new life with freer opportunities, thus easing the pressure at home, where life is to be altered not fundamentally, but in details. Even the visionary communism of pantisocracy was to be practiced, not in England itself, but on the distant banks of the Susquehanna. The abandonment of emigration as a major proposal is one of the clearest signs of a strong movement toward a basically new society. In Carlyle, emigration, like many other ideas of the Lake Poets, is still prominent. He clings to the feudalism of the romantics and makes an advance beyond their ideas largely through eloquence and passion rather than by new proposals. He would legislate to improve conditions of life and work, and he would provide abundant education for all who can learn. He would end unemployment by the regimentation of labor under strong leaders and train the population in obedience and coöperation, giving them a sense of union and brotherhood. Emigration of the superfluous would supplement all other measures. Carlyle's attitude is gloomy, and his fear of the consequences of inaction is very great. His demands are more fiercely insisted upon, and the degree of control which he advocates is more extreme than what had gone before. Yet no one shows more obviously than Carlyle how ill at ease the poet must feel in the practical sphere. There is something almost pathetic in the sum total of his reforms, which in themselves hardly imply a change of the prevailing order. Yet he is full of ominous warnings to society about what will happen if they are ignored, and their language will always ring in human ears. Kingsley says that he follows Carlyle chiefly, but under the influence of F. D. Maurice he went beyond Carlyle's example, especially in his earlier years. He was able to declare himself an active Chartist and to accept the term "socialism" as part of the label "Christian socialism." He desired a change greater than that demanded by his forerunners, although his devotion to the established church made

complete rebellion impossible. While Kingsley proposed great reforms in popular living conditions to be prosecuted by the government and urged the organization of labor into coöperative associations, in his maturity he fell back into a kind of Tory conservatism.
He, too, urged emigration to escape the troubles of life in England.
Yet Kingsley, like his predecessors, moved as far toward the altera-
tion of society as the past and his own background would allow.
Even within the kind of universal religious brotherhood which he
envisioned, Kingsley was able to propose enormous improvements
in the "condition of England," and at least in demanding health
and beauty of environment for all men, he was not outdone even by
Ruskin and Morris. It was really Arnold who first saw clearly the
possibility of reforming society in such a way as to change completely the lives of the "populace." This strikingly intelligent man—
the most intelligent of all the men we have considered—was the
first to abandon the feudal concept in favor of the state. He was opposed to "Socialistic and Communistic schemes" which tended to
lower and coarsen the ideal of well being for all, simply because
all were to partake of it. Arnold was also the first of these humanitarians to consider the mass of men themselves as the means of their
own salvation and that of society. He was aristocratic rather than
democratic, yet he saw in democracy a hope for the future. He desired a genuine social equality based upon culture, since culture does
not recognize classes. He was the first to believe that a high civilization for all was obtainable only if there was a general equality of
material possessions. Such an equality was necessary for culture, the
sum of all human perfections. Arnold saw that people would have
to be prepared for equality by education; when sufficient progress
toward individual perfection had been made, the state might then
be given a freer hand to equalize the conditions of men. Arnold is
thus conservatively afraid of too rapid progress by an uneducated
democracy. But once a high standard of excellence had been set up,
he would let the state work for conditions in which this standard
could become applicable for all men. Arnold does not consider it
his business to say by what details this evolution should be perfected. His contribution is that of general principles, the chief of

which is that of equality based on culture, marking a tremendous advance over the thought of his predecessors.[1] Even Ruskin, for all his complicated schemes was still thinking partly in feudal terms, although his proposals bring us to the very brink of the rebellion of Morris. He clung to the notion of property and the right of every man to possess what he had worked for; he believed that poor men would always exist. He professed disbelief in socialism, although in *Fors Clavigera* he says that he is a communist of the old school, which really dates back three thousand years and is quite different from what his contemporaries were advocating. He considers More's *Utopia* an example of old communism and finds many of its provisions acceptable. In addition to Carlylean leadership by the wise and strong, Ruskin was ready to accept large-scale interference by government and employer on behalf of justice for all men. He marked out a series of schemes which provided, "from the cradle to the grave," for such direction of the material, spiritual, and intellectual welfare of each individual that no one could possibly suffer the degradation which made the "condition of England" what it was. All this was to take place in a land of great beauty and cleanliness, from which a race of superior Englishmen would rise. And yet the final step had not been taken, although envisioned by Arnold. Ruskin still could not escape the feudal obsession of Coleridge and Southey through Carlyle. There was still the belief in established religion and property to maintain a link with the past. Ruskin went as far as he could to make society unrecognizable without repudiating its framework entirely. It remained for Morris to take the last step in a period more receptive to revaluation than the prosperous days of Ruskin's prime. It is not easy to adopt either socialism or fascism when times are good; these two theoretical opposites flourish only when men are desperate. Morris wanted to move the greatest possible distance from a society which allowed the world to become ugly and most men to be unhappy. He built up a new concept of society and read into it the positive virtues which would make for beauty and happiness. His plan included

[1] For a good summary see the chapter on Arnold in Vida D. Scudder, *Social Ideals in English Literature*, New York, 1898.

Ruskin's beautiful world, but it repudiated established religion and private property and so broke with the existing order once and for all. While the work of Morris would have been unacceptable to Coleridge and Southey—they could not follow Robert Owen completely because of his infidelity—it was nonetheless the fulfillment of a tendency which had come after them and which in Morris reached the point toward which it had been progressing for three generations.

It is an impressive fact that the man of letters was thus able to arrive at the concept of a new society largely on grounds and through an inspiration which would be valid only for himself and has little to do with professional or scientific study of economics or sociology. The poet knows little of these studies and cares less; but he does understand man, and he is concerned for the dignity of man, which he will defend whenever it seems to be threatened. He will fight for the values of which he is a principal custodian in whatever terms are imposed by the age in which he lives. In the nineteenth century he took up the criticism of social evil and the ideas which he associated with it, because this was the area in which the corruption and waste of human power were most obvious. His work became a kind of gigantic play, a tragedy of waste with man himself as protagonist in which the ruin and devastation are caused by some of the very qualities which make up one side of the greatness of man: the ingenuity and energy, the capacity for conceiving and doing which by a fatal perversion were turned back upon man himself to waste and degrade his powers. But if by this criticism the man of letters develops plans for a new social system, however ingenious and impressive, he has not really accomplished what his destiny calls for. The world has shown itself entirely capable of planning new societies and economies; in this field the man of letters is not likely to offer something which would never be suggested by anyone else. But he does have something to give which the world will get only from its poets and other spiritual leaders—a true analysis of any danger to its humanity, the powerful assertion of the permanent facts and needs and desires of the nature of man and his proper destiny on the earth. The man of letters is desperately

needed in every age as a defender of human dignity when the latter
is threatened, as a spiritual leader to remind man of what is ever-
lastingly expected of him because of his humanity. If all the plans
offered by these writers for the practical working out of their aim
of justice were actually outlandish and unworkable, we should still
have to regard them as our great and useful servants. If what is temporary, controversial, and journalistic in their work should be forgotten because men do not need further instruction along these
lines, the core of their meaning will be forgotten only at our peril.
Because in the end, the most useful part of what they have to offer
us lies in the poetry and theology of their message, even at the so-
called practical level.

There is poetry here, to some degree, in the metaphorical sense
that the actual visions of the future are figures of speech to clarify
what man is constantly hoping for. The reforms and ideal social
constructions are the figures by which writers dimly shadow forth
the vague aspirations of mankind toward justice and peace in a
world whose every detail denies the hope of fulfilling the dream.
We have poetry here which expresses what is true of man in terms
which have no chance at all of becoming true. What is true is that
man has always supposed or hoped that he could make a better
world for himself to live in, a place which would enable him to
realize fully all the impulses that make him a man. He has wanted
to believe that he is not so weak or depraved or foolish as his actions
make him out to be and that he has within him the possibility of
elevating his life. These poets have simply given form to this universal belief and by describing the kind of world that might exist
if this faith and hope is ever realized, have encouraged man to go
on believing and hoping. The language and the terms used in describing this world are not scientific or exact. To take them all literally would be to miss their general human applicability and usefulness. They are like the terms used in the Bible, as endlessly repeated
by Matthew Arnold in *Literature and Dogma* and elsewhere. The
language is fluid and literary, not rigid or scientific. And because it
is literary, it corresponds more nearly to a human truth than the
language of science. It is

language *thrown out* [says Arnold of the Bible] at an object of consciousness not fully grasped, which inspired emotion. Evidently, if the
object be one not fully to be grasped, and one to inspire emotion, the
language of figure and feeling will satisfy us better about it, will cover
more of what we seek to express, than the language of literal fact and
science; the language of science about it will be *below* what we feel
to be the truth.

Thus, the high, optimistic view of human nature, the vast assumption that men will act unselfishly, mercifully, and justly is, in "the
language of figure and feeling," expressed in an effort to put into
some real form the human dream which is "an object of consciousness not fully grasped." It is absolutely necessary that men hear
such language in every age, because the human dream is always
there and always needs to be renewed in the face of all the evidence
that seems to make it ridiculous and pathetic. If the poets and the
other spiritual leaders fail to give form to it, it is bound to die away
before the evidence of reality. There must be optimism and faith
before any real effort toward the reform of society; man has to be
convinced that he is not the depraved fool he seems to be. He must
be made to feel that his vague desire for betterment is not an absurdity, but that it can come to reality in some such form as the poets
have offered. These men in turn know full well what the obstacles
to fulfillment are and how tragically ludicrous the difference is between what is really possible now and what they say is possible in
the future. Yet by their effort they show that there exists in man
something of the very quality which their efforts are intended to
develop in others. It is the quality of men who go on in battle knowing that they have no chance, yet they fight for what they consider
more precious than life. They demonstrate human dignity in fighting for what cannot possibly profit themselves; so also the poet who
tries to make the human dream credible, when by his very nature
he is best able to see how near defeat he is before he has even begun.

If it has not already been refuted, we may digress at some length
to examine a standard criticism of optimistic humanitarianism, under the general term "sentimentality." Perhaps an age like ours,
which has to face more than its share of unpleasant reality, is inclined to level this charge at any hopeful view which seems to over-

look the score against it. We consider humanitarians good, noble people, but we do not take them very seriously as thinkers. Witness the political fate of the men whose honest fidelity to the human dream has cost them any real chance to work practically toward realizing it. These Victorian poets too cannot be hailed as profound thinkers, although we shall have trouble finding in our own world anyone more intelligent than Matthew Arnold. Yet these men are not sentimental humanitarians. They can be defended because of the nature of their own thought and feeling and because in and near their own time their principles were shared to some extent by men of entirely different character, who cannot be charged with inability to think soberly. The work we have been studying is not inspired by mere feeling; it is unified by ideas which are great and timeless. These ideas have to do with the value of men and with what is needed to protect and expand this value. Compassion and sympathy are associated with humanitarianism, but it is a rational sympathy entirely worthy of the human dignity which is its inspiration. Allied to this, however, is a persistent indignation because men are suffering uselessly, because they are conducting their human business with perverse blindness to the waste of a precious thing. These poets are the angriest men in the nineteenth century, but their anger, too, is justifiable and rational; it is saved from mere rhetoric and is balanced by their sympathy. Again, their compassion would be mere sentimentalism without their anger, their great unifying principles, and their high ideal for mankind. They have within themselves the balancing contradictions which create the sound unity of great persons and great achievements. Their optimism must therefore be strong, because they have set a high ideal by which mankind is to raise itself upward. If they were merely sentimental, they would aim far lower and ask for change only in the details of human feeling. But they are aiming at an impossible height and are demanding the most difficult of all reforms, a change of man's inner self. Their confidence that the world can be renewed by this change is necessary to offset the discouragement which men must feel when they see how far reality is from perfection. The reformer must at once discourage men by offering a high ideal

and yet make them believe that it can be achieved. Far from sentimentalism, therefore, is the hopeful expectation of coming good;
it preserves the humanitarians from becoming another futility, a
means of pressing downward upon men who are already fallen and
falling and who need the strength of optimism and humaneness.

It is also desirable to remark that these men were not writing in
an atmosphere created by their own separate feelings. Entirely aside
from their Christian spiritual principles, they were developing ideas
and attitudes for which the most respectable precedent already existed and which were being urged by some of their own contemporaries, such as the philosopher Kant in the preceding century
and T. H. Green in the Victorian age itself. They were reinforced
by the work of J. S. Mill, a transitional thinker who began as a utilitarian follower of Bentham, against whose ideas the poets rebelled,
and who arrived finally at something like the humanitarian position
himself.[2]

Kant's *Fundamental Principles of the Metaphysic of Morals* contains the classical statement of that human dignity and oneness
which the humanitarian poets were preaching to the nineteenth
century in their own terms. Kant says that any rational being exists
as an end in himself, not as a means "to be arbitrarily used by this or
that will." Rational beings are called persons because of their nature
as ends. The practical imperative follows from this: "So act as to
treat humanity, whether in thine own person or in that of any other,
in every case as an end withal, never as means only." The meaning
of the words "human dignity" is contained in this principle. In the
kingdom of ends everything has either value or dignity. If it has
value only, it can be replaced by some other equivalent thing; if
man is an end in himself, however, he has more than relative worth
or value—he has dignity. He is capable not only of observing moral
law but also of laying down the universal law which he calls upon

[2] For the view that late Victorian humanitarian socialism is really inherent
in its apparent opposite, Benthamite utilitarianism, see A. V. Dicey, *Law and
Public Opinion in England*, London, 1905, pp. 68, 184, 187, 304, 308–9. Dicey
also shows that the humanitarian hatred of cruelty and pain was shared by
men of all philosophies and creeds, from Benthamite freethinkers and Whig
philanthropists to Tories and Evangelical reformers. See pp. 106–8.

himself to observe. He is "a legislating member in the kingdom of ends" and obeys only those laws which he himself gives. "Thus morality, and humanity as capable of it, is that which alone has dignity." This demands in turn that every person should develop those "capacities of greater perfection which belong to the end that nature has in view in regard to humanity." As a creature who is an end in himself, "he necessarily wills that his faculties be developed"; otherwise there can be no advancement of humanity as an end. This principle eventually became Matthew Arnold's guide in the criticism and reform of his age. It is based again on the moral imperative of Kant, one of the great philosophical justifications for believing in the oneness of mankind. Just as it is impossible for man to will that his human powers remain undeveloped, so it is impossible for him to will that no love or sympathy be shown among men. He cannot will that a selfish mode of action of his own should become a universal law, because he may need the love and sympathy of others and would be contradicting his own will in depriving himself of what he desires. Thus, he cannot will the disunity of mankind, because as a man he needs other men. He can do nothing to violate the natural desire for happiness of himself and all other men. Kant admits that humanity might go on existing even though no one contributed to the happiness of others. A negative value would also result if men never intentionally withdrew anything from the happiness of others. But in order to advance humanity as an end in itself, everyone must do all he can to adopt and to forward the ends of others as his own. The law of duty is applicable to all men as such; it is therefore impossible for anyone to separate himself from others without contradicting his own humanity.

These principles were reinforced and clarified in the middle and later Victorian age by the Oxford school of philosophers, whose greatest figure was T. H. Green. The insistence on every man as an end, on the individual worth of persons, is related directly to the authority of Kant. In *Prolegomena to Ethics* Green points out that Bentham's formula does not allow an absolute value in the individual person; therefore it is inferior as a rule of conduct to Kant's imperative. But Green's demand for human oneness in society is clearer and less forbidding than Kant's. He saw also that no man can be what it is possible for him to be unless he is unified with other men. There are no persons without society, and there is no society unless every person "finds satisfaction for himself in procuring or witnessing the self-satisfaction" of others. A man cannot even think properly of himself as a person unless he is in a society with other persons whose ends he considers the same as his own. Any permanent well-being which he seeks for himself must include the well-being of others. One thinks constantly of Matthew Arnold, especially when reading the *Prolegomena to Ethics;* a passage concerning the perfect moral condition for men, except for its terminology, might well have come from an Arnold essay: "the ideal of a society in which everyone shall treat everyone else as his neighbour, in which to every rational agent the well-being or perfection of every other such agent shall be included in that perfection of himself for which he lives"—the realization of this would be perfect morality.

In addition to such philosophical acceptance of the humanitarian principles we have been studying, there is a wealth of parallel thinking outside the literary area in the Victorian age which, if it does not always accept the same doctrine, is generally sympathetic in aim. Carlyle and Ruskin may have exaggerated their isolation from the world around them; often men of similar good will were moving toward similar ideals, fighting on the same front for different reasons and on different terms. Such were John Morley, Leslie Stephen, Frederic Harrison and the English Positivists, and other contributors to the *Fortnightly Review.*[3] The best representative of these writers, indeed, of the fundamental changes taking place in Victorian thought, is J. S. Mill. He at once reflected and caused the transition in England from Benthamite individualism to a modified collectivism. He is of interest alongside the literary humanitarians, not only for his well-known movement toward collectivism, in succeeding editions of *Principles of Political Economy* and elsewhere, but also for his own pity and anger, his optimism and belief in humanity, which so often remind us of Carlyle, Ruskin, and Arnold.

[3] An excellent study of these men and their ideas is Frances Knickerbocker's *Free Minds; John Morley and His Friends,* Harvard Univ. Press, 1943.

He is not so violent or so outspoken, and he comes gradually and more tentatively to their off-repeated propositions. Nonetheless in *Utilitarianism, On Liberty*, his *Autobiography*, and the later editions of the *Principles of Political Economy* Mill speaks for the value of the individual man and the necessity for human oneness. The right of men to an education which will aid their natural desire for a harmonious development of all their faculties; the fact that men seek happiness which is impossible unless their human capacities are satisfied; the need for changing the inner feelings and thoughts of men before their outward circumstances can be improved; the capacity of men for unselfishness and sympathetic union with their fellows; the certainty that "all the grand sources . . . of human suffering are in a great degree . . . conquerable by human care and effort"—all these familiar convictions show an alliance which strengthens the cause of the humanitarian men of letters, whether or not they recognize their ally. Thus, for all the poetry of their message, they rise above vague feeling or sentimentality and are seen to be allied with sober philosophy and a considerable area of nonliterary opinion which seems to come directly from the camp of their enemy.

Finally, the message of these men is theology, because it is part of a timeless effort to perfect the human spirit. Their work recommends for the life of man on this earth the same qualities which have been demanded as a preparation for life in the next world. Their fundamental doctrine is that of both the sages and the saints. They sought a moral deliverance, as Arnold said, "a deliverance from the pride, the sloth, the anger, the selfishness, which impair the moral activity of man—a deliverance which is demanded of all individuals and in all ages." They followed in so doing—for the most part consciously—the path already worn by other men who had been called upon to perform the same function for their own times. Arnold once remarked, when pointing out a similar direction in Goethe and Burke, "it is wonderful how great men agree." He wanted nothing better for his own countrymen than agreement with the simple preaching of the wisest and best of former men. The English should learn the necessity " 'to live,' as Emerson says,

'from a greater depth of being.' The sages and the saints have always preached this necessity; the so-called practical people and
men of the world have always derided it. In the present collapse
of their wisdom, we ought to find it less hard to rate their stock
ideas and stock phrases, their clap-trap and their catch-words, at
their proper value, and to cast in our lot boldly with the sages and
with the saints." And all the accumulated wisdom of the wise and
the holy could offer nothing more useful than the simple statements perpetually repeated by one after the other of these poets.
Most of them clung to the traditional belief in religion; in so doing
they were, perhaps, more closely attuned to the needs of mankind
than William Morris, who followed their same inspiration, while
thinking only of life on this earth. Sir Richard Acland implies that
if there is to be a change to the era of common ownership for which
he is now working, it will have to be carried on with the addition
of religious faith. There must be an emotional appeal such as that of
religion; religion is the force most likely to move the largest part
of mankind. Common ownership must have the aid of some great
emotional urge to insure its acceptance by the masses; if it can com-
bine a new faith in God with its abstract principles of well being,
it will have a wider appeal than the forbidding sternness of Marxism or a like scientific construction.[4] The humanitarians did well
therefore to adhere to religion, and William Morris weakened his
case for the very people he most wanted to help—as most radicals
have done before—by separating his essentially spiritual doctrine
from established religion. To have invoked religion would not have
interfered with his hopes for the improvement of life on this earth,
as it did not in the work of Carlyle. Even the demand that happiness be renounced had nothing to do with the pre-Renaissance notion that the destiny of man was not for this world but for another
and that man would prejudice his chances in the new life if he
sought happiness in this. Carlyle's demand for renunciation does not
assume any other life for man beyond this world. He simply considers it beneath man's high calling to think only of his own welfare

[4] Richard Acland, *What It Will Be Like in the New Britain*, London, 1942,
pp. 13–14.

and peace; to seek "happiness" here is a waste of man's great capability. His duty is to make the fullest use here and now of his human faculties. Any "happiness" he knows will be a by-product of such effort. Carlyle has at least this in common with Morris, that he sees man's struggle for perfection as directed to elevating life on the earth, not beyond it. In either case, whether the sages and saints were thinking of progress in this life or effort toward another world, they all centered the perfection of man within himself, not in the schemes and devices with which man constantly deceives himself and by which he tries to avoid the harsh labor of self-discipline. It may be argued that our sad human inconsistency afflicts even the men who wish to lead us. If it is true that the details of outward reform will take care of themselves once men have achieved inward perfection, why the numerous practical measures which are outlined? An answer might be that the suggested reforms are only possible ways of doing things, efforts to show how men may practically apply their newly learned good will and fellow feeling. Actually, there is a mutual working of cause and effect, by which evil circumstances are the cause of wrong human feelings, which feelings in turn make evil circumstances worse. Nevertheless, the plans for external improvement assume that man will first improve himself, just as he will receive aid in this self-perfection from the better circumstances he is striving for.[5] The poets never compromised with this fundamental human necessity; that man is forced to seek fulfillment first within himself is part of his greatness as man and part of the penalty he must pay for what he is. He tries constantly to avoid this and needs therefore to be reminded that there is no escape from the law of his being.

Thus, the humanitarians have been most immediately and permanently useful to us at the level of poetry and theology rather than that of practical reform. We must be grateful to them for having written out of compassion, love, and sympathy for other men and for having by their own example shown what it means to feel the oneness of mankind. Their work is a function resulting from their inability to lose the sense of unity with others; they were

[5] *Ibid.*, p. 8.

forced to speak out, because they saw other men suffering and the knowledge that complete human fulfillment was denied to any part of humanity made them unhappy in themselves, for they, too, were men. Hawthorne, coming from America to write of *Our Old Home*, is overcome by the same feeling of personal loss when he sees the squalid misery of the English poor. "If they are to have no immortality," he cries, "what superior claim can I assert for mine? . . . Let the whole world be cleansed, or not a man or woman of us all can be clean."

Our own age must be especially grateful for a reminder once more of the very things we profess to believe. The concept that all men have a right to share, in so far as they are able, in the beauty, power, and happiness of life—the idea that unless all are free and expanding, then no one may say that he has what human perfection is possible to him—these are among the most important and useful truths that can be offered to society in our time. The principal danger to our civilization has come from our failure to act upon these principles: we have not followed them among ourselves at home or abroad. So long as we permit the degradation of the lives of individuals among us, so long will the remainder fail in their human purposes. So, also, if we complacently think of remote peoples as unconnected with us and refuse to see that slavery and oppression everywhere are equally offenses against us—for we, too, are men—we shall have war and all the insults to human dignity and oneness which it involves.

Bibliographical Notes

THE AIMS OF THIS WORK have been elementary analysis, exposition, and search for the unifying principle in a large body of literature. The specialist in nineteenth-century England will not learn a great deal from page to page; he may, however, profit from the organization and unity imposed on some rather turbulent materials. It is hoped that the interested general reader and the undergraduate student who is just beginning serious study of the Victorians will profit most from these pages. Since this is an introductory elementary study without controversial issues, it has seemed best to abbreviate the apparatus of bibliography and reference. In the following pages the reader is given a list of the main sources for each chapter and some needed supplementary works. These references will guide him to the primary reading in the areas of nineteenth-century literature under discussion.

The very abundance of material as one approaches modern times also helps to make unnecessary a heavy freight of reference. The problem in nineteenth-century studies is one of selection and interpretation; for every statement made in Chapter I, for example, the evidence is so vast and so easy to find that it seems unnecessary to do more than list the general sources which happen to have been used here. The very same points may be made from an entirely different set of "blue books," government reports, and other contemporary works. Again, in the chapters dealing with the men of letters themselves, the quotations are chosen from many possible ones to illustrate ideas which are not matters of controversy. It has therefore seemed unnecessary to give a page reference for each of these quotations; the reader is referred to the main works from which the passages in each chapter are taken. It is believed that he will recognize them as expressing the typical, characteristic ideas of the author in question. However, when a subject like the relationship of William Morris to Marx is under discussion, direct page references are given to support a view which is not held by everyone.

CHAPTER I

EVIDENCE concerning the wretched living conditions of the English poor a century ago is only too abundant. Here the source most frequently used has been Edwin Chadwick's *Report on the Sanitary Con-*

ditions of the Labouring Population of Great Britain, 1842. Chadwick's conclusions were largely reinforced by the *First Report of the Commissioners for Inquiring into the State of Large Towns and Populous Districts,* 1844, and by the *Second Report* of the same commissioners in 1845. Further details are found in *Local Reports on the Sanitary Condition of the Labouring Population of England,* 1842. The highly prejudiced Frederick Engels produced his *Condition of the Working Class in England in 1844,* trans. and re-ed., London, 1892, which is useful as a general survey. *The Health of Nations,* by Benjamin Richardson, 2 vols., London, 1887, is a good summary of the life and thought of Edwin Chadwick. Sir John Simon's *English Sanitary Institutions,* 2d ed., London, 1897, is an excellent history of the fight for sanitary reform and why it was necessary. See also J. Anthony Delmege, *Towards National Health,* London, 1931.

All this evidence may give, nonetheless, a distorted view of the nineteenth century. It is interesting to read, for example, the testimony of Francis Place in Report of the Select Committee on Education, 1835, pp. 67 ff. Place gives the impression that the condition of the working class had actually improved in the preceding twelve years. See also M. C. Buer, *Health, Wealth, and Population,* London, 1926, for the belief that conditions in the nineteenth century were an improvement over those of the eighteenth century. See M. Dorothy George, "Introduction," *London Life in the Eighteenth Century,* London, 1925.

With customary devotion to duty, investigators also exposed bad working conditions. Charles Wing's *Evils of the Factory System Demonstrated by Parliamentary Evidence,* London, 1837, is a useful abridgment of official reports. A short but well organized discussion is by C. T. Thackrah, *The Effects of the Principal Arts, Trades, and Professions . . . on Health and Longevity,* 2d ed., 1831. A more frequently quoted work is that of James P. Kay, *The Moral and Physical Condition of the Working Classes Employed in the Cotton Manufacturing in Manchester,* 2d ed., 1832. Of several reports by commissioners on mines and collieries, the most useful is Commissioners Appointed . . . to Inquire into . . . the Mining Districts, *Report,* 1850. For many years Henry Mayhew gathered an immense variety of information, finally brought together in an illustrated work *London Labour and the London Poor,* 4 vols., London, 1862. The special problems of women in industry have been ably described by Wanda F. Neff, *Victorian Working Women,* New York, 1929.

A standard work on the earnings of labor in this period is Arthur L. Bowley's *Wages in the United Kingdom in the Nineteenth Century,* Cambridge, 1900. The system of truck is exposed in Select Committee on Payment of Wages, *Report*, 1842. For changes in earnings over a period of years, especially in skilled work, see the Board of Trade, *Labour Statistics; Returns of Wages . . . between 1830 and 1886* (1887). On food see the *Report . . . on the Adulteration of Food, Drink, and Drugs*, abridged, 1855. The suffering caused by the high cost of living is described in *The Hungry Forties; Life under the Bread Tax*, ed. by Mrs. Cobden Unwin, London, 1904.

Official records of unemployment in this period are wanting. Some figures are given by Arthur Redford, *Labour Migration in England, 1800–1850*, Manchester, 1926. The monumental work of Sidney and Beatrice Webb on the English Poor Law is now the standard reference on this subject. See also Herbert V. Mills, *Poverty and the State*, London, 1886.

The general state of education and the resulting neglect of lower-class training is surveyed in Select Committee on Education in England and Wales, *Report*, 1835. The extent of drinking among workers is revealed in Select Committee of Inquiry into Drunkenness, *Report*, 1834. The Select Committee on Criminal and Destitute Children, *Report*, 1853, studies the consequences of neglecting the very young. Another standard source, frequently used here, is the *Reports* of the Children's Employment Commission, 1842 ff. See also *The Perils of the Nation; an Appeal to the Legislature, the Clergy, and the Higher and Middle Classes*, 2d ed., London, 1843.

The quantity of Victorian benevolence is to be seen in *Low's Handbook to the Charities of London*, London, 1870, and in *The Annual Charities Register and Digest*, London, 1890. This second book is very informative, with a bibliography of works on charity and poverty, a long introduction carefully indexed, and a section of interesting advertisements describing the aims and needs of various charitable organizations. See also Donald O. Wagner, *The Church of England and Social Reform since 1854*, New York, 1930; Charles Bosanquet, *London; Its Growth, Charitable Agencies, and Wants*, London, 1868; Helen Bosanquet, *Social Work in London, 1869–1912*, London, 1914.

The standard work on factory laws is that of B. L. Hutchins and A. Harrison, *A History of Factory Legislation*, 2d ed., London, 1911. See also *The Case for the Factory Acts*, ed. by Mrs. Sidney Webb, London, 1901. A good brief summary of housing legislation is contained in the first report of the housing commissioners (1884) already referred to. Industrial problems in this period are dealt with by Beatrice Webb in *My Apprenticeship*, London, 1926, and in the report of the Industrial Remuneration Conference, London, 1885; both volumes are sympathetic toward the worker's problems. The rise in wages and the standard of living is studied by George H. Wood, "Real Wages and the Standard of Comfort since 1850," *Journal of the Royal Statistical Society,* LXXII (1909), 91–103. See also J. H. Clapham, *Economic History of Modern Britain,* Cambridge, 1932, II. Improvement in education is discussed by Henry Craik, *The State in Its Relation to Education,* 2d ed., London, 1896, and by Henry Binns, *A Cenutry of Education,* London, 1908. Many excellent general works are also available for study of this period. See especially E. L. Woodward, *The Age of Reform,* Oxford, 1938; R. C. K. Ensor, *England: 1870–1914,* Oxford, 1936; and Gilbert Slater, *Growth of Modern England,* 2d ed., London, 1939.

CHAPTER II

THE ECONOMIC theories here analyzed will be found in the works of Adam Smith, Thomas Malthus, David Ricardo, Jeremy Bentham, Herbert Spencer, and John Stuart Mill. Brief excerpts from their works illustrating the several laws under discussion are contained in Donald O. Wagner's *Social Reformers,* New York, 1934, a useful condensation and work of reference. See also the *Encyclopedia of the Social Sciences.* A good study, if somewhat prejudiced, of the special difficulties faced by the laborer in selling his commodity is that of Dr. Lujo Brentano, *The Relation of Labor to the Law of Today,* trans. from the German, New York, 1897. The tenth volume of Sir William Holdsworth's monumental *History of English Law,* London, 1938, makes clear the practice of laissez-faire in England before the work of Adam Smith.

CHAPTER III

THE ORDER in Chapter III has been imposed upon Coleridge's ideas from without. There is no coherent work or series of works in which Coleridge states his view of social evil, its cause, and his belief in human dignity and oneness. This is somewhat true of the other writers as well, although none of them approaches the disorganization of Coleridge. Yet after reading in the prose works, letters, and miscellaneous remains of Coleridge one may piece together a consistent set of ideas which recur frequently and admit of the interpretation given them in Chapter III. Much of the necessary material may be found in the *Complete Works,* ed. by W. G. T. Shedd in 7 vols., New York, 1884, and in *Political Thought of Samuel Taylor Coleridge,* a selection by R. J. White, London, 1938. Of importance are the two "Lay Sermons."

1816–17, "The Friend," "Aids to Reflection," and "The Constitution of Church and State." A great deal of indispensable material was reprinted in Coleridge's *Essays on His Own Times*, forming a second series of *The Friend*, ed. by his daughter in three volumes, London, 1850. Two pieces not widely known, but important for Coleridge's view of early humanitarian legislation, are *Two Addresses on Sir R. Peel's Bill*, ed. by Edmund Gosse and privately printed, 1913. These are reprinted at the end of Lucy E. Watson's, *Coleridge at Highgate*, London, 1925. Some of Coleridge's best ideas are scattered among *Notes, Theological, Political, and Miscellaneous*, ed. by the Reverend Derwent Coleridge, London, 1853, *Table Talk and Omniana of S. T. C.*, Oxford, 1917, and *Letters, Conversations and Recollections of S. T. Coleridge*, ed. by T. Allsop in 2 vols., London, 1836. See also *Letters of Samuel Taylor Coleridge*, ed. by Ernest Hartley Coleridge in 2 vols., London, 1895, and *Unpublished Letters of Samuel Taylor Coleridge*, ed. by Earl Leslie Griggs, in 2 vols., London, 1932.

Most of the standard analyses of Coleridge's ideas have a somewhat different emphasis or principle of unity from what is attempted here. See especially Alfred Cobban, *Edmund Burke and the Revolt against the Eighteenth Century*, New York, 1929; Crane Brinton, *Political Ideas of the English Romanticists*, Oxford, 1926; John H. Muirhead, *Coleridge as Philosopher*, New York, 1930.

CHAPTER IV

SOUTHEY's ideas are concentrated in a few volumes and are more accessible than the ramblings of Coleridge. The *Essays, Moral and Political*, 2 vols., London, 1829, contain a number of characteristic pieces, such as "On the State of the Poor" and "On the Means of Improving the People." Less well known but equally important are *Letters from England by Don Manuel Alvarez Espriella*, trans. from the Spanish, 2d ed., 3 vols., London, 1808, and usually called simply the *Espriella Letters*. Macaulay's typical essay in the *Edinburgh Review*, I (1830), 528–53, emphasizes the importance of *Sir Thomas More: or, Colloquies on the Progress and Prospects of Society*, published by Southey in 2 vols., London, 1829. Indispensable also are *Life and Correspondence of Robert Southey*, 2d ed., by the Reverend Charles Cuthbert Southey, 6 vols., London, 1849, and *Selection from the Letters of Robert Southey*, ed. by John Wood Worter, 4 vols., London, 1856. See also *The Correspondence of Robert Southey with Caroline Bowles*, ed. by Edward Dowden, London, 1881.

As a social or political thinker, Southey is usually discussed along with Coleridge. In addition to the titles listed for Chapter III, the article by William Heller, "Southey's Later Radicalism," *Publications of the Modern Language Association*, XXXVII (1922), 281–92, should be mentioned. A fine estimate of Southey and of his importance in the nineteenth century as a whole adds to the already great riches of A. V. Dicey's *Law and Public Opinion in England* . . . London, 1905.

CHAPTER V

WITH Carlyle begins the massive achievement of the great Victorians. His *Collected Works* in the Edinburgh edition, New York, 1903, fill thirty volumes. Those devoted to *Critical and Miscellaneous Essays* contain many important expressions of his ideas. Attention is called especially to "Signs of the Times," "Characteristics," "Chartism," "The Nigger Question," and "Shooting Niagara." The indispensable *Sartor Resartus* and *Past and Present*, because of their importance in Carlyle's work, have been carefully edited several times. *Sartor Resartus* was first completely edited by A. MacMechan, Boston, 1896; more recently it has been annotated by C. F. Harrold, Garden City, 1937. The standard edition of *Past and Present* is that of A. M. D. Hughes, Oxford, 1918. The volume containing *Latter Day Pamphlets* in Carlyle's collected works should be read for some of his typical ideas on the "condition of England," its causes and cure. Carlyle's letters are also very important and have been frequently used for Chapter V. See especially the two volume edition by Charles Eliot Norton of *Letters of Thomas Carlyle*, London, 1888; the *New Letters of Thomas Carlyle*, 2 vols., London, 1904, ed. by Alexander Carlyle; and the same editor's *Letters of Thomas Carlyle to John Stuart Mill, John Sterling, and Robert Browning*, London, 1924.

Great quantities of work have been done on various aspects of Carlyle and his achievement. The two most ambitious lives are by D. A. Wilson, *Life of Thomas Carlyle*, 6 vols., New York, 1923–24, and by J. A. Froude, whose work appeared in two parts of two volumes each: *Thomas Carlyle; a History of the First Forty Years of His Life*, London, 1882, and *Thomas Carlyle; a History of His Life in London*, London, 1884. Froude has written one of the great biographies in English, but he is supposed to favor Carlyle's wife against the man himself. This is true only in detail; the book as a whole gives an impressive picture of a great but fallible human being and should be read by anyone making a serious study of Carlyle. Among the books more closely related to Chapter V, see Emery Neff, *Carlyle and Mill*, New York, Columbia University Press, 1924; F. W. Roe, *The Social Philos-*

ophy of Carlyle and Ruskin, New York, 1921; Benjamin Lippincott, *Victorian Critics of Democracy,* University of Minnesota Press, 1938; and Professor Emery Neff's most recent study of Carlyle as a whole, *Carlyle,* New York, 1932.

CHAPTER VI

MUCH OF Kingsley's humanitarianism is now found hidden away in forgotten sermons, articles, and speeches. In addition to the novels *Yeast,* written 1848, published 1851, and *Alton Locke,* 1850, the tract *Cheap Clothes and Nasty,* 1850, and the article on *The Water Supply of London,* 1850, have been relied upon in Chapter VI. The period when Kingsley wrote as "Parson Lot" and contributed to *Politics for the People,* 1848, and *The Christian Socialist,* 1850, is to some extent represented in *Charles Kingsley: His Letters and Memories of His Life,* ed. by his wife in 2 vols., London, 1901. More frequently reference has been made to the miscellaneous pieces found in Kingsley's *Health and Education,* Newport, 1893, and *Sanitary and Social Lectures and Essays,* London, 1902; the titles of these collections are self-explanatory. Another broad selection from Kingsley's work on social and literary subjects is the *Miscellanies,* 2 vols., London, 1859. Many quotations have been taken from Kingsley's sermons also, especially from the *Sermons on National Subjects,* first series, London, 1852, *Sermons for the Times,* New York, 1856, *The Water of Life and Other Sermons,* London, 1867, and *Village, Town and Country Sermons,* London, 1894.

A number of books have been written about Kingsley as a humanitarian reformer. The most useful are by the Reverend M. Kaufman, *Charles Kingsley; Christian Socialist and Social Reformer,* London, 1892, and W. Henry Brown, *Charles Kingsley; the Work and Influence of Parson Lot,* London, 1924. See also Charles E. Raven, *Christian Socialism; 1848–1854,* London, 1920, Stanley E. Baldwin, *Charles Kingsley,* New York, Cornell University Press, 1934, and Margaret Farrand Thorp, *Charles Kingsley; 1819–1875,* Princeton University Press, 1937.

CHAPTER VII

THE IDEAS PRESENTED in Chapter VII are found endlessly repeated throughout Arnold's prose work. Here the principal sources have been *Culture and Anarchy,* 1869, which contains the famous essay "Sweetness and Light"; *Literature and Dogma,* 1873, a work whose purely theological side has been less useful than its demand for unselfishness as the rule of human life; *Mixed Essays*, 1879, which has been indispensable, especially for its pieces on "Equality," "Democracy," "The Future of Liberalism," "The Incompatibles," "Irish Catholicism and British Liberalism"; and the volumes of *Essays in Criticism*. From the 1st ser., 1865, of these essays special use has been made of "The Function of Criticism" and "Pagan and Mediaeval Religious Sentiment"; from the 2d ser., 1888, Arnold's views on the importance of poetry are taken from "The Study of Poetry" and "Wordsworth." A volume of *Essays in Criticism*, 3d ser., Boston, 1910, contains "The Modern Element in Literature" and "Johnson's Lives," two essays quoted to show Arnold's belief in humane letters as essential to education. The essay "Science and Literature" in *Discourses in America*, 1885, has contributed to the same purpose. Miscellaneous criticism, social, religious, and educational, has also been taken from the essay "Numbers," in *Discourses in America*, the group of satirical letters called *Friendship's Garland*, 1871, the now seldom read *St. Paul and Protestantism*, 1870, *Last Essays on Church and Religion*, 1877, and *A French Eton*, 1864. Arnold's letters are somewhat disappointing as an expression of his thought. They have been edited by G. W. E. Russell, New York, 1900; the *Letters to Arthur Hugh Clough*, ed. by H. F. Lowry, Oxford Press, 1933, are more important for their views on poetry.

Lionel Trilling's excellent *Matthew Arnold*, New York, 1939, is now the standard work on Arnold. Not many other studies are useful for the matters under discussion in Chapter VII. See also Robert Shafer, *Christianity and Naturalism*, Yale University Press, 1926; the study of *Victorian Critics of Democracy*, listed under Carlyle; Charles H. Harvey, *Matthew Arnold; a Critic of the Victorian Period*, London, 1931; Dover Wilson's essay on Arnold in *Social and Political Ideas of Some Representative Thinkers of the Victorian Age*, London, 1933.

CHAPTER VIII

RUSKIN is himself a source for any inquiry into the loss of England's natural and urban beauty during the nineteenth century. The details given in Chapter VIII, however, were found with the help of Elwood H. McClelland's *Bibliography of Smoke Prevention*, Pittsburgh, 1913. Most of the information was taken from Augustus Voelcker, "On the Injurious Effects of Smoke on Certain Building Stones and on Vegetation," *Journal of the Society of Arts*, XII (Jan. 22, 1864), 146–53, "The Noxious Vapour Commission," *The Chemical News*, XXXVIII (Oct. 11, 1878), 181–82, "The History and Workings of the Alkali Acts," *ibid.* (Sept. 27, 1878), 158–60, and various reports of the Rivers Pollution Commission, 1867—.

Ruskin's own enormous labors have been gathered into an edition by E. T. Cook and Alexander Wedderbrun in thirty-nine volumes, London, 1903–12. Although Ruskin's earlier work has to do chiefly with the criticism of art, a number of passages in *Modern Painters*, 1843–60, were relevant to Chapter VIII. The essay on "The Nature of Gothic," in *The Stones of Venice*, 1851–53, has been indispensable. *Unto This Last*, 1862, Ruskin's first organized effort to reform Victorian society, and *Fors Clavigera*, 1871–84, a series of ninety-six letters to workingmen, have also been extensively used. Of almost equal importance are *A Joy Forever*, 1857, *The Crown of Wild Olive*, 1865, and *Munera Pulveris*, 1872; somewhat less use has been made of *Time and Tide*, 1867. These works are merely most extensively used in preparing Chapter VIII and do not by any means exhaust Ruskin's monumental achievement. No special reference has been made to his personal correspondence, which could hardly be more candid in expressing Ruskin's ideas than are his uninhibited published works.

In addition to the analyses by Roe and Lippincott (Chapter V), Ruskin's ideas are discussed by G. Hislop, "Social Teaching of Ruskin," *Economic Review*, XXIV (1914), 30–38, and by John A. Hobson, *John Ruskin: Social Reformer*, London, 1898. See also *Ruskin the Prophet and Other Centenary Studies*, ed. by J. H. Whitehouse, London, 1920; George M. Jones, "The Social Ethics of Ruskin," *Quarterly Journal of the University of North Dakota*, XXIII (1932–33), 252–75; R. V. Collingwood, *Ruskin's Philosophy*, London, 1922.

CHAPTER IX

LIKE CARLYLE AND RUSKIN, Morris was enormously productive. His daughter has edited the *Collected Works of William Morris*, London, 1910–15, of which Vols. XXII (1914) and XXIII (1915) contain most of the important lectures and essays referred to in Chapter IX. Special use has been made of "Art and the Beauty of the Earth," "How We Live and How We Might Live," "Useful Work v. Useless Toil," and "Dawn of a New Epoch." These and other typical expressions of Morris's ideas were written mostly in the 1880's after the period of his best poetry. *A Dream of John Ball*, 1888, and the Utopian romance *News from Nowhere*, 1890, have also been extensively used. Much information was found in the biographical, interpretive volumes which May Morris has recently added to the *Collected Works*. The second of these, *Morris as a Socialist*, Oxford, 1936, gives an invaluable record of the poet's radical activities. It contains abundant quotations from Morris, and together with Vols. XXII–XXIII of the *Collected Works* it provides all that is necessary for an understanding of the great humanitarian's ideas. Some useful secondary works are J. W. Mackail, *Life of William Morris*, 2 vols., London, 1899; A. Clutton-Brock, *William Morris, His Work and Influence*, London, 1914; and the work of J. B. Glasier, quoted in the discussion of Morris, *William Morris and the Early Days of the Socialist Movement*, London, 1921.

CONCLUSION

AN IMMENSE OUTPOURING of literature in the nineteenth century comes under the general heading of "humanitarian" and is more or less related to the work of these seven major figures. Most of the material in the following list is not based on coherent principles, however; it protests against various aspects of "the condition of England," and as a rule does credit rather to the personal decency and good feeling of the authors than to their understanding of what human dignity means.

Among the writers of verse, Ebenezer Elliott attracted attention with his *Corn-Law Rhymes*, 1831, of which Carlyle wrote a fairly sympathetic review. The chartist agitation and general distress among the lower classes in the "hungry forties" inspired numerous minor poems. Among these Mrs. Caroline Norton's *A Voice from the Factories*, 1836, and the well-known poem by Mrs. Browning, "The Cry of the Children," 1844, show the sympathy aroused by the sufferings of young factory workers. See also Mrs. Norton's *Child of the Islands*, 1845. With Thomas Hood's famous poem *The Song of the Shirt*, 1843, most readers are already familiar, but a longer and more powerful contemporary work is less well known. This is Thomas Cooper's *The Purgatory of Suicides*, 1845, a poem in ten books, or cantos, dedicated to Carlyle and written while the author was imprisoned as a chartist agitator. A group of miscellaneous poems by Gerald Massey, *Cries of Forty-Eight*, 1848–49, are inspired by sympathy for the poor, whose effort to help themselves reached a climax in the chartist agitation of 1848. Of interest also as a curiosity, since he was once compared with his fellow countryman Burns, is the work of the Scottish weaver Willie Thom. His *Rhymes and Recollections of a Hand-Loom Weaver*, 1845, depict the sufferings of the poor and plead for their rights.

The great humanitarian novelists produced work of much greater distinction than did these poets, who are representative of a crowd of versifiers now quite properly forgotten. The work of Dickens hardly requires recommendation, and the reader may only be reminded, among other titles, of *Oliver Twist*, 1838, *Little Dorrit* (1855–57), and especially of *Hard Times*, 1854, in which Dickens made his only effort to deal specifically with the problems of a factory laborer. The work of Kingsley in his novels *Yeast*, 1848, and *Alton Locke*, 1850, has already been mentioned. Disraeli's *Sybil*, 1845, reveals its humane purpose in the subtitle *The Two Nations;* this refers to the rich and the poor, who are finally brought to close sympathy and understanding. The novels of Mrs. Gaskell may still be read with interest, especially *Mary Barton*, 1848, a story of the laboring poor in Manchester, and *North and South*, 1855, a noble plea for the poor and one of her best performances from an artistic point of view. The reader may supplement these with Mrs. Francis Trollope's *Michael Armstrong*, 1840, Charlotte Elizabeth's (Mrs. Tonna) *Helen Fleetwood*, 1841, and Charlotte Brontë's *Shirley*, 1849. Of the novels produced toward the end of the century, one of the most interesting is *Workers in the Dawn*, 1880, by George Gissing, a work showing flashes of power and containing a fierce indictment of the "condition of England." For useful discussions of the novel as a social document see C. B. Proper, *Social Elements in English Prose Fiction*, Amsterdam, 1929, which stops at 1832, where M. Cazmian began with his *Le Roman social en Angleterre*, Paris, 1904, a work which deals mainly with Disraeli, Kingsley, Mrs. Gaskell, and Dickens. See also Wanda F. Neff, *Victorian Working Women*, 1929, a work which analyzes many novels and poems dealing with the problems of women in industry.

A number of autobiographical works produced in the early and middle Victorian era are also of some value. One of the most interesting is that of Thomas Cooper, 1872, author of *The Purgatory of Suicides*. A longer and, perhaps, more informative work, a narrative beginning in 1815, is Samuel Bamford's *Passages in the Life of a Radical*, 1842, which was republished with his *Early Days*, 1848, in two volumes, 1893. Other interesting lives are those of William Lovett, whose *Life and Struggles of William Lovett*, 1876,—see new edition by R. H. Tawney in two volumes, New York, 1920—gives an insight into Chartism, and of Charles Knight, *Passages in a Working Life*, 3 vols., 1864–65.

Index

40
42.40
48

3.65
3265
96

0
55
15

42.47
4407
8

RE CLASSIF NO 820.9034

CUTTER NO Sch 33

CHECK DUP SHELF

SEND FOR LC 78-143883

MARK SPINE

MAKE POCKET

PULL CAT BOOKS JUL 31 1972

ACCESSION BOOK

ADD ACC NO TO CDS

WHITE

CORRECT CDS

ADD ON UNIT

OVERSIZE